Legends by the Lake

Ohio History and Culture

Legends by the Lake
The Cleveland Browns at Municipal Stadium

by John Keim
With a Foreword by Jerry Sherk

The University of Akron Press

Series on Ohio History and Culture

John H. White and Robert J. White, Sr., *The Island Queen: Cincinnati's Excursion Steamer*

H. Roger Grant, *Ohio's Railway Age in Postcards*

Frances McGovern, *Written on the Hills: The Making of the Akron Landscape*

Keith McClellan, *The Sunday Game: At the Dawn of Professional Football*

Steve Love and David Giffels, *Wheels of Fortune: The Story of Rubber in Akron*

Alfred Winslow Jones, *Life, Liberty, and Property: A Story of Conflict and a Measurement of Conflicting Rights*

David Brendan Hopes, *A Childhood in the Milky Way: Becoming a Poet in Ohio*

John Keim, *Legends by the Lake: The Cleveland Browns at Municipal Stadium*

© 1999 by John Keim

All inquiries and permissions requests should be addressed to the publisher,
The University of Akron Press, Akron, OH 44325-1703

Manufactured in the United States of America

First Edition 1999

04 03 02 01 00 99   5 4 3 2 1

The paper used in this publication meets the minimum requirements of American National Standard for Information Sciences—Permanence of Paper for Printed Library Materials, ANSI Z39.48-1984.∞

Library of Congress Cataloging-in-Publication Data

Keim, John.

    Legends by the lake : the Cleveland Browns at Municipal Stadium / by John Keim with a foreword by Jerry Sherk.

       p. cm. — (Ohio history and culture)

    Includes bibliographical references.

    ISBN 1-884836-47-X (alk. paper). — ISBN 1-884836-48-8 (pbk. : alk. paper)

    1. Cleveland Browns (Football team)   2. Cleveland Municipal Stadium (Cleveland, Ohio)   I. Title.   II. Series.

GV956.C6K45   1999

796.332′64′0977132—dc21   99–25712

To my greatest gifts, Matthew and Christopher, so they may someday understand, and share, their dad's passion . . .

And to Browns fans, who already do. They deserve the best.

Table of Contents

Paul Brown, left, and Otto Graham

Foreword

I loved Cleveland Stadium. It was history. It was huge. When you talk to other players, many have the same story: You would visit the stadium for the first time and, while your attorney would talk with the Browns people, you would walk up into the stadium, into the second deck, and you would look over and see the vastness.

And fall in love with it immediately.

You felt the history, and you knew before you walked in that you had a chance to be part of history. You knew about the play-off games, and you knew about Lou Groza and Jim Brown. You knew you were part of a good family.

The locker rooms weren't luxurious, but that didn't matter. They contained memories that provided everyone a sense of history. I remember seeing pictures from the 1950 championship team and seeing Groza and those guys against the lockers, and it gave you a sense of the people who were in those lockers before you. That became part and parcel of being with the Browns. There was an unspoken sense of greatness about that locker room.

Another memory was very vivid: walking down the tunnel. It was a leap back in time. Real primitive. The guys all had their stuff for war on, all the pads, and you'd hear the clomp, clomp of the spikes on the wooden plank that was sunk and disintegrating because it had been there for so long, and there were these little light bulbs hanging down.

It was dark and cramped, but you knew there were eighty thousand people just over your head waiting for you to come out of that chute. It was real quiet, but your system was on fire, and your adrenaline was just pounding. Then the first person would come out of the dugout, and the crowd would just start roaring. They would see the Browns' colors and just go crazy. That was an experience none of us will ever forget.

Memories like that are why Brian Sipe and I made a forty-five-minute movie on our journey across country from California to Cleveland for the last game, meeting Browns fans and later interviewing greats such as Brown, Groza, Marion Motley, Bill Willis, and Dante Lavelli. Each one talked about the stadium in glowing terms.

As we toured the locker rooms with the cameras, we were able to reminisce and say the truth. This is where history took place.

But the one thing I heard several times in the video is that people would say it wasn't so much about the team, it was about family. They would talk about the times they went to the stadium, and the worse the weather was, the more fondness they had for it. It wasn't so much the victories, but the last-second defeats.

One man told us, "I was with my son when Brian threw the interception and someone took a picture of us and my eyes were watering." I expected the guy to say what a crummy time it was and instead he said, "No one can take that moment from us." We heard over and over again about fathers and sons or daughters going to that stadium. It wasn't just a sporting event. It was a family event.

—Jerry Sherk
Browns defensive tackle, 1970–1981

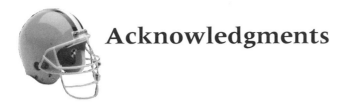

Acknowledgments

This book, recalling some of the Browns most memorable home games, as well as some of the best players, would have been impossible to complete without an army of help, for which I am eternally grateful. Talk about taking a village. This truly was a community effort.

My wife Kerry's constant support and encouragement, not to mention her editing, allowed me to pursue such a time-consuming project. I'm lucky, and blessed, to have her. My brother Bob performed a variety of roles. He edited, chased down photos, researched stories, and provided direction. This book is better because of his help.

My friend and part-time editor Dan Duncan became my personal library and kept me energized with his excitement for the Browns. My dad, with his season tickets (bleachers, section fifty, rows twenty-six and twenty-seven), enabled me to cultivate a strong interest in the Browns and a love for Cleveland Municipal Stadium. Some of his old clippings came in handy. My mom, brothers Chris and Neil, and sister Mary Jo provided support.

I would also like to thank Tom Cammett of Hiram College, as well as the public relation staffs of the Browns (Laura Paquelet and Jason Ferrante), Baltimore Ravens (Kevin Byrne and Francine Lubera), and Washington Redskins (Mike McCall and Phyllis Hayes), and Robin Palmer and Jim Murphy of the *Willoughby News Herald,* and Ray Yanucci of the *Browns News/Illustrated.*

Also, thanks to the former Browns, without whom there's nothing to write, who generously shared their time and memories: Rob Burnett, Earnest Byner, Gary Collins, Vince Costello, Thom Darden, Doug Dieken, Hanford Dixon, Galen Fiss, Frank Gatski, Otto Graham, Lou Groza, Gene Hickerson, Michael Jackson, Joe "Turkey" Jones, Jim Kanicki, Leroy Kelly, Ken Konz, Dante Lavelli, Dale Lindsey, Dave Logan, Clay Matthews, Mike McCormack, Walter Michaels, Frank Minnifield, Bobby Mitchell, Dick Modzelewski, Bill Nelsen, Ozzie Newsome, Greg Pruitt, Sam Rutigliano, Frank Ryan, Dick Schafrath, Marty Schottenheimer, Jerry Sherk, Jim Ray Smith, Don Strock, Paul Warfield, John Wooten, Felix Wright.

And to the media who shared their time: Greg Brinda, Dan Coughlin, Tony Grossi, and Gib Shanley. And to Chuck Heaton, Russ Schneider, and Mike Trivisonno, all of whom I talked to for an earlier project, and Vince Erwin, aka D-Dawg. Also, the photographers Tim and Tom Cammett, Ron Kuntz and Wally McNamee, who shared their work. And comedian Drew Carey.

My friend and occasional coauthor Rick Snider always provided sound advice. Thanks as well to another friend and sometimes coauthor David Elfin, *Journal* sports editor Paul Bergeron, Cleveland State University archivist William Becker, and friend Todd Baldau.

Finally, the staff at the University of Akron Press, especially Elton Glaser and Beth Pratt. This was a different venture for them, but they attacked it with an enthusiasm that made me feel special. Without them, this book wouldn't be possible. And many thanks to Sara Lickey for polishing my copy.

By now, the Academy Awards would have booted me off the stage. But the efforts of many made this a meaningful project. And for that I'm blessed. Thanks to all.

Legends by the Lake

Ohio History and Culture

Introduction

 The stunning end numbed a city and froze the players' emotions. The Kardiac Kids had spent 1980 crafting close win after close win, revitalizing a city and a franchise. No one expected it to end, at least not so soon. But quarterback Brian Sipe threw an interception, quieting Cleveland Stadium and sending the fans' hearts plummeting with the temperature.

The best Browns season in nearly a decade, and the most exciting one in much longer, ended in pain, and Cleveland was forced to face reality: the city still was struggling to escape its bankruptcy, its river-burning image; the baseball Indians offered no hope, and the basketball Cavaliers offered even less. And it was well below zero outside.

Tackle Doug Dieken, in his tenth season, understood the situation. The city had depended on the Browns, and the Browns had failed to come through. So when his brother Bob suggested they drown their sorrows, Dieken said no. He couldn't face the fans.

Finally, Bob Dieken persuaded his brother to drop by Victoria's Station in Rocky River. They sat down in a booth, and Dieken avoided eye contact with other patrons. But the fans had something to say, interrupting Dieken's remedy for heartache.

"You just wanted to pound as many beers as possible, but before you had a chance to do it, people kept walking over and saying, 'Thanks for a great season,'" Dieken recalled. "I was like, 'Hey, we let you down today.' But that's what makes football in Cleveland so great: the fans."

They're why grown men who fought wars and played football without face masks cried when Art Modell announced he was moving the franchise to Baltimore. These players had turned into fans themselves and understood what the Browns meant to the community. In a word, they meant everything.

"It was like losing a relative," Hall of Famer and season-ticket holder Lou Groza said.

Or worse.

"I've been married forty-four years to the same person," former Browns coach Sam Rutigliano said, "and [the move] would be tantamount to me coming home from lunch today and finding a note that says, 'It's over.' My kids, my grandkids, everything we did. This love affair is down the drain, and she never gave me a reason. That's how I and a lot of people in Cleveland felt about the Browns. It's a unique [relationship], and this last happening [the move] has proven it. I'm not sure any other city would have responded the way Cleveland did."

When the tears stopped, the fans took action, fighting the NFL as no other jilted community had, via letters, faxes, rallies, and TV. Then they celebrated a victory, one that no other city could boast. A new team would return by 1999, with the history, and colors, intact.

It wasn't hard to understand why the fans responded to the team's leaving in this fashion and why they executed their plans with such verve. Ohio is football, from Massillon High School's storied tradition to Ohio State. At some level, football gets in the blood. Then stays there. Fridays were for high schools, Saturdays for Ohio State, and, for fifty seasons, Sundays belonged to the Browns.

"The Browns were a blue-collar team with no logo, and Cleveland is the cradle of football," tackle Jerry Sherk said. "Football was almost invented here."

What made the fans so passionate is the players, the ones who spent decades building and maintaining a winning tradition and creating a frenzy that endured even during the bleak years.

"The Cleveland Browns are part of the fabric of the people of northeast Ohio," defensive tackle Jim Kanicki said. "Anyone tells you anything different, they're wrong. This was their team. Modell didn't own it. They invested their time, their money, their feelings. You could walk up and down the street and they knew who you were. They'd talk to you. These were the best fans in the world. I found out how good the Browns fans were when I went to New York [after the 1969 season]. These fans lived and died with their team."

Kanicki offered proof of their devotion: In 1963, two days after President Kennedy was assassinated, the Browns drew 55,096 fans to their game against the Cowboys.

"That's not to say that football was more important [than the President's death]," Kanicki said. "But [going to the game] was something that had to be done. They weren't as excited, but they were there. Everyone felt horrible, but they were there because they *had* to be there."

A similar feeling attracted 55,875 fans to the Browns' last-ever game at Cleveland Stadium. At that time, they were headed to Baltimore, along with the name, colors, and history, barring a miracle. The fans went to say goodbye to the Browns, and to friends they had sat with for years.

"After so many years, you had friends from security to the vendors to the people next to you," said Vince Erwin, aka D-Dawg, the dog-mask-wearing bleacherite who had had season tickets since 1978. "Everyone was crying. It was like a death, like a funeral. They had to run us out there an hour after the game ended. They actually escorted us out of there."

But they came because that's what many of these fans had been doing for years. They came throughout the 1970s despite not making the play-offs between '73 and '79, finishing second or third in attendance in four of those seasons. In 1979, the Browns ranked second and played before 92 percent of the stadium's capacity for a 9–7 team. The fans came in 1991 when the Browns, coming off a 3–13 season, finished 6–10. Yet an average of 71,469 fans attended the games.

In 1994, the year after coach Bill Belichick angered Cleveland by releasing homegrown quarterback Bernie Kosar, the fans wanted to stay away. The Browns averaged less than seventy thousand for the first time since '85. But local TV ratings averaged 42.4, a number unequaled for Super Bowl viewership in some cities.

The Browns offered hope. After all, the city and the team had forged a relationship that transcended sports. For years, Cleveland sought an identity. For years, the Browns provided one. It wasn't just about winning. During the Paul Brown years, from 1946 to 1962, the Browns won a certain way. They played hard-nosed football, slamming fullbacks through the middle. They won minus troublemakers who might tarnish the team's golden image. That pleased this blue-collar city, which prides itself on hard work.

They also were approachable, living on the same streets as their fans. They didn't live in some detached, gated community.

Former *Cleveland Plain Dealer* writer Dan Coughlin recalled getting a letter more than ten years ago from Mike Holland, a former Lakewood resident, telling him of something quarterback Otto Graham had done in 1955. Holland, then in the sixth grade, had invited Graham, in his last season of pro football, to attend one of their St. Luke's football practices at Lakewood Park.

Graham showed up, telling the stunned group, "I got your letter and you asked me to stop by, so I'm stopping by."

"It's one of those moments that would never happen today," Coughlin said. "But it's a moment that every kid on that team remembered."

Graham's teammates were involved in the community, mainly because they couldn't survive on their football salaries. So Bill Willis worked in city administration and Dante Lavelli opened a furniture store and Lou Groza sold insurance. All were future Hall of Famers. Their teammates held jobs as well. And they stuck around after their playing days ended.

"You will not believe how many ex-players live in Cleveland," guard Gene Hickerson said. "We have these Monday golf outings for fund-raisers, and you can go there and see eight or ten Hall of Famers. Every Monday, you can run into them somewhere. Cleveland is a super city. It gets blasted on TV, but you know something, let them blast us. It keeps all the crap out. This is one of the best places I ever lived in my life."

Safety Felix Wright played more than a decade after Hickerson retired, but he stayed, too, even after playing in Minnesota when his Browns career ended.

"The reason why a lot of guys stay is the people here capture you," Wright said, "and make you Cleveland's own."

The Browns also won, especially under Paul Brown. The Browns dominated the All-America Football Conference, winning all four league titles. Then the NFL welcomed them, much to the NFL's chagrin as the Browns kept winning. They demolished the NFL champs, Philadelphia, in the season opener then defeated the Los Angeles Rams, who had moved from Cleveland five years earlier, in the final. And a passion was born.

"When the Browns started winning in the old AAFC, people really got into football," said Greg Brinda, a Cleveland sports radio talk show host since 1980. "For whatever reason, the Rams never caught on. But after the war, Paul Brown got a lot of Ohio State players, and that helped. When you start winning automatically, it really forms a terrific relation.

"The postwar time is an interesting time in America. There was more leisure time, more money spent, and Cleveland was one of those cities that fell in love with a franchise. Then they beat the Eagles in '50 and contended for the championship six of the next seven years. That cemented the tradition. From that point on, it was incredible."

"The fact that we were winning," Groza said, "came from the fact that we had a good following. It's always nice to play under those conditions where there's fan satisfaction."

The Browns' reach stretched well beyond Cleveland, creating large pockets of fans throughout the state and region. Radio stations in Erie, Pennsylvania, and parts of New York, West Virginia, and Kentucky all carried the Browns' games into their last season before the three-year hiatus. Trains from across the state would deliver fans to the games.

In the 1950s, Ohio had two teams: Ohio State and the Browns. Paul Brown helped shape both, sustaining a mania in Columbus and starting one in Cleveland. Football, and the Browns, jelled the state.

"Paul was completely organized and things ran smoothly and the city appreciated that," linebacker Walt Michaels said. "They talk about Green Bay, how it's a small town and how you can walk the town the day of the game and everyone's at the game. Well, on the day of the Browns' games, I always thought the entire Cleveland police force was there also. Maybe they weren't doing any protecting, but they were there to watch. It was a way to see the game."

Then came the 1960s, and more winning as the Browns gained in importance, in part because the Indians, a contender throughout the previous decade, began their free fall. During the 1950s, the Indians were the favored son as they won a record 111 games in 1954, interrupting the New York Yankees' American League reign. But their best finish the following decade came in 1968 when they finished a distant third. A 10–0 start in 1966 caused a ruckus that soon faded, and Rocky Colavito's return in 1965 stirred up interest.

But the Browns' success more than made up for the Indians' failure. Even when Paul Brown was fired, in 1962, fans kept coming, and two years later they outdrew the Indians, 658,878 to 653,293.

"The Browns were it," Brinda said.

"The Indians were dull, dull, dull," Coughlin said. "They were unfashionable; the Browns were fashionable."

They had Jim Brown, arguably the NFL's best player. He, too, was a snug fit in Cleveland. He was a star, yet one who worked hard, withstood pain, and never complained about his work load. The more work for Brown, the better.

When they won the NFL championship in 1964, they became even bigger. From 1960 to 1964, the Browns attracted nine crowds of eighty thousand or more. In the last five seasons that decade, they drew twenty-one such crowds. From the last home game in '68 until the sixth home game in '70, the Browns played before thirteen straight crowds of at least eighty thousand.

"It was our town," linebacker Galen Fiss said. "I don't know what it was like in other towns, but that's what I always told other people. I loved Cleveland. I never spent a winter there; the latest I was there was December 27. But I loved the town because the people really made a fuss over you, and you were part of them. It was a healthy, loving relationship both ways—the players to the town and the town to the players."

"To say I was a Cleveland Brown," said quarterback Bill Nelsen, who helped put the Browns in the 1968 NFL championship, "it was something special. But what else was in Cleveland those days? This was the city. This was northern Ohio. The Indians were like a minor league team. You had Ohio State and the Browns.

"When I was traded there [in 1968], someone asked me, 'Do you know the history of the Browns?' I said, 'No.' I had grown up in Los Angeles and knew the greatness, but not the history. So I was given a book about the history. The relationship between the city and the team was fantastic and something people grew to love."

The 1964 championship was the Browns' last, and, until the Indians won the American League championship in 1995, no major sports team in Cleveland had won anything. A generation of fans grew up without seeing the Browns win the ultimate game, yet it didn't dampen enthusiasm. Besides, they knew all about the '64 team even if they never saw them play.

They had no choice. Rutigliano still meets fans who grew up in Cleveland and whose fathers had taken them to games. The league is full of transient cities, as linebacker Clay Matthews found in his sixteen-year tenure. Cleveland is anything but transient, a stability that leads to generations of Browns fans.

"For a greater percentage of the people there," Matthews said, "not only did their mom and dad root for the Browns, but so did their grandfather and maybe further back than that. It's more ingrained in the community."

Or, as defensive end Joe "Turkey" Jones said, "It seems like they breed little

Browns babies there. You had to be a Cleveland Browns fan. When I went back a couple years ago, it was an eye-opener. I didn't understand the magnitude when I was playing. But there are some die-hard fans, and that's their entertainment. They believe in their Brownies."

They had to, especially in the 1970s when Cleveland was ridiculed night after night, about everything from the Cuyahoga River catching fire to Mayor Ralph Perk's hair doing the same to Mayor Dennis Kucinich leading the city into bankruptcy. One thing after another provided comedic material.

Along came the Kardiac Kids in 1979–80, earning their nickname through a penchant for close games. During those two seasons, twenty-six of the Browns' thirty-three games were decided by a touchdown or less. The Browns won sixteen of those games, including a 27–24 win in 1980 at Cincinnati that gave them their first division title since 1971, ending the worst drought in franchise history. The Browns had saved the city, boosting Cleveland's self-esteem with their pizazz and creating an image that cooled the national jokes. The Browns had the handsome, California cool quarterback in Sipe and the glib coach in Rutigliano. They were exciting. And they were Cleveland's.

"The car industry was winding down, so many jobs were lost, and the area was devastated," tackle Jerry Sherk said. "Cleveland was a joke. But the Browns made a statement that said things were otherwise because the Browns epitomized Cleveland. The Browns really said this place had class."

So the fans clamored to say thanks. More than thirty-five thousand welcomed the Browns at Hopkins Airport after the team's victory over the Bengals, creating a scene those involved won't forget.

"When we got off that plane, I realized it was more than just winning," Rutigliano said. "It was more than just having a play-off team for the first time in ten years, and it was more than just dethroning the Pittsburgh Steelers [division winners from '74 to '79]. You truly shared it [with the city]."

A few years after the Kardiac Kids had faded, their memory endured. "I would be at autograph signings in 1984," Dieken said, "and there would be a four-year-old kid, and I'd ask what his name was, and it seemed like one out of three was named Brian."

As in "Brian Sipe."

Rutigliano was so taken by Cleveland that he has maintained his Waite Hill home, which sits about a mile from Modell's former residence. Rutigliano spends three to four months in Cleveland and plans to live there when he retires. Even he, a native New Yorker, would bristle at the phrase, "Mistake by the Lake," that was Cleveland's derisive alias.

"You can match Shaker or Chagrin Falls or any of the suburbs of Cleveland with any place in America," Rutigliano said. "It's one of the real nice communities in America. I really mean that. It's a great place to grow up and raise a family. I want to go back because I learned to love it. Cleveland is home to all three of my kids."

Other players who left still return once or twice a year. The place meant something to them, and the city's attitude touched their hearts.

"There's a spirit that people have when they have to fight for their own identity," Sherk said. "Clevelanders have had to struggle a bit, and it's created a strong character and strong allegiance. When I think about Cleveland, I not only think of the beautiful areas, I also think of the strong character the people have there, the loyalty for their families and the loyalty they have for their sports teams."

That loyalty rubbed off on the players. Receiver Dave Logan attended Colorado University and returned to Denver after his playing days to host a radio talk show. Whenever the Browns played the Broncos in the AFC championship, Logan would get the same question: Who are you going to root for?

The answer was easy.

"I make no bones about it," Logan said. "I say Cleveland. I live here, I grew up here. I want Denver to do well. When it comes to playing, my heart's in Cleveland. I was a Cleveland Brown.

"In 1987, I was at the [Browns-Broncos championship game in Cleveland]. I was just going crazy thinking, 'We've got to find a way to stop [the Broncos].' I was pulling for Cleveland like crazy."

Nothing pleases Clevelanders more than to hear someone, especially a professional athlete, say good things about their city. Which is why quarterback Bernie Kosar, a Youngstown native, became an icon in the 1980s when he declared his desire to return to northern Ohio and play for the Browns after leading the University of Miami to a national title. After guiding the Browns into three AFC championship games, Kosar's popularity skyrocketed. It was unmatched by anyone in the city. Maybe even the state.

"That's just the way Cleveland is," cornerback Frank Minnifield said. "They love their own. They said to themselves, 'This is one of ours.' They would do that for any player from Cleveland."

That doesn't mean they always went easy on Kosar or any other players. Hardly. When they were bad, the fans singed their ears.

"[In 1975], we only won three games," running back Greg Pruitt said, "and I'm going to a restaurant, and the mailman is putting mail in my box, and he looked up and said, 'Hey, man, when are you all going to win a game?'

"If we had a bad game, we'd be standing in the end zone near the bleachers catching punts and kickoffs, and if I had a bad game the week before, they would let you know every play you did bad. They'd yell, 'You drop another one like that and you can't come here next week.' It was almost like the fans expected a certain kind of play from you and they wouldn't take anything less. They couldn't fire you or trade you, but they could sure let you know how they felt about it."

Woe was the Monday after a loss when callers lit up talk shows.

"If they lost a game on Sunday, the phones wouldn't stop ringing until Wednesday," Brinda said. "That's how incredible it is. There's nothing like it, and everyone has an opinion. As great as the love affair is with baseball and the Indians and the stay-at-home managers that we have, there's nothing more passionate than the calls with the Browns."

Safety Thom Darden grew up in Sandusky rooting for the Browns and played in Cleveland for ten seasons. Former coach Nick Skorich would tell the players that the city would rise or fall Monday based on Sunday's result. But it wasn't until Darden retired and worked downtown that he understood the depth of the fans' feelings.

"You could see it on Monday," Darden said. "People would be downtown, and they would be despondent if we lost, but happy if we won. People would talk about it all day long at work. That was amazing to me. Then it would cease, and on Friday it would start all over again."

That's what the passion created. That's what winning created. Some might leave Cleveland, but Cleveland doesn't leave them, which is why the Browns Backers was believed to be the largest sports club in the world, boasting a membership of more than sixty-five thousand fans with more than two hundred chapters. The distance didn't matter: clubs existed in Italy, England, and Japan.

One spring weekend in 1998, Kanicki visited his son at Fort Knox, Kentucky, when someone knocked on the door. It was a thirteen-year-old fan whose father had sent him down the hall to collect a few autographs.

"He had all this stuff from the '50s, '60s, and '70s," Kanicki said. "It was amazing."

But it wasn't surprising.

"They always have the Browns and the tremendous history," Sherk said. "And history says you just don't get any better than that."

For years, it didn't get any better than the Browns and Cleveland. A football team lifted a city on its shoulders, elevating it to heights it never imagined. But when the team needed a boost, the city delivered. That's why the Browns will be back. It's also why all of them cling to their past.

"It was a great time," Hall of Fame tackle Mike McCormack said. "And a great love affair."

1 **Cleveland Municipal Stadium**
1931–1996

Chipped concrete greeted customers walking through a concourse as gray as a February day. Pillars blocked views for thousands of fans, who craned their necks to catch the action. Bleacher fans had a clear shot—but beware of the splinters in the aging, weather-pounded end zone seats. Forget about fresh paint, unless, of course, the dirt field needed another coat. And Lake Erie's biting winter winds left noses red and teeth chattering.

Then there were the bathrooms. No urinal available? Try the sink. Everyone else did.

So why was Cleveland Municipal Stadium so beloved? Because of the Browns, and the fifty years of memories they provided. Maybe it wasn't pretty and maybe it should have been replaced long ago. But how do you tear down the house you grew up in, even if it is a dump?

"It wasn't the best thing going," linebacker Galen Fiss said, "but there was just a lot of tradition that lived there."

When parents took their child to a game, they could point to where Lou Groza kicked that field goal in 1950, where Gary Collins caught those touchdown passes in '64, where Brian Sipe threw that interception in '81, where John Elway started that drive in '87.

They could close their eyes and see Paul Brown in his felt hat or Jim Brown carrying the ball or Bernie Kosar throwing it. Or they could hear the crowd chanting, "Super Bowl! Super Bowl!" before Elway's ninety-eight-yard death march. Not every recollection is pretty. But it is a memory and, most likely, a shared one, connecting people in a way nothing else could.

The more the Browns won, the more people liked the place and forgot about its aesthetics. Pretty soon, Cleveland Stadium became one of the toughest places for opponents to play.

"It was big, it was cold, but it got noisy," said linebacker Walt Michaels, who also returned as a New York Jets coach. "The people of Cleveland were just fantastic, blue collar all the way. I enjoyed every bit of it."

Crowds approaching eighty thousand became routine, and, though only the bleachers were close to the field, they could be intimidating. Just ask any teams

Cleveland Municipal Stadium, the Browns' home from 1946 to 1995

that had to deal with the Milk-Bone-throwing crowd of the Dawg Pound of the '80s and '90s. Former Chicago coach Mike Ditka marveled at the support when his Bears squad played here for a *Monday Night Football* game in 1989. From 1968 to 1970, the Browns played before at least eighty thousand fans thirteen straight times at this building, hard by Lake Erie. In their history, the Browns drew eighty thousand or more sixty-five times and more than seventy thousand showed up 198 times. Lack of support didn't prompt Art Modell to move the franchise.

"Not too many teams came in whose stadiums were larger," running back Bobby Mitchell said. "We could see that it bothered them. When you walked into Cleveland Stadium, people right away felt they were going up against something awesome." The size even awed the host team.

"The first game we played there, I came out on the field and just felt like a midget," Lou Groza said. Groza stood six-foot-three and weighed 255 pounds. He's no midget.

The stadium, built in 1931 at a cost of $3.5 million, housed more than just the Browns, of course. The Indians played there, though for several decades not many seemed to know, except when free tickets were involved. Even then, it was a struggle to coax fans to their games. The Indians' brass complained that no one wanted to come to the city to watch a baseball game. But they came for the Browns.

The Indians did not win a pennant in their last thirty-nine years at the stadium and were serious contenders only once in that stretch. But they did provide a few memories. They won two World Series games there, in 1948, en route to the title, and they won a record 111 games, in 1954, and stopped Joe DiMaggio's 56-game hitting streak in Cleveland in 1941. Forty years later, Len Barker pitched a perfect game in front of nearly seventy-three thousand empty seats. Still, the Indians often relied on promotions, not wins, to pack Municipal Stadium. Someone once remarked that while other stadiums did the wave, Indians fans could only perform the undertow.

Others flocked to the sandy-brown brick building to see the Beatles, the Rolling Stones, Bruce Springsteen, the Beach Boys, and Pink Floyd. They all played concerts at the stadium. Pelé played a soccer match there, Max Schmeling fought there in the stadium's first event in 1931, and more than ninety thousand jammed into the stadium to witness the closing ceremonies of the Seventh National Eucharistic Congress in 1935.

But nothing, or no one, is linked more to the stadium than the Browns, who won three AAFC championships and three NFL titles at home. Former Browns coach Sam Rutigliano felt the ghosts of Cleveland past whenever he walked onto the turf. Rutigliano had grown up in Brooklyn and watched the New York Giants play at Yankee Stadium. He appreciated old-time football and couldn't believe his good fortune, rising from a high school coach to the leader of the famed Browns.

"All of a sudden on a September afternoon, in 1978, I come through that tunnel and I'm the head coach of the Cleveland Browns," Rutigliano said. "And I'm thinking about Dante Lavelli and Lou Groza and Otto Graham and Marion Motley and all those great players."

In Rutigliano's second year, all those players returned for a celebration of the Browns all-time team. Rutigliano stood at the fifty yard line as the players were introduced, his heart racing.

"I thought to myself, 'Here I am in this place that was built in 1931,'" Rutigliano said. "All the time I was there, that was always [on my mind] every single time I went on that field."

Dick Modzelewski had a word for the stadium: junk. As a New York Giant, he was forced to dress in a cramped locker room. And shower with no hot water.

The Browns celebrated six titles at Cleveland Stadium, including this one in 1954.

"We used to go in there and tell the players, 'If you want to meet the press, meet them outside because the place is going to flood,'" said Modzelewski, who was traded to the Browns in 1964. "Sure as hell, if you stayed, the water would come up to your ankles. And the coaches, our little box that they put us in. We were close to the shower, and we had to hurry up and shower, jump in our clothes, and get out of there quick."

"It was really bad," said former Browns coach Marty Schottenheimer, who returned with Kansas City in 1989. "You literally hung clothing on nails that were hammered into the wall. There was no room. When you stepped out of the coaches' locker room, you stepped right into the shower, and water would splatter over the edge of the shower and into the coaches' locker room. It was terrible."

But both enjoyed playing there.

Modzelewski: "Cleveland Stadium was like Yankee Stadium for nostalgia."

Schottenheimer: "It was fun to play in an old stadium. It was different because, having been there as part of the home team, it had a special place in my heart. If I didn't have that connection, I wouldn't have particularly cared for it."

Not everyone liked Municipal Stadium. After the Browns beat Houston in the 1988 regular-season finale, forcing a rematch in the same place the following week, Oilers general manager Ladd Herzeg complained to the NFL. His beef: Assistant coach Doug Shively was nailed in the back of the neck with an ice ball from a bleacherite during pregame warm-ups. Herzeg wanted to warm up from the other end.

Twice during the 1980s, officials had teams switch directions to avoid the hurled debris from the Dawg Pound.

"I don't want to come back to this rat hole," Oilers receiver Ernest Givins said after that 1988 game.

But the Oilers' staff included at least one fan: coach Jerry Glanville. In 1996, he told the *Cleveland Plain Dealer*'s Tony Grossi, "It was a place I wished to be the coach of the home team because the crowd was so good. We always went in as the bitter enemy, but the crowd never realized we wished we were the home team."

Another former Oiler disagreed with Givins as well.

"It was fun playing there," cornerback Cris Dishman said. "They would always have us warm up in front of the bleachers. The Dawg Pound would throw snowballs and they'd put all kinds of stuff in it—glass, eggs. They'd throw dog biscuits. After the game, we were told to keep our helmets on. It really was fun.

"I enjoyed the excitement, especially when they would play the songs [after a touchdown] and the whole stands were rocking. And Glanville, he'd put a little extra fire on the week before we'd go there. He'd talk about how dirty the city was and give the fans something extra to come and boo him."

But even some Browns didn't like the stadium, at least the bumpy field. Most of them, however, were receivers and didn't like the slippery sod planted on the infield dirt after the Indians completed their season. If it rained in the winter, the resodded portion would be soft while the rest of the field was hard. Receiver Michael Jackson said running from the soft part to the hard area once caused him to pull a calf muscle in pregame warm-ups.

Receiver Gary Collins said, "It was ugly. The mistake by the lake."

Receiver Dante Lavelli said it was a great place to play most of the season.

"It was where football really was football," he said. "Grass, mud, cold. The only bad thing was, in December it got very cold. A football game shouldn't be decided by weather. I wish they would have built a dome stadium."

But a dome would have ended a tradition, welcome or not, of braving the elements. On the other hand, had a dome been in place in 1981, the Browns would have kicked a field goal, rather than risk a pass that Oakland intercepted.

Still, the weather added to the stadium's charm. Linebacker Dale Lindsey, while an assistant coach in Washington, sat in his office one rainy winter day, in 1998, the sort of day that reminded him of playing in Cleveland. Was the weather always bad? No, it just seemed that way.

Linebacker Clay Matthews had similar memories. In the winter of '98, he walked out of a gym in California into a cool, nighttime drizzle.

"I turned to a buddy and said, 'This reminds me of playing in Cleveland,'" he said. "If there is a vision that I could recall from the stadium, it would be a game sometime in the fourth quarter where the game had started at one, but they would have to turn the lights on by the end. And there would be a light rain with a little wind, and it would be just perfect."

Until they returned to their own locker room. But Matthews had it better than those who came before him. He can thank Indians pitcher Wayne Garland, said tackle Doug Dieken. He recalled Garland saying he would install air conditioning in the locker room after signing a $2.3 million contract in 1978.

"Modell got wind of this, and he wasn't going to be embarrassed, so he put air conditioning in," Dieken said. "The home lockers weren't bad, but there might have been only six shower heads and forty, forty-five guys. They finally put a little annex upstairs which [helped]. But if there weren't enough lockers, it went by seniority. That was one of the neat things about it: you earned the right to have your own locker."

An even better thing happened when the Browns left their locker room before the game. That's a memory carved in the minds of just about all who played there. They would walk fifty or so feet through the damp, narrow tunnel, their bodies preparing for a game and their ears readying for the noise. One, maybe two, lights showed the way.

"As you got closer," receiver Paul Warfield said, "you'd come up to the dugout, go up four or five steps and, once you're up, you come onto the field and there would be a tremendous roar. That was one of the greatest experiences I had in athletics. Those fans would make me feel very, very enthusiastic, and all the adrenaline was flowing in every part of my body. It was a great old facility to play in."

Dieken said, "There was nothing that will compare to that walk down the tunnel. It's a time to collect your thoughts, and you can't feel the crowd until you get to that dugout step and then, Boom!, it's like someone turned the TV set on full blast."

That noise shattered ears in big games. At home, the Browns went 10–7 on Monday night, 9–3–1 in overtime games, and 13–6 in the play-offs, including AAFC postseason contests. The Browns finished 238–126–6 at Municipal Stadium. But, for a regular-season game, nothing compared to when the hated Steelers came to town, sometimes, especially in the 1970s, bringing thousands of their own fans.

"You could really feel the crowd," defensive tackle Jerry Sherk said. "And most players fed off that. [Against Pittsburgh], there was a constant roar, even in between plays. That fills your body so full of adrenaline, and it gives you that extra effort. When that roar happens and you're running on a play, if you couldn't get to the ballcarrier, you'd peel back and just drill somebody, even a lineman.

"Sometimes it would feel as if the sound just penetrated you, almost to the point where you could swear that you felt it in the ground if you just stood still. It was so loud, like being in a thunderstorm or in a wind tunnel. It was overwhelming."

Running back Greg Pruitt quickly found out what it meant to beat Pittsburgh in Cleveland. In his rookie season of 1973, Pruitt subbed for injured back Leroy Kelly and scored two touchdowns. His second score, a nineteen-yard run with 1:01 left in the fourth quarter, won the game.

Pruitt was a hero. And the fans celebrated.

"The fans came on the field as if we had won a world championship," Pruitt said. "They were pulling on the goalposts. You've got people patting you on the helmet. I was panicking. If it was one or two or three hundred, fine. But it was thousands."

That swarm prevented Pruitt from a starring role with the media. Pruitt fought through the crowd, finally spotting the dugout that would lead him to the locker room.

"I was finally able to savor the moment," Pruitt recalled. "I said, 'I don't know what I did, but it must have been real important.' Then I thought, 'I'm going to be on TV for weeks after this game [replaying the postgame interview].' So I'm anticipating the questions and rehearsing my answers and I walk up the ramp leading to the locker room. And I'm going to make my big entrance."

Then he opened the door. To the Steelers' locker room. Pruitt retreated back down the ramp, but a throng of fans remained on the field so Pruitt waited for it to clear. By the time he returned to the Browns' locker room, the media had departed.

It was one of these Steelers-Browns games that Rick Patterson of Cleveland wrote about in a letter to the *Akron Beacon Journal* before the Browns' last-ever home game. But his letter had nothing to do about the game. Rather, it showed how Cleveland fans often treated the stadium. They knew they weren't responsible for cleaning.

"At halftime, I joined the crush of mankind waiting to go in the restroom," Patterson wrote. "We were bunched so close together in that line that you could only see the person in front of you. Imagine my surprise when I finally got to the front of the line and found out there was no urinal, just a wall. I was sure glad I had my boots on."

Yet the same fans kept returning, ignoring all that was wrong. Entire sections of fans grew up together.

"Our fans identified with the stadium," tight end Ozzie Newsome said. "They were proud to sit in those seats for thirty years, and their parents had sat in them before they did."

"You'd see the same faces when you walked out of that dugout," defensive tackle Jim Kanicki said. "Young kids and older people that were there every Sunday. I remember one guy named Buddy, an older guy, who would always say, 'Hey! Big Jim!' After seven or eight years, you got to know these people."

And the fans got to know the players, priding themselves on their knowledge. They had witnessed the best football had to offer for nearly twenty years under Paul Brown. They had seen in person one of the greatest quarterbacks ever in Otto Graham. They had watched the NFL's greatest running back in Jim Brown. Fourteen Hall of Famers called the stadium home.

Those memories will be preserved in the fans' minds forever. Chants such as "Here we go Brownies, here we go!" will linger in their ears. That's why they kept coming back, drawn by the ghosts. That's why they braved all sorts of weather. That's why the stadium's dismantling brought tears to many.

"What I remember most is that it was filled with really good, rabid, smart fans," Lindsey said, "who came whether we were winning or losing, whether it was hot or cold, dry or snowy."

They were fans like Phyllis Mesko of Hudson, who, in a 1995 article in the *Akron Beacon Journal* recalled her first Browns game with her father. They sat in the last row of the upper deck.

"The back of our seats had slots where the cold wind blew at our backs," she told reporter Carl Chancellor. "The wind seemed to increase the aroma of the hot dogs and hot chocolate all around us. I was freezing, but my dad never noticed the cold."

It didn't take long to understand the passion unleashed in this building. Quarterback Don Strock played less than one season in Cleveland. He started three games there. Yet he summed up Cleveland Municipal Stadium as well as anyone.

"It was what football was all about," Strock said. "It was just a classic stadium."

2 **Paul Brown**
Head Coach, 1946–1962

 Simple words toppled their egos and a squinty-eyed stare accomplished even more, driving them to perfection. That's all Paul Brown wanted. In 1948, he got it with a 15–0 record, not that the players always liked his methods. They vowed to fight back. They promised to say something the next time. Always the next time.

They never did.

Here's why: Brown won championships. In his seventeen seasons, Cleveland won seven titles, including three in the NFL. More titles meant more cash, not to mention prestige. The players could argue with the methods, but not the results. No NFL team played in more championship games than the Browns in the 1950s, earning them the label of "The New York Yankees of football," a goal Brown sought from the franchise's first season in 1946.

But Brown not only won, he also changed the game, perhaps more than any other coach. He hired full-time assistants; formed the first taxi squad, a five-man group of players who practiced but couldn't play; developed the modern face mask; designed the draw play; developed a blueprint for a championship team that others, such as San Francisco, later copied with an emphasis on speed and offense; signed black players, long before most people had ever heard of baseball's Jackie Robinson; and started film sessions.

"Paul changed the image of pro football, more than any person in history," quarterback Otto Graham said. "In those days, the image was of a great big potbelly guy, smoking big cigars. And when the season was over, the coaches went hunting for months and never got together again.

"Paul organized football. Other teams had to change, and they all followed his leadership. They had to or they couldn't win."

Graham gets rankled when other coaches are mentioned more than Brown in discussions of the all-time greats. Others have more wins. None started two franchises, including one that bears his name and a second, Cincinnati, that has played in two Super Bowls. Those who are called innovators today mostly swipe from the past and tinker. Brown was a true innovator, as much of what he did had never been done.

Also, it's worth pointing out that Vince Lombardi was hired by Green Bay, in

Paul Brown, on player's shoulders, gave Cleveland plenty of reason to celebrate.

large part on Brown's recommendation. And fifteen of Brown's former players or assistant coaches later became head coaches.

"Paul has never gotten the credit he deserves," Graham said. "Lombardi would come to *our* camp and watch practice. He learned from Paul, no question. Paul changed football a lot more than anyone ever thought of doing."

"Lombardi can't even touch him," receiver Dante Lavelli said.

"Paul was so far ahead of the system," guard John Wooten said, "and he had such a great football mind. We can't even try to list all the things that put him ahead of everyone."

Guard Jim Ray Smith played for Brown and then Dallas's Tom Landry.

"Tom was a great person and sharp," Smith said. "But Paul Brown was the coach of all coaches."

Several years ago, Smith, a member of the Cotton Bowl Athletic Association, was at the Big Ten meeting in Chicago when he found himself seated at a table with Penn State coach Joe Paterno. Smith started telling him about Brown's training camps, how he learned more in his first two weeks than he had in his whole career, and how he told college coaches to spend two weeks at one, just to learn.

Then Paterno smiled and said, "I was there for three years when you were playing. That's where I got my ideas."

Brown's ideas paved the way to a successful career, one defined by winning at every level. He started at Massillon (Ohio) High School, in 1932, and compiled an 81–7–2 record. In 1940, his Tigers scrimmaged Kent State University. They scored more than fifty points before Kent State stopped the carnage in the fourth quarter.

Then he did it at Ohio State, winning the 1942 national championship. At the Great Lakes Naval Academy, he took a team patched together before the season that was good enough by year's end to beat Notre Dame, 39–7. Brown later placed that win alongside his greatest of all time.

Those coaching stops cemented Brown's methods for winning, which included no swearing and no smoking and drinking. And no water, even on steamy afternoons.

"Everything was built on a spartan, tough, fight-your-way-to-the-death basis," Brown wrote in his autobiography. "As the attitude seeped into our players [at Massillon], they began to realize they didn't need any comforts on the field."

He carried that philosophy to Cleveland, where the winning continued. Once, the Browns arrived at the stadium at the same time as Baltimore's players, some of whom exited the bus smoking cigars.

Brown told his team, "We can lick any team that gets off the bus smoking cigars."

Which, of course, they did.

But they did that to every team in the All-America Football Conference, which began in 1946. Brown, his war duties complete, was the logical choice to coach owner Mickey McBride's Cleveland team.

When it came time to name the team, the fans chose "Browns," after its already popular coach. Actually, an original contest produced the nickname "Panthers," but another man claimed to hold the rights to the once lowly Cleveland semipro team, so McBride reopened the contest. The naming proved appropriate as Brown symbolized the Browns' success, an efficient master who won.

Brown was way ahead of the other teams when it came to finding talent. He remembered players who had either been with him at his three previous stops, such as fullback Marion Motley and end Dante Lavelli, or had played against him, such as quarterback Otto Graham.

That's why the Browns compiled a 47–4–3 record in the AAFC, winning a championship in each of the league's four years. More of the same followed in the NFL as Cleveland won a title in its inaugural season of 1950 and added championships in '54 and '55. The Browns won twenty-three of their first twenty-seven games in the NFL.

Certainly, they had talent. But Brown also knew how to mold that talent, and he did it through preparation and discipline. Brown learned those traits watching his father, a railroad dispatcher. At a moment's notice, his father had to switch trains from one track to another. Any mishap meant disaster.

"He was always serious-minded, very disciplined and ordered," Brown once said.

The same attributes applied to him. And he never wavered. Brown kicked starting linebacker Jim Daniell off the team the night before the 1946 championship game. Daniell violated the team's rules about drinking and was arrested, news that made headlines the next day. So Brown banned him from the team.

If a player was late for a flight, the plane left, forcing the player to find his own way to the game. In addition to a fine, the player had to pay for the flight. But few violated his rules, because everyone knew the consequences.

"There got to be a saying," safety Ken Konz said. "'There's a right way, a wrong way, and the Paul Brown way.' If you did it the Paul Brown way, you were right. He was a very strict coach, and he expected you to toe the line."

But guard Gene Hickerson said, "He wasn't strict. He just had rules and regulations you had to live by."

Film sessions turned into verbal lynchings.

"You never wanted to get your name mentioned too often," tackle Lou Groza said.

Play for Brown long enough, however, and that would happen, even to a Hall of Famer such as tackle Mike McCormack, whom Brown considered the greatest lineman ever. One game, Baltimore's defensive end Gino Marchetti destroyed McCormack, who didn't realize how good this future Hall of Famer was before they played. The next day, the Browns watched films.

"I dreaded every minute of it," said McCormack, who later coached in Green

Paul Brown, kneeling, ponders his next move.

Bay with Lombardi. "Paul finally stopped the projector and said, 'Michael, Michael. I can't believe you let your parents down. I wonder what your mom and dad would say about that performance.' Holy smokes. And he'd say it in front of all your teammates.

"With Lombardi, he would cuss you and jump all over you and after he got through with you, you felt beat up. But Paul would get on you and say it in such a way that you'd just walk away and all of a sudden realize you're bleeding to death."

Brown's words stung, but they also stuck. The next time Cleveland played Baltimore, the Browns upset the Colts 38–35, and McCormack had a strong day against Marchetti. Brown pointed this out to the squad, too.

Linebacker Vince Costello remembers hearing the phrase, "Either your injury is worse than you think, or you've slipped a lot." All of a sudden, doubt crept in, and Costello said players would second-guess their abilities, perhaps making them work harder.

Brown's zingers worked in games, too.

"One time, in Paul's opinion, I left the pocket too soon," Graham said. "I came off, and Paul sent [backup quarterback] George Ratterman in the game. I was on the bench, and Paul turns to an assistant coach and says, 'Now, at least we have a quarterback in the game with enough guts to stay in the pocket.' I could have killed him. I would have shot him if I had a gun. But I will say this, I went back in the game a few plays later and vowed to myself that I would not leave that pocket if they tore my head off.

"He knew when to kick you in the butt, and he got me fired up. Paul was a very good leader. He was the kind of guy who would have been an admiral in the navy or a general in the army. I always told people that I loved the guy 90 percent of the time and hated his guts 10 percent of the time."

As when Brown insisted, in 1951, that he start calling the plays, taking the responsibility from Graham. Graham didn't like it and occasionally changed the play call, but he didn't despise it as much as fans thought.

Players feared Brown, even as they talked tough. After one season, Smith talked with McCormack and Ray Renfro about changes they felt must be made to win another championship. The latter two suggested they write letters to Brown, and Smith grudgingly agreed. So Smith wrote a letter, outlining ways to improve the Browns. He wrote that six or seven teammates would be doing the same.

"I didn't hear anything back," Smith said, "and on our third day of training camp, I'm walking back to the locker room and Paul walks up and starts grinning and says, 'Your letter is the only one I ever got.' I said, 'What! Those sorry guys.'"

Another time, Wooten injured an ankle playing basketball the day after a game. Teammates told him to tell Brown he injured it in a game, but Wooten opted for honesty. He hobbled into Brown's office, using a golf club as a crutch, and told him the story. Then Brown sent him to the trainer's room, and Wooten figured he was home free. Until he got into the meeting and Brown, in front of the team, informed Wooten that if he couldn't play Sunday, he wouldn't be paid. Wooten embarked on a miraculous recovery that included sticking his foot in water while electrodes were shot underwater and rubbing a pop bottle all night long over his ankle, a remedy passed down from his mother who swore that it loosened up the tear. By Friday, Wooten had recovered.

"To this day, in the morning when I get up, you'd think I was a cripple," he said. "But I played that Sunday. . . . Paul was tough. Every player should have to play one year under Paul."

He expected players to play with pain. During one game, tackle Dick Schafrath recalled receiver Gern Nagler telling Brown his nose was broken. Brown's response: "Get back in the game!" He ordered someone to wrap tape around Nagler's head, covering his nose. Nagler raced back onto the field.

Negotiating contracts proved painful, too. This was a business to Brown—he often said before games, "I hope you're ready to play for your financial lives"—which he reminded those who dared ask for a raise.

"When I signed with Paul, he felt that $1,000 was $10 million," Hickerson said. "I can't knock Art [Modell]. When he took over, that's when our salaries increased."

"In 1956, I led the NFL in punt returns," Konz said. "So I went in to ask for a raise and Paul says, 'That's what I'm already paying you to do.'"

Word of Brown's tactics spread through the league, and out-of-town writers, especially in New York, labeled the felt hat-wearing Brown "cold and brutal." Part of the problem, Graham said, is that when an out-of-town writer would try to get a comment from Brown, the reporter would start by saying, "You don't know me . . ." And Brown would say, "You're right." Then keep walking.

Brown didn't believe in motivating players through rah-rah speeches. He viewed that as a weapon of the unprepared. Brown's teams rarely, if ever, were caught unprepared. He prepared to the tiniest detail, lecturing his players on the proper way to do calisthenics, telling them that jumping jacks were done with arms raised, over the head, and a side-straddle hop. He even dictated how they should run.

Practices were short and crisp under Brown. During two-a-days, Smith said they'd practice for fifty-five minutes in the morning and an hour in the afternoon. During the season, they were on the field for exactly one hour and twelve minutes. They rarely, if ever, scrimmaged. Brown never wavered from his routine.

"If you went back to one of his camps," McCormack said, "on the second day of the second week at 10:00 A.M., and you walked on the field, Paul Brown would be doing the same thing. You got so comfortable with that, and you believed that was the way to win, because of his record.

"Lombardi's way was to work you so hard and prepare you so hard that the only reason you would lose is because the clock ran out on you. With Paul, you just had confidence in what you were doing and how you had been prepared."

One of the players' first acts of training camp was to fill out their playbook. Today, playbooks are filled out for the players. Brown, though, felt his way helped his team learn the plays as well as their teammates' assignments on a particular play. After a week, Brown would test them on the plays. Quarterback Stan Heath once struggled to fill out the playbook, leaving it blank. So Brown cut him.

"Stan was a gifted quarterback," Michaels said. "But Paul said, 'We can't have a man, especially at the quarterback position, who tests like this.' And Paul would look at our books and see how neat we were diagramming the plays. He said it reflects your personality."

Fullback Jim Brown created a stir with a 1964 book in which he said players cheated on the play tests. Paul Brown, in his autobiography, said it didn't matter. To him, repetition was learning, and even if the players were somehow cheating, they still were digesting the plays.

Jim Brown and Paul Brown clashed during their six seasons together, which led to Modell firing Paul Brown after the 1962 season. Jim Brown later said while he had problems with his coach, he, and other disgruntled teammates—notably Bernie Parrish—wanted to work them out with him. But Modell told him he would take care of it. Then he fired Brown.

The bigger clash had been between Modell and Brown. Modell had purchased the team, in 1961, and wanted to be a hands-on owner. Brown wasn't used to an owner hanging around and bristled at Modell's presence. When he fired Brown, much was made of a team revolt. But that might not have been the case.

"We definitely wanted Paul to open up the offense," Jim Brown said in a 1989 book. "But we wanted *Paul* to do something about it. . . . But it's not as if Paul and I were constantly at war. At the end of Paul's reign, we clearly had some problems. They were football problems, disagreements on technique, strategy, winning. Man to man, though, in the six years I played for Paul, he only disappointed me once."

That came during a 1959 game against the Giants when Brown was kicked in the head during a pileup. He struggled to remember the plays and asked quarterback Milt Plum to point out his assignments. Eventually, Plum called time out and told Paul Brown to take out Jim Brown. He did. But at halftime, Paul Brown reminded his star that another teammate had gotten hurt but was back in the game.

Brown returned but later called it his low point under Paul Brown. The two mended their relationship, however, in 1982, when they bumped into one another at the Super Bowl. Jim Brown later played at some of Paul Brown's golf tournaments.

For as much as Paul Brown worked, and berated, his players, most enjoyed playing for him, even as he bruised their egos.

Art Modell, left, Jim Brown, and Paul Brown showed unity in this May 1962 picture, but within a year, Paul Brown was fired.

"I'm glad I came into the league with Paul Brown," running back Bobby Mitchell said. "I needed the father figure, the disciplinarian and a man who believed in family, who said how you should treat your wife and kids. I hear a a lot of stuff about Paul, that he was this or that. But he was an innovator, and he made great ballplayers out of a lot of guys who wouldn't have been that good. I go back to the success of his players away from the field, what he taught us and the manner in which he taught it, and you go all over the country and these guys are doing things he taught them."

Guys like Graham and McCormack and Groza stayed in touch with Brown, who died in 1991. They appreciated his loyalty. When Smith was inducted into the College Football Hall of Fame in the mid-1980s, Brown attended the ceremony, much to Smith's surprise.

"He said, 'When one of my boys has honors like this, I want to be here,'" Smith recalled.

The words touched Smith.

Other words didn't affect him as greatly, but they certainly remain with him. They capture Brown's essence.

"He demanded perfection," Smith said. "He would say, 'This is a business, this is my business.' And you didn't mess with his livelihood."

3 Lou Groza
Tackle/Kicker, 1946–1959, 1961–1967
Numbers 46/76

Lou Groza hopped off the plane in the Phillipines, scared but ready for his first taste of World War II combat. He quickly learned about life in the war. And it wasn't pretty. Moments after stepping off the plane, a soldier within a first down of Groza was shot in the face. Groza witnessed the damage.

"His face was shattered," Groza recalled. "Then someone started going through his wallet and taking the cash out. I thought, 'What kind of animal would do that?'"

He learned war bred many animals during his two years as a surgical technician. The unit he was with set up tents about five miles from the front line and assisted the doctors.

"You were more concerned about not getting run over by the Japanese," said Groza, who also served in Okinawa. "We couldn't run away. If we had wounded, we had to stay with them. I saw a lot of men wounded with severe injuries. Loose legs, guts hanging out, stuff like that. It's a tough thing, but you get hardened to it, and you accept it as part of your being there."

After that experience, kicking a football doesn't seem so difficult. Maybe that's why Groza did it so well and never seemed to be nervous. Certainly, he didn't appear that way when he kicked the game-winning sixteen-yard field goal in Cleveland's first NFL championship in 1950. Nor did he seem that way seventeen years later when he was still booting the ball through the uprights.

Of course, that wasn't all he did. Groza started at left tackle for twelve seasons until first retiring, after 1959, because of a bad back. When he returned, in 1961, Groza only kicked. But he never considered himself only a kicker.

"I went to the Hall of Fame as a tackle," he said.

Added Paul Brown, in his autobiography, "He's in the Hall of Fame as much for his play as a lineman as for his placekicking."

But kicking is what got Groza noticed. And noticed. Even Groza understood that the guys who scored got the press. When he retired for good in '67, no one had scored more. He finished with a then record 1,349 points. His four seasons in the All-America Football Conference increased his total to 1,608. The more he scored,

the more people watched him. The more they watched, the more they liked his entire game.

The folks in Martins Ferry, Ohio, couldn't have been surprised. After all, Groza was just doing what he had done as a kid. He led Martins Ferry to the state basketball title in 1941 and was named all-state in football and basketball. And he captained both those teams as well as the baseball team, earning the nickname "Big Chief."

As a kid, Groza hung around his older brother Frank, fetching the footballs Frank used to boot. Soon Frank Groza taught his younger brother how to kick.

"I used to get a kick out of kicking the ball over the telephone wires when we would play touch football in the street," Groza said. "I liked to see how far I could make it go."

Turns out his kicks went pretty far, especially once he went to Ohio State. There, he played three games on the freshman team—kicking five field goals, including a forty-five-yarder—and would cause eyes to widen when he kicked. Two of those eyes belonged to Buckeye coach Paul Brown.

"We would practice away from the varsity field, and our field was right below [Ohio] Stadium where they had the training room," Groza said. "I kept noticing that [Brown] would look out the window."

He must have seen something he liked. Groza left for the war the next year, but Brown would send him footballs to stay sharp. In jungle clearings, Groza and his war buddies would kick the footballs, wearing out several balls. But Groza said he didn't think he was preparing himself for pro ball.

Rather, he planned to return to Ohio State. However, by the time he was discharged, his class had graduated and he was twenty-two. Brown also was gone, headed to Cleveland to start his new team. So Groza signed a contract with Paul Brown and the Browns two days after he was discharged in February 1946. Groza eventually earned his degree from Ohio State.

Brown may have known Groza could kick far, but even he was surprised to see the rookie, then just a kicker, warming up on the sidelines every time Cleveland crossed midfield.

"You don't think you can kick one from there, do you?" Brown asked him.

"I think I can," Groza answered.

Then Groza showed he could, drilling field goals from forty-nine, fifty-one, and fifty yards, the latter in a driving rainstorm in Miami. Writers started calling him "Groza the Toe-Za" which soon became the more famous "Lou the Toe."

"From that time on," Brown said in his book, "he was always a great potential weapon when we were inside an opponent's 49-yard line. I know that Lou won more games in clutch situations with his kicking than any player in the game's history."

No one did it better during most of Groza's career. The straight-on kicker retired

Lou Groza attempting
a field goal

as the NFL's all-time leading scorer, a mark since broken. But he still holds the record for extra points (641) and extra-point attempts (658).

In 1953, Groza made 88.5 percent of his field goals (twenty-three of twenty-six)—at a time when 53 percent was the average. That mark remained the best mark in pro football history until Washington's Mark Moseley made 95.2 percent of his kicks in 1982.

Groza's mark is more astounding considering the conditions in which he kicked. Much wider hash marks provided harsh angles to the uprights, which were at the front of the end zone, no domes existed during his career, and defenders could be hoisted on teammates' shoulders to try to block the kick.

Plus, Groza doubled as a tackle, a position he moved into full time in 1948. He did so with one year of college ball, interrupted by three years of service, and only two years of pro ball. But he excelled, making nine Pro Bowls.

At tackle, his right foot was fair game for opponents.

"Guys would yell out, 'Step on Groza's foot!'" he recalled. "We were playing the Lions once, and the guy I was playing against was going back to the line of scrimmage after a play. He came over and stomped on my foot in the huddle and ran back to the line of scrimmage laughing."

Groza usually had the last laugh. In 1948, the Los Angeles Dons' Lee Artoe hit Groza's nose on the game's first play. On the next play, Groza nailed Artoe in the face, slamming into the mask he was wearing to protect him and cutting his chin.

Groza's best asset was his speed, as the 255-pounder ran the forty-yard dash in 4.8 seconds, making him effective in pulling situations and lead flips. His wit was just as fast. Even now, when reminded he was fast, Groza said, straight-faced, "Oh, I thought you meant with the girls."

But a back injury nearly ended his career in 1960. A year later, thanks to the rival AFL, the NFL rosters expanded, allowing teams to carry specialists. Groza was working with the Browns' kickers when owner Art Modell asked if he could still kick. Groza said yes. Brown was convinced, and Groza returned for another seven years, even making the game-winning kick in his first game back at Municipal Stadium to beat St. Louis. However, Dick Schafrath had replaced him at tackle.

By this time, Groza had become a successful insurance agent as well. While others would head out for a beer after practice in training camp, he would return to his room to check on business. In 1998, Groza still was selling insurance.

He also became a father figure to many of the players and often would invite the younger guys to his Berea home for dinner. They remembered his practical jokes—like dead rats in teammates' shoes—but also his lessons.

"He preached to all the players, 'When a kid asks you for an autograph, you better give it to him. If not, I'll make you do it,'" said guard Jim Ray Smith. "He believed that you meet the same people on the way up that you do on the way down, and you want to make sure you have a good relationship with them."

Groza, whose jersey number 76 is retired by the Browns, might not be the greatest Brown of all time, but he might be the most significant. Consider: He's the only Brown to play in all thirteen of their championship games, including four in the AAFC and nine in the NFL. And he was the only one to play with, or for, twelve of Cleveland's thirteen Hall of Famers.

Groza's touch even extended into the 1970s and '80s as he recommended the Browns draft a tight end from Illinois named Doug Dieken and move him to tackle.

"When you talk about the ambassador of Cleveland Browns football, it's Lou," Dieken said. "It's an honor to be around him."

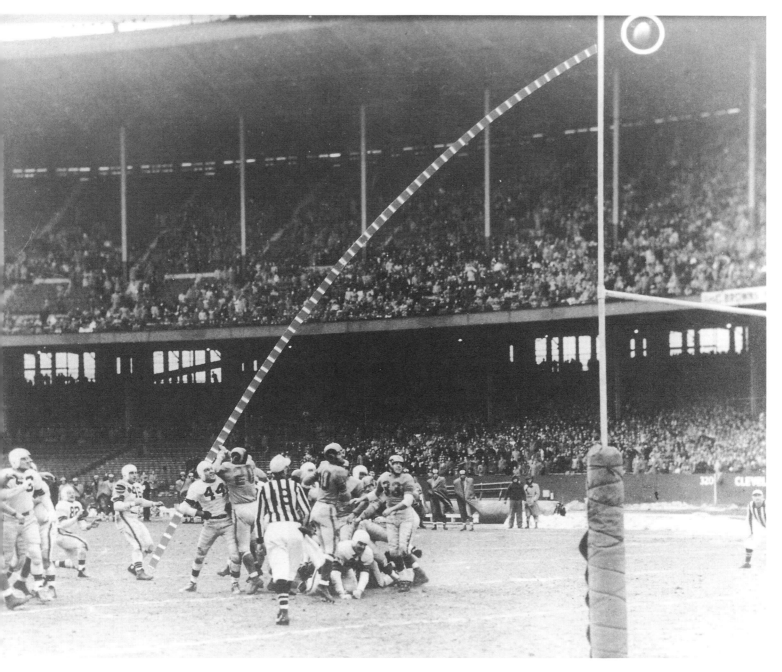

Lou Groza kicks the game-winning field goal with twenty seconds remaining in the Browns' first-ever NFL title game.

4 **New League, Old Result**
1950 NFL Championship

Browns 30, Rams 28
December 24, 1950

 The ball squirted out, rolled around on the frozen ground, and was smothered by the defense. And quarterback Otto Graham walked off the field, his heart dropping, his confidence, not to mention the Browns' title hopes, fading with each step. A blindsided hit had jarred the ball from his hands. But Graham could clearly see what would happen next: Los Angeles would win the NFL championship.

Those who had snickered at Cleveland's entry into the NFL would be redeemed. And Graham retreated to the bench, where he figured he'd watch the Rams run out the final three minutes for a 28–27 win. His shoulders sagged.

Graham was one of eleven original Browns who endured four years of the All-America Conference, waiting for this chance. They put up with the wisecracks and insults and disrespect from dozens in the NFL. This was their opportunity to silence every critic once and for all, some of whom remained even after a 10–2 regular season.

And Graham fumbled the ball. Now he shouldered the blame for an apparent loss. Time remained; hope didn't, at least for Graham.

"I've been dejected before," Graham said. "But I've never been that dejected. I had cancer about twenty years ago, and it was life-threatening. I assure you I didn't feel half as badly when I learned that as I did when I dropped that ball. I thought, 'Here we are, in the NFL, playing in the championship game and Graham, you blew it.' If I could have found a hole, I would have crawled in and hid."

Instead, he found himself standing next to coach Paul Brown, whose famous stare could melt hardened souls and whose biting comments could shrivel large men in a matter of seconds, making molehills out of mountainous egos.

Brown, though, had no such things to say to Graham. For some reason, Brown still felt good. So he patted his quarterback on the shoulder and delivered a line Graham hasn't shaken to this day, "Don't worry, Otts, we're still going to get them."

Suddenly, Graham snapped to attention. The bad feelings fled his body, and a shot of adrenaline surged through when the defense stopped the NFL's best offense in three plays, forcing a punt.

Then Graham charged back onto the field. Then he led the charge down it, driving hard toward the goal line, knowing he had football's best clutch kicker on his side. Knowing that once the Browns crossed the fifty yard line, tackle-placekicker Lou Groza became football's best weapon. Knowing they still could win one of the most entertaining games in NFL history.

For four years, Brown had prepared to beat the NFL while leading Cleveland to championships in the AAFC. More than a year before the merger, Brown had tinkered with alignments that might pose problems for NFL teams. But he never uttered a word about the NFL to his players. Didn't have to. Instead, he posted newspaper clippings on the bulletin board, full of stories poking fun at their league.

"They were saying we were a minor league," Groza said.

After the AAFC was formed, NFL commissioner Elmer Layden, when asked if the NFL would play any games against these new teams, cracked, "What new league? Let them go get a football first and then play a game."

Brown remembered that comment. He never forgot this one, too, from Eagles coach Greasy Neale shortly after the merger between the leagues: "We don't want Cleveland to win, because it will make the NFL look bad." Neale's NFL brethren shared notes on the Browns, conspiring to beat them.

Neale stoked Brown's internal fire even more when he said no team from the AAFC could match his Eagles, which won the '49 title. And Neale insisted on sticking the needle in even more by saying the Browns' passing attack would be no match for his defense when they met in the season opener as the NFL paired the champions from both leagues. Brown was ready for this debut and wanted to be an instant success. That's why he sent letters to all his players in the off-season, asking them to report to camp in top shape, ready for the battles ahead.

The Browns would be a primary target, just like in the AAFC. No one could derail Cleveland in the AAFC, as the Browns won all four league titles. In one twenty-nine-game stretch from 1947 to 1949, Cleveland went 25–0–2 and won eighteen straight. The Browns lost only four times in four years. Their dominance buried the league as attendance dwindled, even in Cleveland. In 1946, the Browns drew five crowds of fifty-seven thousand or more. In 1949, they attracted five crowds of thirty thousand or less.

The rest of the league couldn't match Cleveland's success. It wasn't enough for Brown. The goal was getting to the NFL, where four straight league championships meant zilch. When the players finally reported to camp in 1950, Brown reminded them of the mud slung in their direction.

"Our players were so keyed up," Brown later said, "they were ready to tear into it when training camp opened."

They didn't do it with rah-rah practices. In the week leading up to the first game in Philadelphia, Brown remembered an eerie quiet settling in during practices. Perhaps even Brown didn't realize how affected they were by four years of disrespect.

"After four years of reading this stuff," Graham said, "I assure you, there's never been a team in the history of sports that was better prepared emotionally to play a game than we were. We could have played them for a keg of beer or, in my case, a chocolate milk shake, just to prove we were a good team."

They proved it all right. And it didn't take long. The Browns grabbed a 7–3 lead late in the first quarter, built it to 14–3 at halftime, and rolled. Cleveland won, 35–14, shocking, and impressing, Neale.

"It was like taking candy from a baby," Graham said.

The rest of the league noticed, but there wasn't much they could do as only the New York Giants beat the Browns. But they did it twice. The Browns would have to beat the Giants in a play-off after both finished 10–2 in the American Conference.

The Browns won, thanks to two Groza field goals, the second coming with fifty-eight seconds remaining, snapping a 3–3 tie. A late safety provided the Browns an 8–3 victory. But it was middle guard Bill Willis who saved the game for Cleveland. Late in the game, Giants running back Gene "Choo Choo" Roberts, his team trailing 3–0, broke through the middle from the Browns' forty-seven and sped on the frozen turf toward the end zone. Willis shot out of nowhere and tackled Roberts at the four. The defense held, and New York settled for a field goal. That finish set a tone that would carry the Browns one week later.

The drama was set before the kickoff. The franchise that had bolted Cleveland five years earlier for Los Angeles, five weeks after winning a championship, had returned to play once more for a title. It didn't matter that only three players, including quarterback Bob Waterfield, had even played in Cleveland. This game was an easy sell. The old Cleveland team versus the new one, playing in only its first NFL season. But it wasn't the only angle.

The Rams had one of the NFL's best-ever offenses, scoring 466 regular-season points—an NFL record until 1981—while posting a 9–3 record. They had receiver Tom Fears and his eighty-four catches, an NFL record until 1964; they had the quarterback tandem of Waterfield and Norm Van Brocklin and their combined twenty-nine touchdown passes; they had Elroy Hirsch and Glenn Davis, both with forty-two catches; and they had five players who could run the 100-yard dash in under ten seconds.

Cleveland, though, had allowed the second fewest points in the league. Still, many wondered if the Browns had enough talent to win. Or, rather, maybe they hoped the Browns didn't have enough.

"A lot of people still doubted us," receiver Dante Lavelli said.

The weather certainly helped the Browns. A light rain and temperatures rising to 29 degrees slightly thawed the field, which had frozen to a depth of six inches. But it was still a mess, and Cleveland's players decided to wear sneakers instead of cleats, just like the previous week. Only four Rams wore sneakers, however.

"If you wore spikes, it was like wearing golf spikes on a marble floor," Graham said. "There was no traction at all. The rumor going around for years and years was that Paul Brown had someone contact all the sporting goods stores in Ohio saying, 'Don't sell any tennis shoes to the Rams.' I doubt very much if it's true, but it's a good rumor."

Actually, the Rams had more sneakers. They just didn't want to wear them.

"We often wondered if we were right, because all the Browns wore them," Fears later said.

But one play into the game, no one thought that put them at a disadvantage. On Los Angeles's first play, Waterfield sent Fears on a decoy route across the middle, keeping Davis in the backfield for an extra second. When Fears drew attention from the linebackers, Davis released and caught a pass wide open at the Rams' forty-five. No one caught him, and Davis easily completed an eighty-two-yard touchdown. One of the sneaker-wearing defensive backs, Tommy James, slipped in pursuit.

The lead didn't last long as Graham led a six-play drive, running for twenty-one yards and completing three passes, including a thirty-one-yard touchdown toss to receiver Dub Jones. But the tie didn't last long, either, as Waterfield needed only eight plays to snap it, handing to fullback Dick Hoerner for the final yard and 14–7 first-quarter lead.

But on this frigid day, in front of 29,751 fans, no advantage was safe. And all leads were quickly erased. This time, the Browns used their own decoy, receiver Mac Speedie. He had pulled a muscle three days earlier, but only Cleveland knew of the injury. All Los Angeles knew was that Speedie was dangerous.

Besides, if they knew anything about Speedie's background, they would know he wouldn't succumb to a leg injury. As a child, he had a problem that made his left leg an inch shorter and two inches smaller in diameter than his right leg. But he refused to use crutches or wear a brace and spent his childhood doing whatever his friends did. He could ignore a little pain in a championship game.

On the Browns' second scoring drive, Graham passed to Speedie, drawing an interference penalty. Then he hit Speedie for seventeen yards to the Rams' twenty-six. Now, with Los Angeles paying attention to Speedie, who would not play in the second half, Lavelli sneaked behind the secondary and grabbed a scoring pass. Cleveland couldn't tie the game as Hal Herring's snap was high to holder Tommy James.

"When the ball was snapped, the wind caught it, and Tommy had to jump up to grab it," Groza recalled.

Quarterback Otto Graham ran for twelve yards and a first down on this first-quarter run, but it was his passing that led Cleveland to victory.

James managed a pass to Tony Adamle, but Adamle stumbled and dropped the pass in the end zone. Los Angeles then took control. But the Rams couldn't score despite twice driving deep into Browns territory. The blown chances would haunt them. On the first series, safety Ken Gorgal intercepted Waterfield inside the ten. One possession later, Waterfield missed a fifteen-yard field goal.

The Browns made those mistakes hurt. They started it on defense, and they got a boost when end Len Ford entered the game late in the first half. Ford had not played since October 15 because of a broken jaw and had regained only twenty-five of the forty pounds he had lost. Brown did not expect much from Ford, but the defense was playing poorly and needed something.

Ford immediately provided momentum. In consecutive plays, Ford nailed Verda T. "Vitamin T" Smith for a fourteen-yard loss; sacked Waterfield for eleven more yards; and tackled Davis for another thirteen in arrears.

Then the offense clicked, and Graham passed to Lavelli for a thirty-nine-yard touchdown and 20–14 lead early in the third quarter. But Los Angeles answered, stunning the Browns with two touchdowns in twenty-five seconds. Waterfield picked apart the Cleveland defense through the air, completing three passes, the last of which resulted in a thirty-eight-yard gain to the Browns' seventeen. Seven Hoerner runs later, Los Angeles led, 21–20.

More trouble followed on the first play after the kickoff. Marion Motley, one of the few Browns who wore cleats, tried to reverse his field on a handoff and raced thirteen yards back to the seven where he bobbled the ball and fumbled. Los Angeles end Larry Brink picked it up and scored. Motley's biggest role in this game was keeping pass rushers off Graham with his blocking. But the fumble annoyed Brown.

"Marion told me he could run all right in cleats," Brown said after the game. "There was nothing I could do. I think he'd have been much better off in basketball shoes."

The Browns weren't finished, and when cornerback Warren Lahr intercepted Waterfield near the end of the third quarter, they embarked on one of the most clutch drives in their history. At least until later in the game.

Graham and Lavelli connected for five passes, including a seven-yarder on fourth and four, pushing the ball to the Los Angeles forty-seven. Later, on another fourth down, Graham snuck forward for three yards and a first down. Then, eight plays later, running back Rex Bumgardner, his arms fully extended and his body falling forward, hauled in Graham's fourteen-yard pass to cut the score to 28–27.

Could they top this drive? They would have to. After picking apart the Rams' defense through the air, Graham took off on a seven-yard run. But it ended in disaster at the Los Angeles twenty-four when a defender nailed Graham from the blind side, jarring the ball loose. When Milan Lazetich, a former Cleveland Ram, recovered, Graham figured he had cost the Browns the game. Until Paul Brown predicted he would get another chance.

"I had seen us battle harder in this game than any Browns team had ever battled before," Brown said in his autobiography. "I was completely confident we could still win and I wanted Otto feeling the same way when we got the ball back for him."

He did. When the Browns returned to the field, Graham was energized. He ran for fourteen yards to the Cleveland forty-six. From there, Graham completed passes to Bumgardner, Jones, and Bumgardner again, good for a combined forty-three yards to the Rams' twelve. Forty-one seconds remained when Graham called time.

Offensive assistant Blanton Collier didn't like the ball's placement on the left hash mark. So when Brown asked for his input, Collier didn't hesitate. Run a sneak toward the middle, he yelled. Then Collier sweated.

"In the next few seconds, I aged a hundred years," he later said. "I just called a running play from automatic field-goal range. What if there had been a fumble?"

Linebacker Tony Adamle, right,
eagerly awaited Groza's kick.

There wasn't. Graham fell down in the middle for a yard, and the sideline celebrated as the offense left the field and the field-goal team entered. Brown shouted, "Stop it!" But he understood their excitement. He knew there wasn't a better clutch kicker than Groza.

Groza lined up, closed his ears to the noise—and chants of "Lou! Lou!"—and whipped his right leg through the ball. He sent the ball through the uprights with twenty seconds to play.

"I just lined up for the kick and kicked it," Groza said. "I didn't get rattled about it. I never thought I'd miss any kick. [But] what made it tough was that I had a tennis shoe on my left foot and a football shoe on my right, and I took the cleats off the bottom so it had a flat sole. I felt like a cat where you put paper on his paws and he's trying to walk around. It was a funny sensation."

Followed by one of ecstasy.

But the Rams still had one more chance. They returned the kickoff to the forty-six, and on first down, Van Brocklin heaved a pass for Davis, the famed Heisman Trophy winner with incredible speed, inside the Cleveland ten. It never reached him. Lahr hauled in the interception at the five and his momentum, in addition to Davis, carried him into the end zone, causing anxious moments for the Browns.

"Sometimes officials make horrible mistakes," said Graham, who completed twenty-two of thirty-three passes for 298 yards and four touchdowns. He also ran twelve times for ninety-eight yards. "That official could have ruled it a safety and given them two points which would have tied the game."

But he didn't, and it ended the game, prompting thousands of fans to storm the field, including a young Don Shula who watched from the bleachers and would be drafted by Cleveland a year later.

The Browns hustled to the locker room, where they gathered for pictures and watched Groza kiss his muddy shoe for photographers. Two days later he would be driven around his hometown of Martins Ferry, Ohio, in a fire engine. NFL Commissioner Bert Bell entered the locker room and told Brown, "You are the greatest team ever to play football." Years later, Brown still called this the greatest victory he'd ever seen, in part because eleven future Hall of Famers participated.

And also because of the path Cleveland traveled. They had wiped out any doubts about their standing in the league. The AAFC jokes vanished, replaced by awe.

But Graham knew how close they had come to finishing with nothing but heartache. With nearly fifty years to reflect, he still returns to the seconds after he fumbled the football. A pat on the shoulder and a few words changed his outlook, restored confidence to his voice and more. One moment altered a championship.

"If Paul Brown had not done that," Graham said, "we would have lost the game."

	1	2	3	4	Total
Rams	14	0	14	0	28
Browns	7	6	7	10	30

FIRST QUARTER
LA - Davis 82 pass from Waterfield (Waterfield kick). Rams, 7–0
C - Jones 31 pass from Graham (Groza kick). Tie, 7–7
LA - Hoerner 3 run (Waterfield kick). Rams, 14–7

SECOND QUARTER
C - Lavelli 26 pass from Graham (kick failed). Rams, 14–13

THIRD QUARTER
C - Lavelli 39 pass from Graham (Groza kick). Browns, 20–14
LA - Hoerner 1 run (Waterfield kick). Rams, 21–20
LA - Brink 6 return of fumble (Waterfield kick). Rams, 28–20

FOURTH QUARTER
C - Bumgardner 14 pass from Graham (Groza kick). Rams, 28–27
C - Groza 16 FG. Browns, 30–28

5 **Marion Motley**
Fullback, 1946–1953

Numbers 76/36

He saved touchdowns one series and his quarterback's behind the next. He ran for long touchdowns and short ones—in the same game. He had sprinter's speed crammed in a lineman's body. And when he retired, Marion Motley set a standard for a Paul Brown fullback, one that even Jim Brown couldn't match.

Motley also set a standard for any player. Even now, some longtime NFL observers consider him perhaps the best ever to play the game. That's because Motley could swallow running backs while playing linebacker and pound through offenses as a runner.

"He is the greatest fullback ever," Paul Brown said after a 1946 game in which Motley rushed for 133 yards and three touchdowns.

His opinion didn't change even after coaching Jim Brown.

"If Jim had worked on his blocking," Brown later said, "he would have been as great as Motley."

Sports Illustrated's Paul Zimmerman went a step further. In his book, *A Thinking Man's Guide to Pro Football,* Zimmerman called Motley (who, in 1968, became the first black elected into the Pro Football Hall of Fame) the greatest player ever. He based his reasoning on Motley's play at linebacker, especially his first two seasons in the All-America Football Conference when he started at that position. But he continued to play linebacker in the NFL as well in that era of small rosters.

Philadelphia quickly learned of Motley's defensive prowess. In the Browns' first NFL game, the Eagles had first and goal at the six. On first down, they tried a smash up the middle. Motley stopped them. So the Eagles ran the same play. Motley stuffed it again. Philadelphia didn't learn. The Eagles ran the play twice more, getting stopped by Motley on both occasions. Four plays gained three yards.

When Motley ended his career with Pittsburgh, in 1955, it was as a linebacker.

"I've always believed," Brown said, "that Motley could have gone into the Hall of Fame solely as a linebacker if we had used him only at that position. He was as good as our great ones."

Of course, his name was made on offense. There, Motley gained 4,712 yards in eight seasons and averaged 5.7 yards per carry. In the AAFC, Motley gained 6.2

yards every time he ran, including an 8.23 yards average in 1946. Motley is the last player to lead the NFL in rushing with 140 or fewer carries, a feat he accomplished, in 1950, when he averaged 5.8 yards a pop.

He could run over people and past them. In the navy, Motley routinely raced the world record holder in the 440-yard dash, Grover Klemmer. Over seventy-five yards, Motley was his equal.

"He was pretty big," center Frank Gatski said. "And pretty bad."

While his yardage total isn't spectacular by modern standards, it was huge at the time. It stood out even more considering Motley didn't play pro ball until he was twenty-six.

Brown had known about him for years, dating back to their days as rivals with Motley at Canton McKinley High School and Brown at Massillon. After that, Motley played at the University of Nevada, where he also ran track and threw the javelin. He even boxed in college, losing his only bout in the Reno Golden Gloves.

Football was his calling, and Motley wound up playing for Brown at the Great Lakes Naval Training Center during World War II. But after the war, Motley, married with four kids, took a job in a mill near his hometown of Canton.

When he heard about the new league, Motley wrote Brown for a tryout. Brown said no, they already had enough backs. However, Bill Willis, the first black to play for the Browns, reported for a tryout, and ten days later Motley was invited to do the same. "I think they felt [Willis] needed a roommate," Motley often said. "I don't think they felt I'd make the team. I'm glad I was able to fool them."

Brown, though, later said that he knew all along that he wanted these two players. But he wanted to avoid a media frenzy during training camp because of the racial issue and waited until the last possible minute to sign them. No matter. Motley only wanted a chance.

"I knew this was the one big chance in my life to rise above the steel mill existence, and I really wanted to take it," Motley said in the book, *Great Teams, Great Years: Cleveland Browns.* "I had no doubt that I could make the team because I had played against some of the best competition around during the war and I measured up pretty well."

Brown said, "No other pro football team was interested in him at the time. That was their loss. No one ever cared more about his team and whether it won or lost, rather than how many yards he gained or where he was asked to run."

Joe Spencer, who played with Motley, in 1949, remembered one day counting his pennies and trying to figure out the cheapest way to get home from practice. Suddenly, Motley, by this time a star, pulled up and said two words, "Get in." After that, every day they rode together.

But life wasn't always a smooth ride for Motley, who dealt with his share of racism on and off the field.

"My hands were always bloody," Motley said in the book, *Iron Men.* "But if either Willis or myself had been hotheads and gotten into fights and things like that, it would have put things back 10 years. Sometimes I wanted to just kill some of those guys, and the officials would just stand right there. They'd see those guys stepping on us and heard them saying things and just turn their backs. That kind of crap went on for two or three years until they found out what kind of players we were. They found out that while they were calling us, 'niggers,' I was running for touchdowns and Willis was knocking the shit out of them."

Motley did his share of knocking as well, especially against the blitz, which endeared him to Brown, not to mention quarterback Otto Graham. Defenders weren't too thrilled with this ability, since it meant crashing into the six-foot-one, 238-pound Motley. The Browns often let Motley handle defensive ends by himself.

"Motley really built the passing attack for the Browns because of his blocking," receiver Dante Lavelli said.

"You rush Graham," San Francisco end Gail Bruce said in *Iron Men*, "and put on a move and beat your man and there's Motley waiting for you. Next play, you beat your man with a different move and there's Motley, waiting again. Pretty soon you say, 'The hell with it. I'd rather stand on the line and battle the first guy.'"

Motley's runs are legendary, handed down from generation to generation. They sound exaggerated. They weren't. The Hall of Fame has one film in which Motley grabs a swing pass, barrels over players down the sideline, loses his helmet, and keeps running.

In a 1950 home game against Pittsburgh, Motley gained 188 yards on eleven carries. On one long run, Lavelli remembers that, "Eleven guys had a shot at him and no one brought him down." Tackle Lou Groza understood what the Pittsburgh defenders were going through.

"We were scrimmaging [in 1946], and I tackled Marion head-on," Groza said. "Have you ever gotten hit where you saw a big flash? From that point on, instead of hitting him head-on, I tried to tackle him from the side. He was a load and he was fast."

The trap became Motley's play, but the draw became his legacy. In one 1946 game, Graham got in trouble in the backfield after colliding with Motley. The defenders charged at Graham, so he flipped the ball to Motley, who ran through an open hole for pro football's first draw play. Brown quickly worked this into his game plan.

"When he got up a head of steam, he was going to run over everybody," linebacker Walt Michaels said. "He was very tough. The difference between him and Jim Brown, in all fairness Marion had spent years in the service. Jim had about five years of get up and go that Marion didn't have. Marion was beat on in the service. There's a difference when you're going into your tenth year at age thirty-five and going into your tenth year at age thirty or thirty-one."

But Motley remained a force late in his career. Dick "Night Train" Lane, a Los Angeles Rams defensive back, said he'll never forget his first encounter with Motley in 1952.

"He looked like a big tank rolling down on me," Lane said. "But you've got to take him on. I hit him with my head in his knees, and he came down. I saw a few stars, but I felt good because I tackled Marion Motley."

6 **Bill Willis**
Middle Guard, 1946–1953

Numbers 60/45/30

Quarterbacks changed their stance and centers hurried their snaps. Or complained to the officials. Running backs learned to fear this lineman's speed, even when they appeared safe. Just ask New York's Gene "Choo-Choo" Roberts. On a frozen field, in a 1950 play-off game, Roberts eyed the end zone on a breakaway run. Suddenly, four yards shy of a touchdown, a defensive lineman dragged down the Giants' fastest back. Middle guard Bill Willis just happened to be faster.

It was his quickness that riled centers and helped him become a Hall of Famer. At 214 pounds, Willis had to be quicker. The Browns boasted in their media guide that when Willis shot out of his crouch, he was moving at seventy miles per hour.

"No one could block him," receiver Dante Lavelli said. "He was across the line before the other guy was making the blocks."

It didn't take long for the Browns to discover that. In Willis's first intrasquad scrimmage with Cleveland, which also happened to be his first day with the Browns, he was matched against center Mo Scarry.

Scarry never had a chance. Willis pounced on Scarry time and again, forcing a bad snap each time. Scarry, starting a trend soon to be followed by other centers, resorted to screaming about offsides. Brown obliged Scarry and checked to make sure Willis wasn't jumping early. He wasn't. Later, Brown asked Willis how he was so disruptive.

"He told me that he watched Mo's hands," Brown said in his autobiography. "As soon as they tightened to snap the ball, he moved. I was so intrigued with this explanation I got right down on my hands and knees along the line of scrimmage to be sure Bill wasn't offsides. He wasn't, but he moved with the ball so quickly, it was hard to determine."

Another time, after Otto Graham arrived in camp, Willis's quickness caused Scarry to snap early then bolt into his pass protection. Graham wasn't used to this and couldn't get away in time. Scarry stepped on his foot, causing Graham to shout in pain.

"In the beginning, he annoyed everybody with his quickness," Lavelli said.

No one more than his opponents. In the 1946 season opener, Brown said the

Miami Seahawks never made a good center exchange because of Willis. Ed McKeever, coach of the All-America Football Conference's Chicago Hornets, once said his staff studied numerous films of Willis and found he followed a set pattern. It didn't help.

"There is no way to beat Bill," McKeever concluded.

Willis forced his own coach to alter his quarterback's stance behind center. Rather than have them parallel to center, Brown made his quarterbacks place one foot slightly behind the other, allowing them to push off quicker from behind center. Soon most teams adopted this stance. The complaining about Willis's being offsides rarely ceased. Occasionally, he would get flagged, but that would make him laugh.

"He would say, 'They just can't see me,'" linebacker Walt Michaels said. "Many times I thought they called him offside simply because he was the first guy to move, but the ball was already snapped."

When Willis retired after the 1953 season, his replacement, Mike McCormack, knew all about him even though they had never played on the same team. McCormack even recalled a photo sequence in a New York paper after a Browns game against the Giants.

The sequence went like this: Willis drove into center John Rapacz and knocked him back; quarterback Charley Connerly bobbled the ball; Willis dropped into coverage; and Willis intercepted the pass.

The thing is, Willis nearly missed out on a Browns career. It had nothing to do with his being black, though he would be the first African-American to play for Cleveland. Rather, Willis, who had spent the previous year as a coach at Kentucky State, had agreed to play for Montreal of the Canadian Football League. He had waited for Brown, his coach at Ohio State, to call when he went to Cleveland.

But Brown waited, later saying he wanted to avoid a training camp media circus because of Willis's race. It nearly cost Brown as Willis initially turned him down. Brown persisted, however, and several phone calls later finally convinced Willis to come for a tryout before heading to Canada, practically guaranteeing him a roster spot. Willis never reached Canada.

The Browns benefited, never more so than in the 1950 play-off game versus New York. The Giants had the ball on the Cleveland thirty-six in the fourth quarter, trailing 3–0, when Roberts broke free, chugging for a killer score. Willis, who ran track at Ohio State and once was one-tenth of a second off the Big Ten record, took off after him.

"I knew it meant the ball game," Willis said the next year. "I just had to catch him. But I didn't think I had him in time. I thought we'd both probably be over the goal line. I just closed my eyes and grabbed for him."

And tackled him, saving a touchdown. Four plays later, the Giants kicked a ty-

Bill Willis

ing field goal, but the Browns went on to win, 8–3. A week later, they won the championship.

It's easy to remember Willis for such standout plays. Also for being a football pioneer as his middle guard spot in the Browns' five-man line evolved into the modern-day middle linebacker. But Willis, as well as teammate Marion Motley, also was a pioneer because of his race. He and Motley played professional football one year before Jackie Robinson broke baseball's color barrier.

"They made it easier for other black players to enter professional football," Brown said.

Not without setbacks, however. Willis and Motley once received threatening letters before a game in Miami, causing both to remain in Cleveland. Another time, quarterback Otto Graham remembered going to a Miami hotel. When a hotel employee spotted Willis and Motley, he said they had to stay elsewhere. So Brown told his team to leave, forcing the hotel to change its policy on the spot. The entire team stayed together. Willis no longer grants interviews, but Lavelli said race wasn't an issue among the team.

"Paul Brown always had blacks on his team [dating to high school]," Lavelli said. "We didn't even notice it."

Brown said he believes his history with blacks persuaded Willis to change his mind about going to Illinois when Brown went to Ohio State. Through it all, Willis impressed everyone, *Cleveland Press* reporter Regis McAuley once wrote, with his, "charm, dignity and social grace."

Perhaps that's why Willis was in demand as a public speaker, often cracking up crowds with his imitation of an announcer calling off the weights of much larger linemen, *Press* columnist Bob August wrote in 1977. When the announcer would get to Willis, some thirty pounds lighter than his counterparts, the announcer would say, "At 214 pounds . . . BIG Bill Willis!"

Willis went on to hold a variety of jobs with the city and later the state. He quit football after being appointed assistant recreation commissioner of Cleveland and eventually served on the Ohio Youth Commission. McAuley even tried, but failed, to persuade Willis to run for mayor of Cleveland.

Those feats added to his already long list of accomplishments. But football put him on the map. Willis's quickness helped put the Browns on the football globe. Despite what McKeever thought, Willis said he never followed a routine, except early in the game. He'd start by testing his opponent's strength.

"Then I like to make contact with the opposing quarterback," Willis said. "Just to let him know I am in the game."

As if they didn't already know.

6 Dante Lavelli
Receiver, 1946–1956

Numbers 56/86

The ball stuck to his fingers, resulting in first downs, touchdowns, and a nickname. "Gluefingers" they called him. The evidence backed it up. Once, receiver Dante Lavelli claims he snagged every pass thrown his way—for the season. No one doubts that it happened.

"I can't remember him dropping a single pass," coach Paul Brown said in his autobiography. "Either in a game or practice. The reason was his great concentration on the ball and the best pair of hands I've ever seen on any receiver. They had an almost liquid softness which seemed to slurp the ball into them. He always seemed to catch every ball that was thrown near him."

Lavelli worked at developing his hands, performing simple tasks that later became the seeds of his success. A young Lavelli would stand outside church after mass, waiting for his friends to arrive so they could go play baseball. To combat boredom, he would toss a ball against the wall and catch the hard return, looking it into his hands.

Other times, he would challenge friends to hit a Ping-Pong ball past him. Lavelli would then snatch it from the air. All the while, he honed his hand-eye coordination. "It makes your hands soft to grab the ball," Lavelli said of his Ping-Pong antics. "The balls are very light, they go in different directions. Try to catch a Ping-Pong ball once."

Those soft hands made him a capable infielder, too. The Detroit Tigers wooed Lavelli after high school, wanting him to play second base in the low minors. He declined. Ohio State was his next stop, after reneging on his decision to attend Notre Dame when Paul Brown went from Massillon to Columbus to coach the Buckeyes. Lavelli figured he would be a running back at OSU. But after one practice, Brown moved him to end. Injuries limited him to three games with the Buckeyes, and World War II ended his college career.

In Europe, Lavelli fought in the Battle of the Bulge and at Bastogne, where dead bodies littered the streets. Lavelli said his squad of twelve was the only one from its platoon to survive the war.

When the war ended, a broke Lavelli again considered signing with Detroit. He

Dante Lavelli

also was drafted by the Cleveland Pipers of the National Basketball Association. Once more, however, Brown induced him to join his team, the Browns of the All-America Conference. A $500.00 bonus convinced Lavelli. Also, he had watched the New York Giants play and saw former OSU teammate Sam Fox play for the Giants.

"He was behind me at Ohio State, and he was starting for the Giants," said Lavelli, whose signing angered OSU officials because he had two years of eligibility remaining. "I said, 'If he can make it, I'll take a shot at it.'"

Lavelli made a wise choice. He became a fixture at right end until he retired following the 1956 season, catching 386 passes, 62 for touchdowns. He grabbed 244 passes, 33 for scores, in his seven NFL seasons. Those numbers are why he landed in the Hall of Fame in 1975.

Lavelli also made a lasting impact in other ways. He says the concept of the NFL Players Association was born in his basement. He and teammates Abe Gibron and George Ratterman and attorney Creighton Miller, a former Browns general manager, would meet on Wednesday nights to discuss their plans. Lavelli once said the players' union idea was why he returned after the 1955 championship.

But pass-catching was his forte. Lavelli and quarterback Otto Graham, along with fellow end Mac Speedie, gave Cleveland one of the best passing combinations ever, first in the AAFC and then the NFL.

The six-foot, 199-pound Lavelli was faster than Speedie, but he used more than feet to get open. He also had smarts and used whatever he could to gain an advantage. Like the goalposts. Sometimes he would cut off a defender by running him into the post.

Twice—against Philadelphia and Pittsburgh—he grabbed the goalpost by his elbow and swung around to change directions on a slippery field and catch a touchdown pass. That trick resulted in the game-winning score with less than a minute remaining against the Eagles in a 21–17 win at home in 1955. On the play, which began at the five yard line, Lavelli, unknown even to Graham, shot toward the post, grabbed it, whirled, and shot toward the right corner—minus the cornerback.

"Dante had great talent for a man of that era," tackle Mike McCormack said. "He always thought he was open, and he would come back to the huddle and say, 'Otts, I was open, I was open.' And you'd look at the film and he wasn't open half as much as he said he was."

Graham said, "Dante's judgment was terrible. If he was one inch off of someone, he would say he's wide open."

Lavelli had a different definition of being open, however. In his mind, if a ball came his way, he would grab it no matter where the defensive back was positioned.

"I would just say, 'Throw the ball near me and I'll get it,'" said Lavelli, who earned his sticky nickname courtesy of Browns radio man Bob Neal. "I was pretty competitive. The best thing is, I could time the jump and I would bounce the ball up in the air and catch it with the other hand. Defenses used to put two guys on me a lot of the time. I'd time my jump and bounce the ball to one side or the other."

If Graham ever got in trouble, Lavelli would bail him out by yelling, "Otto! Otto!" in his high-pitched voice.

"Whenever he got jammed up, he would just listen for me and throw where I was," Lavelli said. "I used to break a lot of patterns that way. Paul Brown wouldn't like it. But when we scored, he'd say it was OK."

Lavelli improvised in an AAFC game against New York. The Yankees' defense anticipated a pass to Lavelli in the right corner and set their scheme accordingly. Midway into his pattern, Lavelli spotted this and broke off toward the posts. Graham, his arm cocked, adjusted and hit an open Lavelli for a score.

Graham came running off the field saying, "Did you see what that crazy son-of-a-gun just did?" Lavelli stood on the bench and smiled.

Lavelli's tactics usually worked, often at perfect times. In the 1950 championship game, Lavelli caught eleven passes, including two for touchdowns in the Browns' 30–28 win over Los Angeles. On one late touchdown drive, Lavelli grabbed five passes.

His feats under pressure earned him another nickname, this one from a Pittsburgh scouting report: "Mr. Clutch."

"If I had to throw a ball to one individual in a clutch situation," Graham said, "I would pick Dante."

With good reason.

"Lavelli had one of the strongest pairs of hands I've ever seen," Paul Brown said in *Great Teams, Great Years: Cleveland Browns.* "When he went up for a pass with a defender, you could almost always count on him coming back down with the ball. Nobody could take it away from him once he had it in his hands."

8 Loose Lip Sinks Niners
1953 vs. San Francisco

Browns 23, 49ers 21
November 15, 1953

 Otto Graham, his lower lip dangling by the side of his mouth, lay dazed on the ground, oblivious to the storm of emotion swirling around him. His Browns teammates charged off the bench, ready to pounce on the San Francisco rookie who dared to injure their star quarterback.

Graham, looking to pad a 10–7 second-quarter lead, had rolled around right end seeking a receiver. When he found none, Graham tucked the ball and ran, as he had hundreds of times before. But no carry ended like this: with a loose piece of lip and a bench ready to brawl.

As he reached the sideline near the Cleveland bench, Graham cocked his left arm to deliver a blow as defensive back Fred Bruney knocked him out of bounds. Then, as Graham skidded along the ground, rookie guard Art Michalik dove and landed his right elbow on Graham's unprotected left cheek. Blood poured from his face due to a three-inch cut. And players raced onto the field, led by captain and center Tommy Thompson, vowing revenge. Coach Paul Brown, steamed as well, managed to hold him back.

Maybe if someone else had been injured, they would have reacted differently. But this was Otto Graham, their leader. Not to mention one of the best quarterbacks in history.

"You're not supposed to hit Otto," linebacker Walt Michaels said. "There was no need for that."

Or, as Thompson said after the game, "They couldn't do that to Otto and get away with it."

They wouldn't. At first, the players shouted at Michalik, who quickly returned to a safer part of the field. Then they decided to shift their energy toward getting the entire 49ers team. They figured the best way to punish Michalik was to beat him. But the Browns weren't sure if Graham would be able to help them do it.

"He looked woozy," Michaels said. "He looked like a boxer who was dazed. We didn't know if he was coming back."

At least Michaels remembered the play. Graham doesn't, save for the initial run.

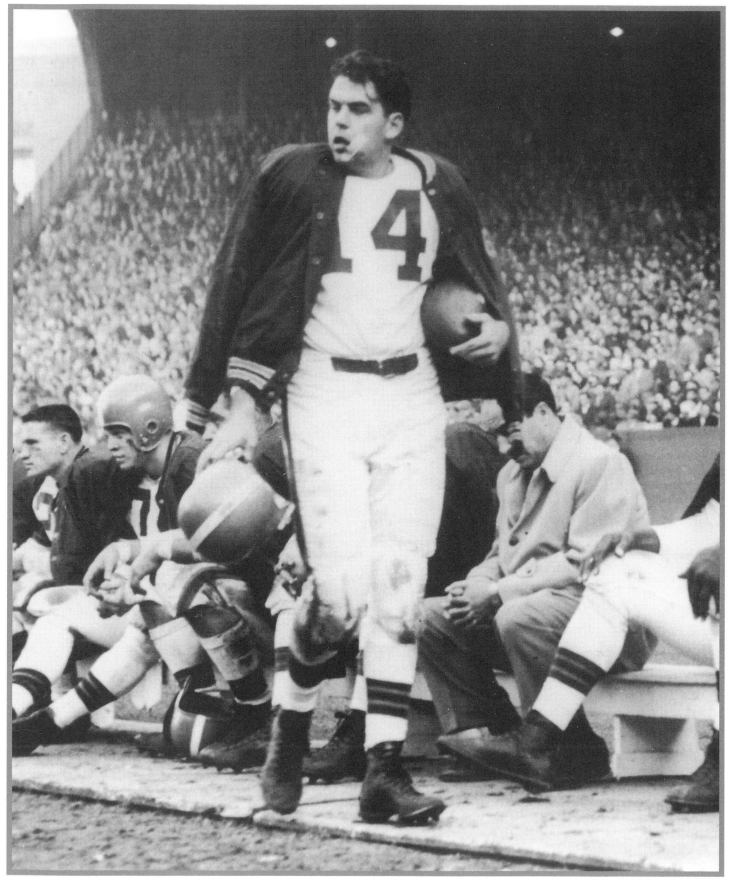

Otto Graham, after receiving fifteen stitches near his mouth, patrols the bench.

But he remembered seeing a picture of teammates dragging him out of the way, hoisting his arms over their shoulders, and taking him to the locker room. By the time he finally regained his faculties, Graham was lying on a table receiving fifteen stitches courtesy of Dr. Vic Ippolito. With no Novocain.

"Vic gave me something to wake up," Graham said. "Before that, I didn't have the slightest idea where I was."

The pain, not to mention a dazed brain, didn't stop Graham, an insurance salesman in the off-season, from trying to drum up business.

"I was lying there, giving [Ippolito] a sales talk while he was sewing me up," Graham recalled.

Pep talks, however, weren't needed. They usually weren't when Cleveland played San Francisco in this era as their matchups became one of football's top rivalries, despite the distance between the cities. In the All-America Football Conference, the 49ers chased the Browns for supremacy. Cleveland always won the war but occasionally lost the battle. Two of the Browns' four losses in the AAFC came against the 49ers. San Francisco snapped Cleveland's twenty-nine-game winning streak with a 56–28 win in 1949. Afterward, a disgusted Paul Brown chewed out his players, who were shocked by the outburst, considering they hadn't lost in two years.

In 1948, when the Browns went 14–0, their toughest match proved to be the 49ers, as well as an unkind schedule. In five days, Cleveland beat New York and Los Angeles, both on the road. Three days later, they beat host San Francisco 31–28, despite Graham playing on a severely gimpy knee. But the 12–0 Browns led the 49ers by only one game, so Graham, despite instructions from his coach not to play, hobbled off the bench to lead the win.

Cleveland's success spoiled the league and had to miff San Francisco, who lost to the Browns in the 1949 championship game and finished second to them three other times in the Western Division. Five of the teams' eight meetings resulted in final spreads of a touchdown or less.

The 1948 game in Cleveland attracted 82,769 fans, a Browns record for twelve seasons. Including the 1953 game, this matchup averaged 61,690 fans in eleven games. Of the six games played in Cleveland, five surpassed seventy thousand.

"That was a great rivalry," receiver Dante Lavelli said.

But when the teams merged into the NFL, the rivalry fizzled because they played each other only once a season. Still, some passion remained as the Browns entered this game 7–0 and in first place in the Eastern Division, while the 49ers were 5–2 and tied for first in the Western Division. So, when Michalik delivered his shot to Graham's face, it was as if someone had doused a dying fire with gasoline, igniting a torch of passion for the players as well as the 80,698 fans in attendance.

The players' focus, already crisp, sharpened even more. In his autobiography,

Brown recalled that he spent most of the time in the locker room, "trying to restore some rationality; we were still involved in a close game, and I was afraid we would lose our poise and the game."

But Brown made sure the players' attention remained on the game. He prevented the players from wandering into the trainers' room where Graham was, and instead they did what they always did: go over their second-half plans.

Still, they didn't know who would be at quarterback. George Ratterman had replaced Graham and was capable of leading the Browns to victory. They nearly scored on the series after Graham was hurt. Something, though, was missing minus Graham. Their answer, the one they wanted, came early in the third quarter. After staying in the locker room for thirty-five minutes, and missing the start of the second half, Graham finally sped onto the field, cheers greeting him with each step.

"When he came out, it was that extra spark," Michaels said.

"That [incident] brought us back," Graham said. "It got the team worked up, and there's no doubt in my mind it was a big factor. They're always trying their best, but at the same time, when something like that happens, their best improves. I'm sure every player on the team worked just a little harder to make sure no one got to me again."

Graham returned wearing an inch-thick plastic apparatus across his face, protecting his wound and eventually leading to the modern face mask. With added protection and incentive, Graham got hot, completing nine of ten passes upon his return. The Browns still led 10–7 when Graham drove them to the 49ers' five yard line. But the drive stalled, and Cleveland settled for an eleven-yard Lou Groza field goal for the only third-quarter score.

The Browns hiked their lead to 20–7 in the fourth quarter when San Francisco running back Joe Perry fumbled and safety Ken Gorgal recovered on the Cleveland forty-six. A holding penalty pushed the ball back to the thirty-three before Graham and Ray Renfro connected twice, the second for a thirty-four-yard score.

But the 49ers had a habit of erasing large deficits that season, rallying from twenty and twenty-one points down to win in two other games. They had one of the best runners, if not the best, in the league in Hugh McElhenny. They had Perry, another dangerous runner. And they had quarterback Y. A. Tittle, whose rights once belonged to the Browns in the AAFC. Cleveland lost those rights in a special draft to help Baltimore stock its roster. After Renfro scored, Tittle reminded the Browns what they once nearly had.

A screen pass to Perry gained eight yards to their own twenty-eight, and a pass to receiver Gordie Soltau tacked on twenty-six more. Then the Browns lost their cool for a moment, giving the 49ers fifteen more yards because of a personal foul, their second of the game. On the next play, Tittle hit McElhenny for a thirty-one-yard touchdown, cutting Cleveland's lead to 20–14 with six minutes remaining.

Halfback Ray Renfro takes a screen pass forty-four yards against the 49ers.

Then disaster struck for the Browns as Ken Carpenter fumbled the kickoff, giving a hot Tittle the chance to grab the lead. Instead, the Browns grabbed him and the game. More accurately, end Len Ford sacked Tittle for a twelve-yard loss on fourth down, giving Cleveland possession on the San Francisco thirty-two.

That was the story of the day for the 49ers. They failed on fourth and goal from the three in the third quarter—Tittle missed on a screen pass to Perry, in part because Thompson was hounding the intended receiver—and Perry fumbled on the Browns' eighteen in the fourth. Cleveland made the last mishap sting when Groza booted a twenty-eight-yard field goal with 3:50 remaining for a nine-point lead. Tittle led another scoring drive, but his eight-yard run came with thirty-five seconds left in the game.

The Browns, and Graham, had pulled off an emotional win. Lost in the emotion around Graham was the fact that middle guard Bill Willis hurt his knee in the second quarter and was used sparingly thereafter. An injury forced starting end Darrell Brewster to be used mainly as a decoy. And starting defensive tackle Derrell Palmer missed the game with a bad knee. But the late hit on Graham served as a rallying point.

"Could I say if not for that play, we wouldn't have won?" asked Michaels, who recovered Perry's fumble. "I doubt that. But it was a contributing factor."

Certainly Graham's passes were a bigger reason. He completed seventeen of twenty-four for 286 of the Browns' 457 total yards. Lavelli caught six of those passes for 137 yards. One 43-yard Graham-to-Lavelli connection led to Cleveland's first touchdown, a 5-yard run by back Billy Reynolds. And a 42-yard hookup by the same pair helped set up a 26-yard Groza field goal.

Michalik, meanwhile, had a rough game. Afterward, he sat at his locker with a towel around his shoulders and his head buried in his hands, shielding two blackened eyes.

"I made a dive for Graham and hit him with my elbow," he said to reporters while eyeing the ground. "I hope he's all right. I sure didn't mean to hurt him."

When the Browns' anger subsided, tempered greatly by the win, they said it wasn't a cheap shot. Even now, Graham doesn't believe it was.

"He was never considered a dirty player," Graham said. "There was a picture of me in the paper the next day with blood dripping down my chin. I looked horrible, frankly. But it wasn't that bad."

And Graham said the lip never bothered him that much, though one wouldn't have known that based on his weekly TV show nearly a week later. During the episode, Graham irritated his wound by talking and, as he read from a cue card, blood dribbled down his chin.

The significance of the injury would come after the season. Brown, long bothered by facial injuries since Ford had his face smashed three years earlier, said he talked to a friend of his, Jerry Morgan, at Riddell, a sporting goods company, about devising a protective bar. Their first attempt failed as Riddell made a face mask similar to the one Graham wore the rest of the 1953 season. There were problems. It cracked in cold weather and it fogged up.

"Your breath would bounce back into your face," Graham said. "It was hard to breathe, and your vision was impaired because it wasn't transparent. You could see everything above and below [the mask], but there was a hell of a lot of field you couldn't see."

So Riddell tried again, with instructions from Brown to keep it light—less than an ounce—and small. This time it worked, as Riddell returned with a one-inch bar that, though other players had worn some type of facial protection in the past, became the first face mask. Within a few years, they added another bar. For years,

Brown received a royalty on every bar that was sold. It was a major invention. But some cling to the supposed good old days of no face masks.

"I'll talk to some old-time players and they say, 'You're not a man until you've had some teeth knocked out,'" Graham said. "I look at them and say, 'You've got to be an idiot. Who the hell wants their teeth knocked out? That's ridiculous.'"

The 1953 season could have been remembered for much more than a protective bar, however. Cleveland kept winning, running its streak to eleven games until blowing a 17–0 lead in the regular-season finale against Philadelphia in a 42–27 loss.

Brown wasn't crushed, later saying, "there had been too much talk about our being the greatest team of all time." Two weeks later, that sentiment was squashed for good when Detroit beat Cleveland, 17–16, in the NFL Championship on a late touchdown pass. But the Browns did prove one thing that year: Mess with Graham, and you'll be sorry.

"We got pretty steamed up when Otto got hurt," Thompson said. "Maybe we had no reason to. But we did."

	1	2	3	4	Total
49ers	0	7	0	14	21
Browns	7	3	3	10	23

FIRST QUARTER
C - Reynolds 5 run (Groza kick). Browns, 7–0

SECOND QUARTER
C - Groza 26 FG. Browns, 10–0
S - McElhenny 4 run (Soltau kick). Browns, 10–7

THIRD QUARTER
C - Groza 11 FG. Browns, 13–7

FOURTH QUARTER
C - Renfro 34 pass from Graham (Groza kick). Browns, 20–7
S - McElhenny 31 pass from Tittle (Soltau kick). Browns, 20–14
C - Groza 28 FG. Browns, 23–14
S - Tittle 8 run (Soltau kick). Browns, 23–21

Otto Graham

9 Otto Graham
Quarterback, 1946–1955
Numbers 60/14

 Cancer couldn't beat him, proving a point his teammates believed many years earlier: Otto Graham doesn't lose. Especially when he was desperate for a victory. That's why championships nearly became an annual event with him at quarterback. And it's why writers dubbed him "Automatic Otto."

Teammates believed in Graham even when the situation appeared bleak. In 1949, San Francisco built a 35–14 halftime lead over Cleveland. Running back Edgar Jones watched coach Paul Brown seethe then told him to relax.

"Don't worry," Jones said. "Otto will bail us out."

He didn't. But the players believed that, with him, they could overcome anything. Besides, history was on their side. Two years earlier, Graham had led Cleveland's greatest comeback when he wiped out a 28–0 deficit against the New York Yankees, throwing two touchdown passes and leading drives for two more to complete the tie.

Championships, however, are why Graham is ranked with the greatest quarterbacks of all time and is in the Hall of Fame. In ten seasons, Graham guided Cleveland to ten title appearances, winning seven.

These games brought out Graham's best. In the Browns' three NFL championship victories, Graham completed a combined forty-five passes in seventy attempts for 670 yards and nine touchdowns. He ran for three more.

Perhaps the 1950 championship game provided his greatest moment. With the Browns trailing by one with less than two minutes remaining on a slightly frozen field, Graham led a fifty-eight-yard drive to the Los Angeles eleven—either running or throwing for all the yards. From there, Lou Groza kicked the game-winning field goal.

Graham's numbers: twenty-two for thirty-three, 298 yards, four touchdowns, and ninety-eight yards rushing. It's no wonder Brown considered Graham "the greatest player in the game's history." His teammates liked him because Graham never tried to place himself above them. Even now, when asked about his leadership skills, Graham deflects the praise and instead embarks on how Brown shaped the team.

"I was blessed with the ability to throw the ball accurately," Graham said.

And da Vinci was blessed with the ability to slap a little paint on a canvas.

Graham's strengths went beyond simply throwing a good pass. Brown spotted these other qualities when he was at Ohio State and Graham, a tailback in the single wing, was leading a Northwestern upset over the Buckeyes.

Graham's magic began in college when he led the Wildcats to a surprising 8–2 record, in 1943, a seven-game improvement over the previous season. He did it with his running and passing, finishing with a Western Conference record 2,132 career passing yards. Graham also earned conference MVP honors in 1943.

Not bad for someone who entered college on a basketball scholarship. As a freshman, Graham wasn't invited out for football. Eventually, after starring in an intramural league, Graham's football talents were discovered by the coaches.

But he continued playing basketball and became an all-American. Graham even played one season with the Rochester Royals of the National Basketball League. Graham, starting his trend in pro sports, won a championship with Rochester. Football, though, offered a better lifestyle than basketball. Graham quickly tired of the travel and constant road trips.

"You lived on trains," Graham said.

Besides, Graham had alternatives. During World War II, Detroit had drafted him in the NFL, and Cleveland, with Brown as coach, had pursued him for the newly formed All-America Conference. Cleveland's attractive offer—$250 per month salary through the end of the war, a $1,000 signing bonus, and a $7,500 contract— caused Graham to shun the NFL and become the Browns' first signee.

Brown wanted Graham to be his quarterback in the wing-T, a spot he had never played in college. But he had played it, in 1944, for the North Carolina Pre-Flight team, where Brown saw him play. And basketball, with its emphasis on footwork, helped prepare Graham's transition.

Brown liked the ball-handling skills and poise Graham displayed, traits that convinced him he had his quarterback. He watched Graham buy extra time in the pocket because of his athleticism, and he saw him tuck the ball and run for more yards. It was everything he wanted to see. The basics of the position were learned. The rest was all Graham's doing.

"I learned the position by myself," Graham said. "No one taught me. But basketball helped me, the spinning and moving. That was a big help. If I was not a basketball player, it would have been tougher.

"When I first played in the T, I put my left hand up because in baseball you caught with your left hand. So I did the same with football. [But] in the Browns camp, they had me put my right hand up because then your hand is on the ball ready to throw right away. I made that switch in a couple of days."

His career numbers suggest he adjusted rather well: 23,584 passing yards and 174 touchdown passes. In the NFL, Graham tossed 88 touchdown passes and threw for 13,499 yards during an era when passing was frowned upon. If his NFL numbers are combined with his All-America Conference statistics, no Browns quarterback threw for more touchdowns, and only Brian Sipe tossed for more yardage.

"Otto was such a brilliant passer," Brown said in his autobiography. "Everyone marveled that Otto could work so well with our receivers, but he had learned to anticipate their movements by watching their shoulders. The intricate timing came from their working together for hours after practice.

"I remember his tremendous peripheral vision and his great athletic skill, as well as his ability to throw a football far and accurately with just a flick of his arm."

But Graham was more than just a passer.

"Otto was the main reason the Browns were called the team of the [1950s]," tackle Mike McCormack said. "He had an awful lot of talent, he was a great guy in the huddle and a great team man.

"He was not aloof, which you see a lot of times today. He was just one of the guys. Otto would have you over to his house. I was single the first two years, and I'd go to his house for Christmas dinner. All the single guys would."

He led in the huddle, too, as in the 1950 championship when he convinced his teammates they would win. Graham wasn't boisterous or a yeller. Nor would he scream at someone who dropped a pass or blew a block, as Detroit's Bobby Layne would. Graham was calm.

"When it got down to it, Otto would say, 'Come on, you guys, we can win,'" receiver Dante Lavelli said. "He wasn't a guy that went up and down. He was very level."

Graham said, "The guys respected me as a person. I didn't drink or smoke or chase women. I would joke and laugh and have fun and was just one of the guys. Because I was the quarterback and doing well, I didn't keep myself above everyone else. Some guys think they're so great and one step above everyone."

Brown and Graham formed a strong relationship, though as time went on they disagreed on who should call the plays. Graham, who began calling his own plays, thought he should continue; Brown thought otherwise. Brown won, most of the time.

In a 1951 game against the Chicago Bears, receiver Dub Jones had scored five touchdowns, one short of tying an NFL record. Late in the game, Brown sent in a play, not designed for Jones. Guard Abe Gibron shouted, "F—— Paul Brown, call your own damn play!" So Graham did and hit Jones on a post pattern for a touchdown.

"Paul never said a word," Graham said.

These days, Graham is retired and living in Sarasota, Florida, attending autograph shows and playing an occasional round of golf, another sport in which he once excelled. He fought off rectal cancer in 1977, leaving him a changed person.

Before, Graham said, he attended charity events because he had to. Afterward, he wanted to go.

Graham looks back on his career and says he was simply blessed. Others say they were blessed to see him play. But Graham does have one regret. He wishes he had stuck to his music. Graham, whose parents were music teachers, played the violin, cornet, and french horn and was in the band in high school and orchestra in college. In high school, he was part of a group that won first place in a national contest in Columbus, Ohio.

"I'm honest when I say I would take every medal and honor earned in sports and throw them out the window," Graham said, "if I had been smart enough to keep playing the piano. When you're seventy-seven, you can't play football, but you can still sit down and be the life of the party and play the piano well and be very enjoyable."

Maybe he can't play football at seventy-seven, but he most certainly could in his twenties and thirties. For ten years, he was the life of the party, at least when it came time to orchestrating championships. And that was music to Cleveland's ears.

10 Frank Gatski
Center, 1946–1956

Number 52

 A former teammate wanted to track down Frank Gatski. One problem: Gatski, a man long known for his economy with words, didn't have a phone at his home atop a West Virginia mountain.

Rex Bumgardner was stumped. But another former teammate, Walt Michaels, provided the help and a number to a local diner.

"I [told Rex] to make sure and call between 7:30 and 8:00 A.M.," Michaels said. "And he said, 'Why?' And I told him that's because that's the diner he goes to every morning. Rex called there, and they said, 'Yeah, he's here.' And Rex said he could hear Frank in the background saying, 'Who the hell knows I'm here?'"

But Gatski was prone to developing habits, ones his friends and teammates relied upon, as when he played for Cleveland. Then, his teammates always knew where he could be found: at the center of the offensive line.

That's where Gatski was from 1946 to 1956 for the Browns. He never missed a game, a habit he formed early. Gatski played every game, and took part in every practice, in high school, college, and the pros, a trend that continued when he played for Detroit for three seasons.

Gatski didn't want the trade to Detroit, but coach Paul Brown didn't want to give him a raise. So he shipped him out. But Gatski, who helped the Lions beat the Browns in the '57 championship, left a strong impression.

"He was there, whether you needed him or not, he was there," guard Jim Ray Smith said.

The Browns usually needed him, however, and benefited from his presence. Gatski, who became a full-time starter in 1948, made four Pro Bowls and finally was elected to the Hall of Fame in 1985. His reliability made him beloved.

"He was as durable and tough as any player I've ever known," Brown once said.

But all Gatski did was what his family had taught him through their own deeds. Gatski was born and raised in the Number Nine Coal Camp in Farmington, West Virginia, where his grandfather and father—immigrants from Poland—and brothers worked.

So did Frank Gatski, putting in his time during summers after high school and then during breaks from Marshall University. But football provided a way out of

Frank Gatski

that existence. After he played three seasons at Marshall, World War II interrupted his career. He was discharged, in 1945, after two years and finished his career at Auburn. A former teammate at Marshall, Sam Clagg, arranged a tryout for Gatski with the Browns. Clagg contacted Cleveland assistant coach John Brickels, a former high school coach in Huntington, West Virginia.

Though Gatski escaped the mines, his memories of them provide a snapshot of why he endured in football.

"It wasn't bad," Gatski said of working in the mines. "The elements were against you, but I never did consider it hard work. That's why football wasn't that hard."

He stopped coal mining during his playing days, but his family continued this dirty work.

"They never missed work," said Gatski, who now has a home phone. "They were all workaholics."

And, he said, they rarely complained, another attribute Gatski carried with him to the Browns. It would have been easy for him to moan about many things, particularly his high school days. At Farmington High School—where Hall of Fame linebacker Sam Huff later attended—players ignored their surroundings and just played. They had to. The field had little or no grass, no scoreboard or bleachers, and no clock.

It got worse. The opposing team wasn't the only thing Farmington had to dodge. "The football field had cowshit on it," Gatski remembered. "Football players don't play in cow pastures anymore. But it makes no difference to a football player. They'll play anywhere. [Besides], most of those boys were from the coal camps where the old man was tough and the kids a little tougher."

By the time he got to Cleveland, accompanied by the nickname "Gunner," Gatski had toughened himself to the rough aspects of football. Which is why he never minded Brown. "You're supposed to be a pro. You're supposed to be able to take that crap," Gatski said. And it's why Brown, as well as Gatski's teammates, marveled at him.

"He was an iron man," tackle Mike McCormack said. "He came to work and just did his job. That was it."

"I went for one day," Gatski said. "And stayed twelve years."

For several years, Gatski was the only center Cleveland took to training camp, an unheard of move then and now. But he was reliable, so why bring in anyone else?

Besides, he liked the work.

One day in the early 1950s, Michaels remembers relaxing with Gatski, both of them members of the Filthy Five group who refused to wash their practice uniforms all season, and a few teammates after a training camp practice. The veterans were sizing up the competition when Gatski chimed in excitedly.

"Frank said, 'I don't know about you guys, but I've got it made. There are no other centers in camp,'" Michaels recalled. "Today if you did that, that center would complain and say, 'I've got to take all the snaps.' Frank didn't care. He would take all the snaps."

Weight lifting wasn't popular in Gatski's era—his strength was natural, and it stemmed from his mining days. Also, Gatski loved bow hunting, which certainly toned his six-foot-three, 240-pound body.

Gatski would bring his bow to practice at League Park, and receiver Mac Speedie would take aim at the clock in center field, which he always missed. Gatski still hunts white-tailed deer with the bow and arrow three months a year. Perhaps that's how he developed such a physique that Brown once said he "looked a bit like L'il Abner with his ready smile."

In his autobiography, Brown remembered a time when some players were working out. Guard George Cheroke was one of the few players who lifted weights, and one day Gatski asked Cheroke what the weights were for.

"You lift them," Cheroke said.

Gatski did just that, lifting the weight with one hand. Then Gatski said, "Now what do I do with it?" Brown wrote that Cheroke looked on in amazement.

That's what Gatski's teammates did with him most of his career, one that included zero broken bones and hundreds of bruises. He was a quiet man who liked to work. Nothing more.

"It couldn't be luck, could it?" Gatski said. "You have to learn how to play the game. Hell, yeah, you've got to be tough, and you're gonna get some licks. But I never even called time all the years I played. I'd wait until the end of the quarter or let someone else call time. I always had a full tank of gas."

11 **Len Ford**
Defensive End, 1950–1957

Number 80

The high-pitched voice startled visitors, who expected a much deeper sound from such a mammoth man. But that wasn't the only time Len Ford caused heads to turn. Nor was it his lone contradiction. On the field, Ford would ram an opponent—then apologize for his violence.

Ford spent one game crashing into Washington quarterback Eddie LeBaron time and again, knocking him to the ground all day. One hit caused LeBaron's nose to bleed and Ford's heart to soften.

"I'm awfully sorry," Ford told LeBaron as he helped him up. "I hope you understand I'm just doing my job."

No Browns defensive end ever did his job better than Ford. The Hall of Fame agreed, and Ford finally made it to Canton, in 1976, four years after his death. He also was named to the NFL's Team of the 1950s by *Sports Illustrated*. He made four Pro Bowls and was named all-Pro an equal number of times.

All this by a player known for his offense when he arrived in Cleveland in 1950. In the All-America Football Conference, Ford starred at end for the Los Angeles Dons, catching a combined sixty-seven passes for 1,175 yards in 1948 and '49.

But he also was a defensive end and, when the Browns selected him in a special draft after the league's breakup, that's where coach Paul Brown stationed Ford, even though Cleveland was stacked at the position. Wise move.

"Lenny was a great pass rusher," linebacker Walt Michaels said. "A lot of times he would just crank it up and run over the tackle. Would Lenny still be good today? I think so. I would say he and [Baltimore's] Gino Marchetti invented the pass rush."

"He was a fierce player," Brown once said, "and something to behold when he uncoiled and went after a passer."

Ford perfected the art of leaping over tackles, especially against the New York Giants' Rosey Brown. That athleticism was honed in Washington, where he grew up and later made all-city in football, baseball, and basketball. In 1948, Ford traveled with the professional basketball New York Rens. It's no wonder the Browns felt comfortable dropping Ford into pass coverage every once in a while.

Len Ford

But he also was strong and sometimes shelved his athletic moves in favor of muscle, overpowering tackles. At six-foot-four and 265 pounds, that wasn't hard for Ford, whose size matches that of today's ends.

"Lenny used to delight in running over guys," tackle Lou Groza said. "He was a real load."

But Ford also gambled in his pursuit of the quarterback.

"He'd say, 'Walt, we've got to get to the quarterback,'" Michaels, who lined up on Ford's side, recalled. "Don Colo was at tackle, and he'd look at Ford and say, 'You'll never get there.' That would rile Lenny up. Then Lenny would turn around and say, 'Walt, protect me. I'm gonna get [the quarterback]. But if they run, we're in trouble.' When he got the quarterback, forget it."

Ford once said pregame conversations with himself keyed his surges during games.

"I tell myself, 'Nobody's going to stop me,'" Ford said. "It's all a challenge, a matter of determination and desire."

Ford displayed that desire in his first season with the Browns. In an October 15 game against St. Louis, Cardinals running back Pat Harder, frustrated by his inability to block Ford on pass plays, smashed the end's face with an elbow. With no face mask to protect Ford, Harder's hit fractured his cheekbone, broke his nose, and knocked out two teeth.

"As vicious a blow as I've seen in football," Brown said.

Ford, after having extensive surgery, was done for the season. Or so everyone thought. In the Browns 30–28 championship victory over the Los Angeles Rams, Ford popped off the bench in the second quarter, wearing a specially designed helmet to protect his face, and played the rest of the game. He was twenty pounds underweight, due to a liquid diet, but still effective.

One series showed his worth. On consecutive plays, Ford snuffed out the Statue of Liberty play and nailed running back Verda T. "Vitamin T" Smith for a fourteen-yard loss, sacked quarterback Bob Waterfield for an eleven-yard loss, and drilled halfback Glenn Davis for minus-thirteen yards.

"Len showed me that day that he really was a man," Brown said.

True to form, Ford never held a grudge against Harder. But he noticed a change in Harder.

"After the incident, Harder couldn't stand still around me," Ford said. "He would just fake a block and get out of the way."

When Ford retired, he was the NFL's all-time leader in fumble recoveries with twenty, nineteen of which came during his eight seasons in Cleveland. The Browns traded Ford to Green Bay in 1958, and he retired a year later.

After that, Ford wanted to practice law—he often studied law books during his playing days—but he never earned his degree. Ford suffered numerous personal problems after retiring, including a divorce, and was hospitalized for a month before dying of a heart attack in 1972.

But that's not how Ford will be remembered. Rather, it's for his performance on the field, as in 1953 when the Browns shut out the New York Giants 7–0, with Ford dominating the contest. After the game, Brown was asked if Ford played like that every game.

"Yes," Brown said.

"I have to do it that way," Ford once said. "The result you get from any endeavor depends upon the effort you put into it. I tell my brother that I wouldn't give him a break on the field. I tell him I would be coming through if I could. I wouldn't give him a break or anyone else. If they can't take it, they shouldn't be out there. I'm going to do my job."

12 Something to Prove
1954 NFL Championship

Browns 56, Lions 10
December 26, 1954

 A dozen or so offensive players gathered in secret, plotting a strategy against their own coach, perhaps the most famous one in football. Less than twelve hours before the NFL championship, they concluded their meeting with a stunning decision. If they didn't like Paul Brown's play, they would change it in the huddle—then deal with the fallout later.

They were tired of losing championship games. They were tired of losing to Detroit, especially in those title games. And they wanted to present quarterback Otto Graham with a retirement gift.

Brown's conservative play calling, they thought, would prevent Graham from leaving happy and prolong their own misery. One week earlier, Graham threw but six passes in a 14–10 loss to Detroit. The game meant nothing. Except to the players, who had grown sick of losing to their northern rivals.

That made it four straight losses to the Lions, including defeats in the past two championship games. Three exhibition losses jumped the total to seven, increasing the frustration. Whispers filled the league that the Browns couldn't beat Detroit. Now the whispers became shouts as the evidence mounted. Those shouts reverberated in the players' ears, who started to believe that Brown's conservative game plans were the main culprit.

"It seemed like every time we got ready to play the Lions," receiver Dante Lavelli said, "he'd go down to basic football and try to get to a three- or six-point lead and hold onto that. We never realized that until after we played them for a couple years.

"He became paranoid. His record was getting so great that he had to make sure he kept winning. That's when he thought everyone was spying on him and watching practice. We could tell [Brown had changed]."

Linebacker Walt Michaels said, "Paul got in a rut, and he got paranoid against Detroit. Everyone thought that."

So they met at 2:00 A.M. in a room at the Carter Hotel in downtown Cleveland the night before the game and declared their intentions.

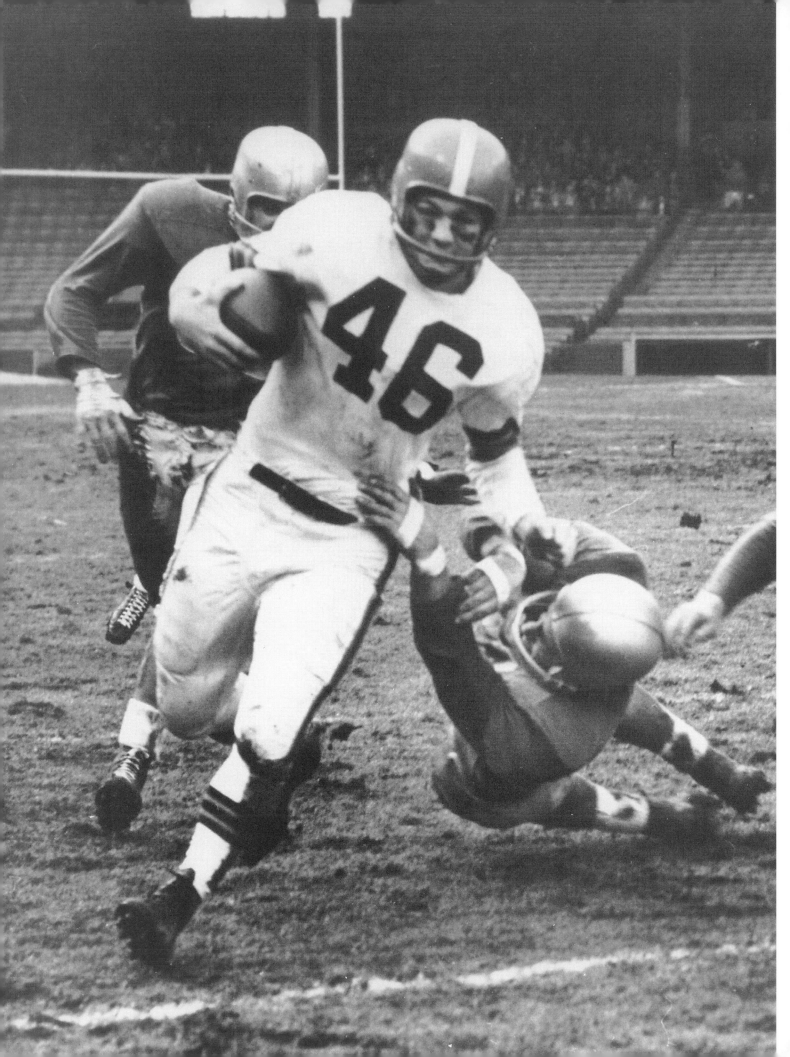

"We decided we would do what we wanted to do," Lavelli said. "Every time he would send a play in, we didn't think it was right because he didn't know what the defensive alignment was, and he'd just send in a play and you couldn't run it sometimes. So we said if Paul Brown sent in plays we didn't like, we would use our own plays."

Not that it would matter.

Graham had his own reasons for wanting to win, some of which spilled over onto his teammates. After the Pro Bowl that January, Graham announced the 1954 season would be his last.

A love for football still burned in his heart, but a dislike of the surrounding aspects sapped his passion. Game day nerves eroded his appetite, leaving him a pregame meal of a couple of oranges or Hershey bars. Graham also tired of the time away from his family, a main reason why he dropped his pursuit of professional basketball after one season nearly a decade earlier.

The thought of enduring more training camps and filling out more playbooks added to his retirement wishes. Besides, a lucrative insurance career, one he had already started, awaited him.

"[It all] gets tiresome," Graham said. "You don't like it, but you have to do it. I also thought it might be smart business to quit on top. At the time, I recalled the fabulous boxer Joe Louis had to box again when he shouldn't have been fighting. I didn't want to have that same reputation. When you put it all together, I decided it was time to quit."

Not everyone believed his decision was final. On the day of the championship game, *Cleveland Plain Dealer* sports editor Gordon Cobbledick wrote, "But still he's a football player, and the only persons who can appreciate the full meaning of that are other football players. They don't quit for any of the reasons Graham enumerated. . . . When he does quit, whether now or a year or two from now . . ."

That was all speculation, however. On this day, Graham believed he was quitting, and, before he did, he wanted to erase the memory of last year's 17–16 championship loss to Detroit. Brown called it Graham's worst game with Cleveland. The numbers agreed: Graham completed two of fifteen passes.

An injured finger on his passing hand, which later became chapped during the game, contributed to Graham's problems. He couldn't control the ball, and his passes sailed high and wide of their intended targets. Graham blamed himself for the loss, once saying he wanted to "jump off a building."

"I was the main factor in losing," Graham said. "If I had played my usual game, we would have won. I could not throw as accurately as I should have, and that's why we lost. There's no doubt in my mind about that."

Also, he hadn't thrown a touchdown pass in the last four games against Detroit. But Graham wasn't alone in seeking redemption. Cornerback Warren Lahr, one of

Billy Reynolds set up Cleveland's fourth touchdown with this forty-two-yard punt return. He also positioned the Browns for their first score with a forty-six-yard kickoff return.

the best in franchise history, was suckered on the last-minute, game-winning touchdown pass in 1953.

"It was almost like he was frozen in his tracks," Michaels said.

On the train ride home, Lahr sat alone, far from his teammates. No one dared say a word to him, and Brown later said he never felt sorrier for anyone in his life. It got worse for Lahr. In the 1954 regular-season finale, he was beaten once again for the winning score. Lahr, though, dug in against this assault on his confidence. Few corners in the league were better, either against the pass or the run. Lahr had to forget the touchdowns and move forward.

"He just got tougher," tackle Mike McCormack said.

The whole team did. But that was to be expected with this bunch, most of whom had been raised in coal-mining country or served in a war or grew up in a rough neighborhood. They were survivors. Any hardship the NFL tossed at them was nothing compared to their past.

Take Michaels, for instance. His father worked in the Pennsylvania coal mines for thirty-five years, and when he would come home, Michaels could see only the whites of his eyes as his body was smothered in dirt. When Michaels grew up, he played football with the condition that he get home in time to saw wood. In the springtime, he would wake up at 5:00 A.M. to pick coal, returning home two or three hours later, pushing a wheelbarrow with a few hundred pounds of coal that he had to crack down to size.

"You show me guys that grow up under those circumstances and I'll show you guys that have a responsibility to what they're doing," said Michaels, a four-time Pro Bowler.

He wasn't alone in this type of story. The roster was filled with such cases. That's why they never backed down from Detroit, despite the four straight losses. It's also why they shrugged off the numerous changes prior to 1954. Gone were two future Hall of Famers, middle guard Bill Willis (retirement) and fullback Marion Motley (released), and coaches Blanton Collier (Kentucky) and Weeb Ewbank (Baltimore). Halfback Dub Jones also retired but eventually returned.

But the additions proved beneficial as McCormack replaced Willis. Also, linebacker Tony Adamle returned after a two-year retirement, though he would miss the championship with a broken leg. Defensive tackle John Kissell returned after one season in the Canadian Football League. New starter Tom Catlin, obtained in the ten-for-five trade with Baltimore, in 1953, helped at linebacker. Cornerback Don Paul, acquired in a trade with the Chicago Cardinals, solidified the secondary.

The Browns handled the changes. Their resolve paid off after losses in two of their first three games, including a 55–27 defeat by Pittsburgh. The loss turned the season around as Cleveland started winning. When the Browns beat Philadelphia 6–0 on a late goal-line stand—spurred by McCormack—their coach felt confident his team was rolling. They would win eight straight.

Even the loss to Detroit—a game that was originally scheduled for October 3, but was switched because of a potential conflict with the Indians and the World Series—didn't faze Brown, who knew he had limited his offense. The players were bothered by the loss, but only because they felt they were superior.

"We were surprised we lost," safety Ken Konz said. "We had the talent, we knew the things they were going to do, and Paul was a great mastermind."

So thirty-three players and a coaching staff ran onto the field with something to prove—to themselves, to the 43,827 in attendance, and to the world. They wasted little time in doing it. First, though, Detroit took a short-lived lead, on a thirty-six-yard Doak Walker field goal, set up by an interception of Graham.

Then Cleveland began its onslaught, getting a forty-six-yard kickoff return by Billy Reynolds. Now it was receiver Ray Renfro's turn. His hands couldn't match Lavelli's or Jones's, Brown once said, but his speed, which forced him to switch from running back, put him in a different class. At North Texas State, Renfro set a Gulf Coast Conference record by running the 100-yard dash in 9.5 seconds. He also was the conference's best in the 220.

Renfro was always capable of long gains with his blazing speed. He would finish his career with a 19.6 yards-per-catch average, still the best mark in franchise history. In 1953, Renfro led the Browns in rushing with 352 yards, averaging 5.9 yards a carry, and was second in receiving with thirty-nine catches. This is what Cleveland expected when it drafted him in the fourth round the year before and watched him return his first punt fifty-eight yards for a touchdown in an exhibition game.

Brown envisioned all sorts of huge plays from Renfro. No one, though, anticipated what he did against Detroit, mainly because Renfro had missed six weeks with an injured knee and wasn't expected to play. Certainly, the Lions didn't think he would and when he did, all they could try to do was use man coverage.

It didn't work. Renfro's thirty-five-yard touchdown catch put the Browns on top for good on this mild December day. Renfro would finish with five receptions for ninety-four yards, limping to the bench after each catch.

"We killed them there," Graham said. "Ray was very fast and a very good receiver."

The players began to forget about their late-night meeting as the Browns' momentum gathered force. It helped that the defense squashed everything Detroit wanted to run. When Paul returned an interception of a Bobby Layne pass to the Lions' eight, the Browns' roll continued. Two plays later, Graham hit end Darrell Brewster for a ten-yard touchdown.

Reynolds chipped in again with a forty-two-yard punt return to the Detroit twelve, setting up Graham's one-yard run in the second quarter.

The defense allowed a five-yard touchdown run by halfback Bill Bowman, but it positioned Cleveland for its next two scores with turnovers. First, McCormack

Cleveland end Darryl Brewster couldn't grab this pass, but the ball was knocked in the air and caught by teammate Ray Renfro at the Lions' four.

stripped Layne of the ball at the Detroit thirty-one, and Graham followed with a five-yard scoring run. Then Michaels intercepted Layne, again giving the Browns possession at the Lions' thirty-one. From there, Renfro cemented the first-half success when he hauled in Graham's pass with fully extended arms for a 35–10 halftime lead.

"All the talk of the Lions' 'jinx' disappeared," Brown later said.

Little changed in the second half as the Browns dominated both sides of the ball again, especially the defense, en route to a 56–10 win. The Browns intercepted six passes—five off Layne—getting two each by Konz and defensive end Len Ford. Cleveland also recovered three fumbles. Layne's magic against Cleveland had disappeared, at least for a day. In the past four games, he had thrown for five touchdowns and run for another.

"They just beat the hell out of us," Layne said afterward.

"The defense wanted to prove something to Paul Brown because of the way they had beaten us [the last two games]," Konz said. "We wanted to prove we had the best defense in the league."

They all proved something and stole the headlines from Cleveland's infamous murder case of Dr. Sam Sheppard. Brown showed everyone that he could beat Lions coach Buddy Parker, his friend and rival. Surely Brown reveled in stomping Detroit and Layne, the hard-partying Texan. Brown frowned on any drinking or smoking. The Lions didn't. Tackle Lou Groza recalled a 1950 exhibition game in Akron when several Lions smoked and drank in the parking lot afterward.

"That ruffled Paul's feathers," Groza said.

Brown's way had succeeded. And the players presented him a game ball after the win. They also gave one to Lahr. Graham showed he was still a master, completing nine of twelve passes for 163 yards. His three touchdown runs set two records—most touchdowns in a championship game and most touchdowns rushing. When Brown removed him late in the fourth quarter, the crowd stood and cheered for five minutes, thanking him for leading the Browns to nine title games in nine seasons.

This was their going-away gift. Or was it? Brown convinced Graham to return the following summer, and he wound up winning another title, his seventh in ten seasons. But the win in 1955 couldn't top this one, not when the Browns considered the path they had traveled in 1954. After beating the Lions, Brown told reporters this was the "finest team I've coached on a given day."

Even Parker said in the locker room that he couldn't believe the outcome. "It has me dazed," he said.

They steamrolled Detroit with a vigor that stemmed from frustration. They knew what had to be done, and they did it.

"The emotional outburst came from within," Brown said afterward. "No one had to stick a needle in them today. They were ready."

	1	2	3	4	Total
Lions	3	7	0	0	10
Browns	14	21	14	7	56

FIRST QUARTER

D - Walker 36 FG. Lions, 3–0
C - Renfro 35 pass from Graham (Groza kick). Browns, 7–3
C - Brewster 10 pass from Graham (Groza kick). Browns, 14–3

SECOND QUARTER

C - Graham 1 run (Groza kick). Browns, 21–3
D - Bowman 5 run (Walker kick). Browns, 21–10
C - Graham 5 run (Groza kick). Browns, 28–10
C - Renfro 31 pass from Graham (Groza kick). Browns, 35–10

THIRD QUARTER

C - Graham 1 run (Groza kick). Browns, 42–10
C - Morrison 12 run (Groza kick). Browns, 49–10

FOURTH QUARTER

C - Hanulak 10 run (Groza kick). Browns, 56–10

13 Mike McCormack
Offensive tackle, 1954–1962

Number 74

The Depression battered his father, knocking him down time and again. Each time, he dusted himself off and kept going. When Michael McCormack Sr. immigrated to the United States from Ireland in the mid-1920s, he figured his skill as a pipe insulator would make life easy. He was wrong.

McCormack soon learned the Irish weren't welcome everywhere. For fifteen years, unions turned down McCormack, preventing him from finding work. Somehow, his family had to survive. So McCormack worked when he could and became creative in finding ways to endure. In the winter, McCormack would walk nearly five miles to Union Station in Kansas City. Then he would walk along the rails, picking up coal that had fallen from the trains.

"He would bring that home to heat the house," said the son who shared his name.

Mike McCormack Jr. studied his father's efforts. Later, McCormack used that effort to pave his path to the Hall of Fame. When it came time to work, McCormack knew what that meant. At the University of Kansas, McCormack's offensive line coach was the legendary Pop Warner. When McCormack was a sophomore, Warner provided him a list of drills. McCormack devoured this information.

"At that time, I was so taken up with the game that I overdid the drills," McCormack said. "The footwork, the turns, the knee bends, a lot of twisting. I would do them almost every spare moment in my living room or in my backyard. [Warner] had said, 'These drills would help make you a better player.' It paid off."

Paid off? Paul Brown thought so. On more than one occasion, including when he delivered McCormack's Hall of Fame induction speech, Brown called him "the finest offensive tackle who ever played professional football."

Brown had kept tabs on McCormack since his college days. At the East-West college all-star game, in 1950, McCormack played both ways, at tackle and on the defensive line. He faced an all-American player on the East team in both jobs. The West won, and McCormack had played well.

Brown noticed. When McCormack returned to Kansas, he heard over and over again about how Brown, as a halftime radio guest, had said the one player who really impressed him was McCormack.

"I always had a soft spot in my heart for him from that time on," McCormack said.

In 1953, Brown finally had an opportunity to trade for McCormack. It became one of the largest deals ever made in the NFL, as Cleveland traded ten players to Baltimore for McCormack and four others.

McCormack was stationed at Fort Leonard Wood in Missouri at the time, serving as an army instructor in the heavy equipment school. While he was out in a field working with students on tractors and road graders, McCormack heard the news. Another student had heard it on armed forces radio. But he didn't know the details. So McCormack had no idea where he was traded. Or for whom. A week later, he found out.

Another year passed before McCormack was able to play for Cleveland. He actually started his Browns career at middle guard, a combination of a nose guard and middle linebacker. All he had to do was replace future Hall of Famer Bill Willis.

How was McCormack?

"He could have very likely been a Hall of Famer as a defensive lineman," linebacker Galen Fiss said, echoing a comment Chuck Noll once made.

"I enjoyed defense more," McCormack said. "Defense is more natural because you get to use your hands, and it's a more physical endeavor. On offense, you were so constrained, and you had to keep your hands in against your chest. You couldn't extend your arms like you can today. You had to do it all with footwork. I was fortunate that the good Lord gave me speed and I was able to run. But I just enjoyed defense."

Brown, though, wanted him at tackle and moved McCormack there, in 1954, when Bob Gain returned from the service. Gain was a middle guard, so McCormack teamed with left tackle Lou Groza as offensive line bookends. They shared one trait: speed. Both 250-pound men ran the forty-yard dash in 4.8 seconds.

"Mike was quick on his feet and he had good balance, and that's what makes a good offensive lineman," guard Jim Ray Smith said. "He was like a boxer in a ring; he always had one foot a little forward."

Brown once said, "He was an excellent pass blocker, but he could also blow people out of there." He also called him a stabilizing factor during his tenure. Teammates remembered his leadership.

"He never made a mistake," running back Bobby Mitchell said. "He always knew where he was supposed to be. But he had tremendous leadership. If captain Mike said something, that was it. It was like God speaking. We all looked up to him. To play the years he played, he must have been pretty gosh darn good, and Paul loved him to death. But when I evaluate him, his leadership gets in the way. He was a tremendous leader."

That served him well after his playing days ended, in 1962—after six Pro Bowls and two championships—as McCormack would coach with Vince Lombardi,

George Allen, and Brown. Allen once called him "the best assistant coach I ever had." Then McCormack served as Seattle's president and later held the same role with expansion Carolina. He took with him the work ethic that made him a Hall of Famer. McCormack routinely worked twelve-hour days and stayed fit with hour-and-a-half workouts. The thing is, McCormack, now retired, never viewed it as work.

"I feel very blessed that I was able to to spend that length of time doing something I loved," McCormack said. "It enabled me to have a good life. I feel very, very fortunate. More than anything, I loved the game. I enjoyed practice. I enjoyed everything."

14 **Jim Ray Smith**
Guard, 1956–1962

Number 64

 His speed created openings for players and stories for himself, most of which guard Jim Ray Smith likes to tell. Like the time, in 1960, when two future Hall of Fame runners, one a former track star, ranked first and second on the Browns in the forty-yard dash. Two-tenths of a second later, Smith pulled in, matching receiver Ray Renfro second for second. Too bad Smith's career flew by just as fast. Otherwise, Smith would have done more than reach the College Football Hall of Fame.

"If he had played twelve or fourteen years, he would have been the greatest offensive lineman who ever played," guard Gene Hickerson said. "He was big, and the dude could run."

That attribute mattered most to coach Paul Brown, and the six-foot-four, 255-pound Smith ran fast, making him valuable in leading Jim Brown around the corners. Brown and Smith rose together, helping each other achieve success. Smith became a starter in 1957, Brown's rookie season, and in the next six years, Smith earned five Pro Bowl berths.

"I've had tackles from Detroit come to me and hug me and kiss me and tell me, 'You're the greatest that ever was,'" Smith said. "Another guy told me, 'When I talk about the Browns, I talk about two players, Jim Brown and Jim Ray Smith.'"

And when the Browns talk about guards, they place Smith at, or very near, the top. Even linebacker Dale Lindsey, who joined the Browns three years after Smith left, knew all about him.

"Any of those old Browns will tell you the best player they had there was Jim Ray Smith," Lindsey said. "They'll say he was the best athlete they ever played with."

Smith first opened eyes in 1958. In the Browns' first four games that season, Smith faced Pittsburgh tackle Ernie Stautner twice and the Los Angeles Rams' Lamar Lundy once. Before the season, linebacker Vince Costello remembered Paul Brown saying to Smith, "We're going to find out how good you are." Cleveland won all three games as the offense scored thirty, forty-five, and twenty-seven points, respectively.

"None of them even smelled the passer," Costello said. "Jim Ray ate them alive."

Jim Ray Smith

The next season, Smith played a key role in one of Jim Brown's greatest games. In a 38–31 win over Baltimore, Brown rushed for 179 yards and five touchdowns. Most of his damage came over Smith, who blew open holes against Big Daddy Lipscomb, one of the most feared defensive lineman of that era. Brown rammed over Smith for three of his scores.

Paul Brown later said Smith "consistently took Big Daddy Lipscomb out of the play. . . . He was one of our greatest guards."

That season, coaches graded Smith's pass blocking at 94 percent, well above the norm. Brown thought enough of Smith to draft him in the sixth round in 1954 as a junior, thereby securing his rights. Smith earned all-America honors as a junior and senior tackle at Baylor—he appeared with the squad on the *Ed Sullivan Show.*

But Smith, who played tackle on both lines at Baylor, didn't arrive in Cleveland until midway through the 1956 season after a one-year stint in the army. And he came as a 218-pound defensive end. The Browns sought a replacement for future Hall of Famer Len Ford. Smith's speed made him attractive. But in his first season, Smith learned the offense during the week and played defense in games. By the next training camp, Smith had gained thirty pounds and found a permanent home on the offensive line.

"They were elated that I didn't lose any speed when I came back with that much weight," said Smith, who started first at right guard then moved to the left side a year later. "[Line coach] Fritz [Heisler] always said, 'You hit that sled like no one else has ever hit it. You had a pop on it.' That's what they were looking for. Paul Brown looked for offensive lineman before defense. If you couldn't be an offensive lineman, you went to defense. And if you couldn't be a defensive lineman, you were gone."

The Browns didn't regret their decision.

"Jim is extremely fast for a big man," Heisler said during the 1959 season, "and I never cease to be amazed at his agility. He has wonderful lateral speed and can bring himself under control for blocks in an instant. Jim does have a good straight ahead boom, too. He's not just an open-field blocker."

Maybe not, but that's where he excelled most. Smith's early days prepared him for this role as he lettered in football, basketball, and track in his West Columbia, Texas, high school. In track, Smith ran on the relay teams and advanced to the state tournament in the high jump. Speed wasn't his only contribution, as he threw the shot and discus as well. Smith packaged those qualities with his attention to technique to become an excellent pulling guard. He also was smart. Smith understood the necessity to find a rhythm with the backs when pulling.

"I remember Jim Brown's rookie year, and I'm pulling for him, and he'd run out there and I'd tell him to slow down a bit," Smith said. "I'd say, 'Let me knock the guy on his can and you cut behind me. You make the touchdown and I get the block.' That's something people don't teach now. The lineman and the running back need to be talking all the time."

One former Lion told Smith that their coaches would show film of him to demonstrate how to play guard. Smith's teammates wouldn't be surprised to learn this.

"He was the prototype offensive lineman," Bobby Mitchell said. "I'd come out with the ball, and he was the first one I'd look for. He was awesome. I've been fussing for years about this guy getting in the Hall."

Perhaps Smith would have reached Canton had he played longer. But his Dallas real estate business was bringing home more money than football. And he was tiring of being away from his family. So he retired, in 1961, only to be lured back by Paul Brown with help from Renfro, tackle Mike McCormack, and linebacker Galen Fiss. Smith made the Pro Bowl again, then said he was done. But the Browns talked him into returning so they could trade him to Dallas. Smith agreed, and Cleveland received tackle Monte Clark in return.

But knee surgeries, in 1963 and 1964, cut short Smith's career and convinced him to retire for good. The Browns survived his departure quite well as Hickerson and John Wooten dominated up front. Smith's name, common as it was, wasn't forgotten.

"He was better than both, by far," Costello said. "Of all the offensive linemen I played with, he was the best."

15 **Bobby Mitchell**
Running Back, 1958–1961

Number 49

The NFL wasn't an option. Not for Bobby Mitchell. Even after he ripped through collegiate all-star games and even as he impressed Paul Brown in training camp, Mitchell had other plans. First would come graduate school. Then the 1960 Olympics. And then he would become a dentist, leaving football far behind.

As a rookie eighth-round draft choice in 1958, Mitchell didn't expect those plans to change. Especially not after he arrived in training camp, competing with more than a dozen other runners. Especially not after one of them, Leroy Bolden, kept putting up big numbers. Mitchell's outlook didn't budge even when he, too, started breaking off long runs.

"I was still upset that I wasn't an amateur and going for the Olympics," said Mitchell, one of the top 100-yard sprinters and high-hurdlers in the country. "And I still wanted to go to dental school. I promised my mother I would, and she was already calling me doctor. So I wasn't caught up in the pro thing. But I just got better and better and better, and the money kept getting a little better. It was so easy. I couldn't believe how easy it was."

So Mitchell stayed. And stayed. He's still not a dentist. More than forty years later, he's still in the NFL as the Washington Redskins' assistant general manager. Though he played only four seasons in Cleveland, Mitchell made an impact. He provided the shake to Jim Brown's power out of the Browns' backfield.

"He became the greatest will-o'-the-wisp runner ever to play for my teams," Paul Brown once said.

Mitchell's Illinois career was filled with long runs—he gained 173 yards on ten carries in an upset over Michigan—injuries, and fumbles. That's why he lasted until the eighth round. But Brown's son Pete attended Illinois and insisted his father watch Mitchell run at a Knights of Columbus track meet in Cleveland. Mitchell remembers that meet well: he stumbled out of the blocks and still won.

Brown was impressed and drafted Mitchell, once timed at 9.7 seconds in the 100-yard dash. Then Brown persuaded Blanton Collier, Kentucky's head coach, to use Mitchell in the East-West all-star game. After a day of long runs, a Canadian Football League coach visited Mitchell in his hotel room.

"The guy had a briefcase full of money and said, 'If I can get you to sign this contract and come to Canada, we'll pay you a lot of money,'" Mitchell said. "For a kid that never had anything, that was very effective. I don't know how I managed to this day to fight him off. I always had good intuition, and something kept saying to me, 'Don't do that. You can do better.'"

From there, Mitchell starred in the college all-star game against Detroit, helping his team, coached by Otto Graham, to a 35–16 win.

"They couldn't get anywhere near me," Mitchell said. "It was easy."

Neither could the NFL defenders as Mitchell won the starting halfback job from Bolden by gaining 114 yards against the Los Angeles Rams in an exhibition game—in the first half. He and Jim Brown both averaged nearly seven yards a carry in the season's first six games.

In the next-to-last game against Philadelphia, Mitchell returned a kickoff ninety-eight yards for a score and later ran sixty-eight yards with a punt for a touchdown in a 21–14 win. One year later, Mitchell rushed for 232 yards—five yards shy of Brown's club record—on only fourteen carries and barely played in the fourth quarter of a home game versus Washington. Such performances served to motivate Jim Brown.

"Paul Brown knew Jim Brown would never let me outplay him," Mitchell said. "Paul would tell me before games, 'You've got to break one, either on the kickoff or first play.' If I broke a run [early] past five yards, Paul knew Jim was going to go to war."

Tackle Mike McCormack said that competitiveness manifested itself in practice, too. Brown, determined to upstage the rookie, beat Mitchell in their first forty-yard dash.

"They would challenge each other," McCormack said. "Bobby would win one, and then Jim would win one. They pushed each other."

Mitchell also ran interference for Jim Brown, his roommate, off the field, particularly with Paul Brown. If the coach was peeved at his star fullback, Mitchell often would receive the anger. Once, in a Los Angeles hotel, Mitchell kept telling Brown it was time to leave for the team bus. Brown ignored the warnings, and when they finally did leave, they were late. Paul Brown stormed off the bus and stalked toward his running backs.

"When he gets to us, he doesn't go to Jim, he flies right into my face," Mitchell said. "And he just chews me out. Jim is just standing there with his arms crossed. Now, Jim knows he's talking to him, and Paul knows he's talking to Jim. They both know I wouldn't be late for anything. But Paul had to get it off, and I had to take it. I got on the bus, and the players said, 'Aren't you tired of taking that?' I said, 'What am I going to do?' And even Jim said, 'Man, I can't believe you keep taking that stuff.' But Paul needed some way to get to Jim without having a direct confrontation.

Bobby Mitchell

"But every time I talked contract with Paul, he darn near gave me what I asked for. He would always say, 'I'm giving this to you not because of the season you had, but because of the type of man you are.' I gladly accepted it."

The Browns gladly accepted him. In his brief Cleveland career, Mitchell gained 5,916 combined yards and scored thirty-eight touchdowns. He averaged 11.2 yards per punt return and 25.0 yards per kick return and scored three touchdowns in both categories. He averaged 5.4 yards—higher than Brown—on 423 carries.

But during the 1961 season, the Browns opened discussions with Washington about a possible trade of Mitchell for Ernie Davis, the Redskins' first round pick from Syracuse, who would never play for the Browns and died of leukemia in 1963. Paul Brown wanted two big backs, and as effective as Mitchell had been, he struggled in late-season games when the field froze, limiting the moves he could use. At the time of the discussions, Mitchell was stationed at Fort Meade in Maryland, returning to Cleveland for the games, and was unaware of the proceedings. Most others knew, however.

"In my last couple games, Jim was acting different [toward me], and I didn't know why," said Mitchell, who now holds an annual Hall of Fame golf tournament to raise money for leukemia in honor of Davis. "It turns out he was so concerned that someone had said he went to Syracuse to try and get Ernie to come to Cleveland. That was bothering him, and he kept saying, 'I never had anything to do with this.' I never knew it had happened until our last game."

He left a championship-caliber team for one constantly rebuilding. And he was switched to receiver. Mitchell also left an integrated team for one in which he would be the first black in franchise history. Washington was considered a southern town, and Mitchell had to deal with the wild expectations of blacks and the hostility of whites. Once, he was spit upon at a restaurant. But Mitchell endured, playing seven seasons for the Redskins, and retired with 14,708 combined yards and ninety-one touchdowns.

"It was a real jolt to come to a town and not be accepted," Mitchell said. "I never went through it to that extent in Cleveland. All these things bothered me. I always wondered how good I could have been if I could have just concentrated on football. I never went on the field without a whole week of problems on my shoulders. Then I'm out there playing with half the guys saying, 'I accept you.' And half saying, 'I don't know.'

"Fortunately, I had four years in the game. I came into the league immature, and Paul taught me about being a man. If I had not had my previous years with Cleveland, I wouldn't have made it in Washington."

16 **Beating the Odds**
1964 NFL Championship

Browns 27, Colts 0
December 27, 1964

 They closed their ears to the world, ignoring a sporting public which shouted the Browns had no chance. Every day, bookies seemed to tack on another point for Baltimore, tilting this game heavily the Colts way. A one-touchdown edge quickly shot to two. But they couldn't budge Cleveland's confidence.

Besides, the Browns could see what the world couldn't. Like coach Blanton Collier coming home after practices in an incredible mood. Or Collier confiding his confidence in reporters. This is what defensive tackle Jim Kanicki saw: practices as crisp as he'd ever seen, or would see, led by fullback Jim Brown. In a typical practice, Brown would carry the ball about five or ten yards, make his move then stop. Not during these two-week workouts.

"He was running like it was The Run," Kanicki recalled. "And the guards and tackles and defensive people were running farther and faster than I had seen previously. Some players on our team felt that they were getting toward the end of their careers and this was their last big chance. I remember our star players being ready to play, and that rubbed off on the other forty-four guys."

So, long before receiver Gary Collins boasted of a blowout win to a local television station a couple days before the game, Kanicki shared his own prediction with his wife, Sandy, after a particularly sharp practice at Fleming Field.

"I remember going home and telling my wife, 'We're going to surprise a lot of people this week,'" Kanicki said. "I'd never seen a team so high and as ready to play as we were."

Little things kept the Browns encouraged, too. The week of the game, linebacker Vince Costello and defensive end Paul Wiggin ate lunch with Kanicki, a second-year player preparing to face a future Hall of Famer. Wiggin and Costello harped on what a good matchup this would be for Kanicki. Jim Parker struggled with linemen who could match his power. The 270-pound Kanicki could do just that.

The more that outsiders said Cleveland had no chance, the more the Browns believed they could win. They checked the rosters and saw Baltimore's all-Pro line-

Receiver Gary Collins catches the first of his three TD passes, leading the Browns to a stunning upset and earning himself MVP honors.

up on offense, which included five future Hall of Famers. Sure, that concerned them.

"But the one thing they didn't have is anyone with a lot of speed," Costello said. Nor did they have Jim Brown and Paul Warfield.

"When you've got guys like that," Costello said, "you don't go into games thinking you're going to lose."

One media member noticed this attitude. The *Cleveland Plain Dealer*'s Chuck Heaton wrote that the Browns would win, following up on his preseason prediction of a championship. Many dismissed his prognostication as homerism. But Heaton called it something else: a wise selection.

"I was going to pick the Colts because they had the great Johnny Unitas and a great offense," Heaton said. "But I was standing outside [the Pick-Carter Hotel where the Browns were staying the day before the game] and I was talking to Bill Glass and Paul Wiggin, and they convinced me they were ready for the game. They were so excited. So I outlined what would happen in my column ["Plain Talk"], and it turned out that's just what happened."

But not everyone had the gift of prophecy. Defensive tackle Dick Modzelewski remembered the precise moment when he knew the Browns would win.

"When the game ended," Modzelewski said.

The Browns played as if they had something to prove. That's because they did. Two years earlier, owner Art Modell made his first stunning move. He fired coach Paul Brown, an ouster many pinned on the players and particularly Jim Brown, and replaced him with Blanton Collier. Contrary to public opinion at the time, it wasn't a move greeted with unanimous cheers.

Two players who left after Brown was canned, guard Jim Ray Smith and tackle Mike McCormack, said they never heard of any planned revolt against Paul Brown. Neither did others who remained, despite what cornerback Bernie Parrish said.

"I read a lot about what people were saying and how they were going to rebel," linebacker Galen Fiss said. "That wasn't true. To my knowledge, it wasn't that strong. We were a little unhappy because we weren't very successful and we had Jim Brown, the best guy in football, so we were trying to find someone to blame other than ourselves. The team wasn't that divided over it. Some had stronger feelings than others, but I was quite shocked when it happened.

"Modell used the players. He wanted very badly to be a players' owner. He rallied the players and used the players in their struggles with Paul. One time, we were riding the train to Chicago and Art was in the car, in the club room, with five or six of us. We were talking about things, and a lot of people were venting their spleens, and he was trying to dig things out. Until later, I didn't realize what was going on."

Guard John Wooten, Jim Brown's roommate, saw the fullback's unhappiness.

"He felt we had become too stereotyped and too predictable," Wooten said. "He was frustrated to the point where he was ready to quit."

In his book, *Out of Bounds,* Brown said, "It's ridiculous to believe that NFL players wield the clout to fire a coach. This is what I know: we did not want to play another season in seat belts. We definitely wanted Paul to open the offense. But we wanted *Paul* to do something about it. In pursuit of the Team Fires Paul Brown storyline, the press may have been, let's say, encouraged by Art Modell."

Whether or not the move was applauded at the time, it was done. And the Browns had to show the world they could survive. They started off 6–0, in 1963, before Wooten said a racial split on the team caused it to tumble as they split their last eight games. Among other problems, Brown rushed for an NFL-best 1,863 yards, but his own teammates voted tackle Dick Schafrath as the team's MVP. Collier took charge.

"He immediately stepped in and [got rid of] the players who caused the [racial dissension]," Wooten said. "That team was whacked up and put back together."

Defensively, Kanicki, Modzelewski, obtained in an off-season trade, and cornerback Walter Beach became full-time starters. Modzelewski came over from Cleveland nemesis New York in a trade he didn't want. But the Giants were dismantling their team, sending all-Pro linebacker Sam Huff to Washington as well.

Modzelewski and his brother Ed, a former Brown, owned a home and a restaurant in Cleveland.

"I was working in the restaurant when [Giants coach] Allie Sherman called and told me," Modzelewski said. "Sam Huff was in the restaurant when he learned they traded him. Everyone said, 'Stay the hell out of the restaurant.'"

Modzelewski, known for his tough play, became a stabilizing and enthusiastic force along the line, and the Browns embarked on a special season, winning nine of their first ten games. For the first time in a regular-season game, Cleveland beat Detroit, 37–21. But St. Louis forced the Browns to win their last game of the season after beating them 28–19.

No problem. In week fourteen, quarterback Frank Ryan threw five passes in a 52–20 rout of Modzelewski's old team to win the Eastern Conference title. Still, the Browns were dubbed "Laugh Champs" as few took them seriously; the Western Conference earned all the praise.

Jim Brown finished the regular season with 1,446 yards rushing. Warfield, the rookie receiver, led Cleveland (10–3–1) with fifty-two catches for 920 yards. Ryan led the NFL with twenty-five touchdown passes. But the defense ranked fourteenth in the league in yards allowed. It would have to be much better against the Colts (12–2). No one had stopped their offense all season as they scored fifty-four touchdowns, an NFL record.

Six Colts, five on offense, would eventually reach the Hall of Fame: Jim Parker, quarterback Johnny Unitas, receiver Raymond Berry, running back Lenny Moore, tight end John Mackey, and defensive end Gino Marchetti. Plus they had a hotshot young coach in Don Shula.

Was there any doubt about this game? Not throughout the country. The line reached as high as seventeen before the bookies settled on the Colts as seven-point favorites.

The Browns and Colts wrestled for control throughout the first half. But it was Cleveland that turned in the first big play, one whose aftershocks lasted all day. In the second quarter of this scoreless game, Unitas, from his own thirty, flipped a screen pass to Moore with blockers in front of him. And a lot of room to run.

Fiss, on the weak side, had taken his usual deep drop on the play, trying to help with downfield coverages. Moore was his responsibility.

"I knew I was in trouble," Fiss said. "He had three lead blockers in front of him. I had to gamble, so instead of taking on the blockers, I shot the gap between two of them, roadblocked the guy, and got away with it. It looked for a moment like it would be a big play. Suddenly, it went absolutely the other way."

He dropped Moore for a five-yard loss. Fiss still occasionally watches the play on tape, and one of his grandsons, a young linebacker, sits with him.

"I'm fully aware of all the attention the hit got," Fiss said. "Maybe undeservedly. Sometimes I heave a sigh of relief that I did make the play."

His teammates felt the same way.

"If he misses it," Kanicki said, "it's gone."

Fiss actually made a number of big plays in this game. He tipped a pass that Costello intercepted. He knocked fullback Jerry Hill onto his fanny on a third-quarter swing pass and played a near-perfect game. But no play resonated like the one when he toppled Moore.

"That's what did the whole thing," Modzelewski said. "We knew we could stop them."

They did. Fiss had plenty of help. The secondary shut down the Baltimore receivers. Cornerback Bernie Parrish claims he diagrammed the defensive game plan, convincing coordinator Howard Brinker to allow the secondary to play tight on the receivers, figuring they weren't fast enough to beat them. Unitas later said the Browns' secondary would play tight when the 20 mph wind whipped in the Colts' faces and would play off when it was at their backs. Whatever the reason, Unitas managed just ninety-five yards passing.

"Bernie doesn't deserve any more credit than anyone else," Costello said. "That book of his, which I have never read, is totally false. I don't want to start a fight with Bernie; we're friends. But he had nothing to do with anything I did or Galen did or anything the linebackers did."

Besides, the line played perhaps its best game of the season, forcing Unitas on

Linebacker Galen Fiss set the defensive tone by stopping Baltimore's Lenny Moore on this second-quarter screen pass as tackle Dick Modzelewski watches.

the move much of the first half and disrupting the Colts' timing in their passing attack. Unitas was sacked six times.

Kanicki especially played well, neutralizing Parker. At his midweek lunch with Wiggin and Costello, the group chatted about how former Pittsburgh defensive tackle Ernie Stautner used to play well against Parker. Stautner attacked Parker and never gave him a chance to get set. That was Kanicki's strength. It also helped to have an extra week to study film.

"I was probably as strong as he was," Kanicki said, "and they didn't give him any help because I was just a young player. And the style of offense they played helped. They didn't run a lot of sweeps. They ran at you, and I was more suited for that type of play."

While Kanicki was establishing himself, Modzelewski and ends Paul Wiggin and Bill Glass also were playing well. That wasn't surprising.

"Everyone thought Parker was going to kill Kanicki," Modzelewski said. "But Big Jim went in there with his big biceps and just knocked the hell out of the guy. I never thought we would [shut them out]. Before you knew it, everything started turning our way. The more it did, the more our confidence shot up."

In early 1998, Kanicki received a taped radio broadcast of the Colts' announcers calling the game.

"Toward the end of the game, they were saying I was a big surprise," he recalled. "They didn't look to me to be a factor. It's thirty-four years later, and I'm riding in a car at fifty-five years old and thinking about how I wish I could do it all over again."

The confidence skyrocketed when the teams were tied 0–0 at halftime. It escalated even more when the Browns finally scored on a forty-three-yard field goal by Lou Groza. Collier set that up with a pregame decision. Because of the wind, Collier decided it was best to have the wind at his team's back in the third quarter.

When the Browns won the toss, they deferred their choice until the second half, taking the wind. The result: a third-quarter punt by Baltimore's Tom Gilburg got caught in the wind and died twenty-five yards from the line of scrimmage near midfield. Cleveland was soon stopped, but the Browns had moved far enough to allow Groza to kick a forty-three-yard field goal, his NFL-record seventh field goal in a championship.

The offense took it from there. On the next possession, Brown, beginning to tax the Colts, ran forty-six yards to the eighteen. Then Ryan called for a hook pass to Gary Collins, who was drawing man coverage while Warfield was doubled up. Collins was also feeling good. The night before the game, he predicted to Wiggin that he would catch three touchdown passes and win the MVP. Baltimore's strategy helped.

"At that point in my career, double-teaming me took me out of the game," said Warfield, who would finish with one catch. "But that was their gamble. We knew we had one-on-one situations with Gary against [cornerback] Bobby Boyd. The timing between he and Frank was great."

When Collins ran the hook route, Boyd had it played perfect. So he broke the route, headed toward the goal posts, and hauled in Ryan's pass for a 10–0 lead. They connected again on the next series as Boyd misread the Browns' formation and played short when he should have been deep. Collins was wide open for a forty-two-yard score and 17–0 advantage. Ryan had all day to throw as the line,

Quarterback Frank Ryan is mobbed by fans en route to the locker room after this victory over the Colts.

led by right tackle Monte Clark, who shut down Marchetti, staved off a Colts' rush that had recorded fifty-seven sacks.

The rout was on, and the 79,554 fans sensed an historical day. After Groza's ten-yard field goal in the fourth, set up by a twenty-three-yard Brown run, Ryan and Collins did it again, this time from fifty-one yards. Boyd actually tipped the ball, but it landed in Collins's hands. Collins finished with five catches for 130 yards and three touchdowns. He was named the game's MVP, just as he had told Wiggin. Meanwhile, Ryan was mobbed by fans, many of whom had booed him earlier in the season, en route to the locker room. There, Collier hugged Kanicki, saying, "You proved me right." But Jim Brown felt the largest relief.

"Unless he wins a championship, even a superstar is never fully accepted,"

Brown said in his book. "Some people use the absence of a title to criticize a successful individual. . . . He's too much of a soloist. Otto Graham announced it to the world about me [before the season]. So it felt GOOD to get that primate off my back."

In their fifteenth NFL season, the Browns had won their fourth title. They would win no more. Wooten is convinced the Browns would have won two or three more titles if Brown hadn't retired after 1965. Other teams were better that decade, the players said. Some said the '65 team was better, others pointed to '68.

"The '64 team was the worst one I played on in the '60s," Collins said.

But none did the job when it counted. The 1964 team did.

"I really didn't think we'd shut them out, that was beyond belief," Fiss said. "But we felt we could win because our offense was strong enough with Jim Brown to handle them and control the ball. If we didn't make mistakes [defensively], we could win. We were underdogs. Everyone said we didn't have a chance. But we didn't believe that for a minute."

	1	2	3	4	Total
Colts	0	0	0	0	0
Browns	0	0	17	10	27

THIRD QUARTER
C - Groza 43 FG. Browns, 3–0
C - Collins 18 pass from Ryan (Groza kick). Browns, 10–0
C - Collins 42 pass from Ryan (Groza kick). Browns, 17–0

FOURTH QUARTER
C - Groza 10 FG. Browns, 20–0
C - Collins 51 pass from Ryan (Groza kick). Browns, 27–0

17 **Jim Brown**
Running Back, 1957–1965

Number 32

They rattle off his stats as if they were their own, protecting his place in history. Other running backs beat his numbers. But none, in his teammates' minds, topped his stature. It's not even close. When arguments ensue about the greatest runner ever, they punctuate the discussion with this: There was Jim Brown. Then there was everyone else. Period.

In nine seasons, Brown rushed for an NFL-best 12,312 yards and 106 touchdowns. He retired in his prime, at twenty-nine, to make movies, one season after rushing for 1,544 yards and twenty-one touchdowns and earning league most valuable player honors.

Walter Payton, Eric Dickerson, and Tony Dorsett surpassed his career rushing yardage—playing two to four more games per season than Brown did—but none got within a whiff of his career yards per carry of 5.2, still the NFL's best. And all played into their thirties. Baseball's Pete Rose has the most hits, but was he the best hitter?

"If Jim had played four more years, who knows where that record would have been," tackle Mike McCormack said.

As a rookie, Brown rushed for a club record 237 yards at home against the Los Angeles Rams—sixty-nine yards coming on a touchdown run that ended without his helmet—en route to his first league MVP trophy. Four years later, he matched that mark versus visiting Philadelphia.

Brown mixed speed with strength. He has four of the Browns' eight longest runs from scrimmage, yet often his greatest runs resulted in only four yards as a mound of defenders swallowed him.

Brown had his faults. He irritated Paul Brown with halfhearted blocking attempts and miffed him by sometimes not giving 100 percent, in the coach's mind, with each practice snap. And Paul Brown thought his star divided his team racially. The coach even said in his autobiography that he sometimes regretted drafting Brown and considered trading him before 1962, which happened to be Paul Brown's last year in Cleveland.

But Jim Brown stayed through 1965, helping the Browns to an NFL champi-

Jim Brown

onship in '64. He retired with eight NFL rushing titles, four more than anyone else in history.

Brown's feats were legendary and spilled into other sporting venues. He was an all-American lacrosse player at Syracuse, and in his first summer golfing, he shot a 77. He made it look easy, but it wasn't. Brown had worked on his golf game, playing up to seven times a week. Some days, his hands bled. What people saw, however, were the results.

"I didn't think it was so great," Brown once said. "I put enough damn work in."

In high school, he built a high jump in his backyard, where he spent hours working on his form. And, for hours at a time, he worked on his running starts, increasing an already quick first step. Brown also scored thirty-eight points per game for the basketball team.

Brown had his reasons for everything he did. He got up slowly every time so the defense never knew if he was injured. He remained aloof from many teammates so they would pass along his behavior to curious opponents.

And when he got hurt, Brown hated for anyone to know. In a 1963 game, New York defenders constantly scraped his eyes when they tackled him. By game's end, his vision was cloudy. Two days after the game, his eyes remained blurry. But the coaches asked him to practice so no one would know he was hurt. Then he dashed off to the doctor's at night.

"If certain guys wanted to think I was otherworldly, I'd be the last man on earth to dissuade them," Brown said. "Mystique is a powerful force."

No one matched Brown's mystique. Why was he great? Listen to his teammates and others, who remain in awe.

Athleticism

Linebacker Dale Lindsey: "He was the best basketball player, the best golfer, and, I'm sure, the best lacrosse player. Whatever it was, he would have been the best of anything he wanted to be. The aura around him was the same as around Muhammad Ali. If there was a guy who could have whipped Ali, it would have been Jim Brown."

Tackle Mike McCormack: "He was just a great natural athlete. You just look at him: thirty-two-inch waist, 232 pounds. [In 1958, Bobby Mitchell's rookie year], he and Bobby were running against the clock. Bobby came out of Illinois as the indoor Big Ten sprint champion in the sixty-yard dash. Paul [Brown] lined the two up together against each other, and Jim beat Bobby in that forty-yard dash. You get a man going that fast with that size . . . He was just an outstanding talent."

Receiver Paul Warfield: "I've never seen a back who has been endowed with all the things needed to rush the football. He was an amazing physical specimen who had the physique and an upper torso of a 250–260 pounder. And he was a finesse player. He never abused his power or strength. He was so nimble on his feet and athletic, and he could do all the things smaller people could do. He could catch the ball out of the backfield with one hand, he would throw the ball, and, on top of that, he was an extremely intelligent player. I was in tremendous awe. You'd see the film and see the things this guy did, and it was incredible. It was almost like no other human being could do them."

Broadcaster Gib Shanley: "He was the second best athlete I've ever seen, behind Secretariat."

Preparation

Warfield: "We were rehearsing our sweep against the [Redskins'] 4–3 defense [in 1964], and Jim Houston was impersonating Sam Huff at middle linebacker. We started the sweep, and [Brown] stopped in his tracks, and told Jim, 'You're coming to my left on this play. Sam Huff never comes that way when I run this play. He always runs to the right.' [Brown] asked if we could line up and run it again and he told Jim, 'Show it to me running to the right. I want to see it in practice so it will help me get a feel for running the play.'"

Guard John Wooten: "I roomed with Jim and knew him a lot different than the others. When we got into big games, he just went into a totally different thing. The preparation . . . he almost withdrew, and I knew all he was doing was getting ready. He'd talk quieter, he wouldn't smile, and he'd read all the time. We'd get into the hotel two days before the game, and he wouldn't say three words. He would sit and read magazines, books, whatever he could get his hands on, as opposed to other times when he would kid with somebody, particularly the young guys. He would read up where those guys were from and say stuff to them. But not before the big games.

"What he would say to me is, 'When we run this play, make sure the line understands this is what we want.' We would meet as an offensive line with the quarterbacks on Saturday night to talk about the plays that we thought were pretty good. And he'd give me the plays he thought would work. He'd say, 'Tell them we've got this play, and we need to run it early so we can see how the defense is going to react to it.'"

Guard Gene Hickerson: "On Thursdays, it was offensive day at practice. That was the one time he used to cut it full speed because timing is everything in sports. If the defensive players didn't get out of the way, he would run them over in practice. They'd always step aside and let him go."

Superman Syndrome

Hickerson: "I don't think he wanted people to see him work out. He wanted everyone to think he was Superman. He's one of the best specimens of a human being I've ever seen. There was not an ounce of fat on him. He weighed more than I did."

Jim Brown got help from his teammates, but he didn't always need it.

Defensive tackle Dick Modzelewski: "Jim got hurt one time, and he was supposed to meet Doc Ippolito at the hospital the next day. They're still waiting for him. The trainers told me if he wanted treatment, he would come in early before anyone else came in so no one else saw him.

"The thing I admired most was the only time he ran out of bounds was to kill the clock in case we were behind. The man ran three or four extra yards and was the kind of guy who would gain extra yards with people on top of him. In Yankee Stadium once [before Modzelewski joined the Browns], he ran the ball through the middle of the line. When you see the film, there is a pile of Giants on top of him, eight or nine of us, and he's still moving. We couldn't bring him down.

"[Another time] Gene Hickerson had me pinned, and Jim ran a draw play. I stuck my hand out and accidently got it caught behind his pad. I couldn't get my hand out. Hickerson knocked me down, and Jim took off, and his feet went out from underneath him and he fell down. The crowd gave me a standing ovation. I took my helmet off and said, 'Thank you very much.' It was a hell of an accident, but it was damn great."

Paul Brown (in his autobiography): "His feet were never far off the ground when he ran, so he was very difficult to knock down. Another key was the unusual muscle structure in his upper thighs that generated his power. . . . In a game, his great second efforts were his trademarks and he never once complained to me even after running twenty-five or thirty times a game."

The Slow Rise

Running back Bobby Mitchell: "That trademark of Jim taking his time walking back to the huddle came from him realizing, 'If I'm going to be the guy carrying the ball, I want to be able to come back each time with a blast.' He'd come back to the huddle and lean over, and everyone would wonder if he's all right. Then he'd get up to the line and *Boom!*

"My rookie year, I would try to get that extra yard because it was a competition thing between he and I. Meanwhile, I'm getting blasted going [for the extra yard] and walking back to the huddle. He pulled me aside and said, 'Hey, man, I'm the big man, you're the little man. So get your butt back in the huddle.'"

Thirst for Winning

Shanley: "Jim Brown just wanted the ball. One game, I don't remember which one, he was just standing near Paul Brown on the sideline and yelled out real loud, 'Tell the man to give me the ball.' They said he didn't block, but when he came out of the backfield, he took two guys with him. That's just as good as blocking."

Warfield: "He wasn't always the easiest person to get to know. But he was a tremendous teammate. He was an unselfish teammate. Rushing titles were important because they were an individual accomplishment. But he wanted to win championships. That's lost in some players today. He could have said, 'I have to rush the ball so I can get to 100 yards.'

"If we were behind in a game and we had to throw the ball three or four times or more to win, that didn't bother him because winning was the most important thing. Today, you hear players cry when they don't get the ball even if they're winning."

Wooten: "He would take over in the huddle. We were in a tight game once, and [receiver] Gary Collins asked for a pass. [Quarterback] Frank [Ryan] was hesitant about calling it, and Jim said, 'Hey, man, give the man the ball. He knows what he has, give him the ball.' He was that kind of a guy."

Individuality

Hickerson: "He was always very warm to [the linemen]. But Jim minded his own business and kept to himself. I used to agitate that dude, but I knew when to stop. I knew when I ruffled his feathers up pretty good. I still agitate him every time I see him. Now that he's getting old, he'll just grin at you."

Mitchell: "Jim wanted you to be a man. He was way ahead of his time. I was immature. If anything bothered him about me, it was my immaturity. He set out to make a man out of me in his own way. Any conflict would come because I couldn't do all the things Jim could do. I felt I couldn't do all those things because I wasn't Jim Brown, and he could do those things and get away with it. I'd be gone.

"Paul Brown used me in the sense that he felt I was the only sobering force for Jim Brown. I could get him to come to the bus on time so he wouldn't be late, and I could somewhat keep him from coming in after hours, all those things Paul didn't want him to do, which no one else had the nerve to do. Jim would play with that because he was such a strong, forceful guy. I was always caught up in that. That's one reason I was his roommate. No one else could live with him, and I had a little influence on him. But I don't want anyone to think I had a lot of influence on him."

Wooten: "He called me two days before he announced his retirement. He said, 'Get with the guys and tell them I'm not coming back anymore. I've done all I can do to try and explain [to owner Art Modell] that I'm ready and will be ready and in great shape. I'm running, working out. But I can't live like that. I've done everything I can to prepare. The movie [*Dirty Dozen*] is just running late. I can't be put in a situation where someone's being unfair to me.'"

The Man

Hickerson: "Jim was very easy to work with. He didn't ask for much, just get out of the way. He didn't need much help."

Modzelewski: "I had never met him before I came to the Browns, but I knew what kind of player he was. My brother Ed [the starting running back in 1956] said he saw Jim run the ball and said, 'I guess I'll be his backup.' Jim had great enthusiasm to win. The man impressed me, and he still impresses me. When you practiced against him and saw how the man got the moves and everything else, it totally impressed me. That was a confidence builder. I always said God made one running back. It was Jim Brown, and he threw the mold away."

18 **Frank Ryan**
Quarterback, 1962–1968
Number 13

Defensive linemen flattened him, drilling his body into the turf. Sometimes, they did worse. One year they separated his sternum. Another time, they ripped up his shoulder. When that happened, Frank Ryan altered his throwing motion and ruined his elbow. So he would take an injection, suit up, and play—then stand his ground while linemen tried to repeat their maimings. This was a man known for his brains?

But Ryan didn't survive in the NFL because he was smart. He lasted because he could hang in the pocket and deliver a bullet at the last minute, allowing his receivers time to break free.

"You just have to ignore the [rush]," Ryan said. "If you worry or think about that, then you're distracted from the concentration that's required. I never concerned myself with the fear of being hit or the fear of the pass rush. I never took pride in getting pounded around or throwing the ball under pressure. I did take pride in throwing a good ball, and I didn't always do that."

For seven seasons, six of which he started, Ryan blocked out his surroundings, including the boos that rang down even in his championship season, and delivered the football. Ryan made three Pro Bowls and twice led the NFL in touchdown passes, including one year with a banged-up elbow. And he brought Cleveland its last football title in 1964.

Coach Paul Brown was gone for most of Ryan's success in Cleveland. But he did foresee it after obtaining him from the Los Angeles Rams in 1962.

"Getting Frank was one of the best trades I ever made," Brown said in his autobiography. "The more I worked with him, the more I wished we had had him a few years earlier because we could have won big with him as our quarterback."

The Browns also reached the championship game, in 1965, but lost to Green Bay. Ryan's last play-off march came, in '67, when Dallas buried Cleveland, 52–14. By this time, Ryan's arm strength had plummeted because of various injuries. And three games into '68, coach Blanton Collier benched him in favor of Bill Nelsen.

"I'm sure my strength and ability to throw had been marred, no question about it," Ryan said. "You always hate to sit down, but it was warranted. I should have

taken myself out two or three years before that, instead of going through the difficulty I had to go through to be an effective quarterback.

"I didn't enjoy football the last five or six years I played. [After 1964,] it was downhill. I was still challenged by it, and I wanted to be effective and had that Texas-bred desire to throw a good ball, so I had a hard time realizing that I had overstayed my welcome too long."

His sternum injury, suffered in 1961, healed fine. But after the '64 championship, Ryan was nailed in the Pro Bowl and separated his shoulder. Part of it may have been his own doing. In the championship win over Baltimore, Ryan threw into the end zone for tight end Johnny Brewer on the last play of Cleveland's 27–0 win. That angered many Colts, including end Gino Marchetti who vowed to get Ryan. Guess who hit him in the Pro Bowl? Marchetti, along with tackles Rosey Brown and Merlin Olsen.

"I give Marchetti credit because I'm sure he wanted to get a lick in," Ryan said. "I can appreciate his ire. [But] I was just trying to get a play into Johnny Brewer because he hadn't caught many passes that year."

Ryan didn't need surgery, but his shoulder was taped up for a while, helping alleviate the injury. Recovering from that injury led to another: while lifting weights, Ryan tore his right elbow.

A constant pain shot through his arm, requiring Ryan to take cortisone injections on Wednesdays and on game days.

"I had injections just so I could have a good practice and have an opportunity to throw the ball without worrying about my arm in the game," Ryan said. "It got worse and worse, and playing with it made it even worse. I never wised up to that, and the medical group with the Browns never wised up to that either."

Ryan had torn a muscle in the attachment to his elbow, yet it took time to diagnose the problem. Soon his throwing motion changed, and his arm strength diminished. Yet his effectiveness continued. In 1966, Ryan tossed an NFL-best twenty-nine touchdown passes, a Browns record until Brian Sipe topped it in 1980, playing two more games.

"You learn to manage your concentration," said Ryan, who spent two seasons as a backup in Washington before retiring. "You just have to do it. There's always someone breathing down your neck to take your place. There have been many fine quarterbacks in Cleveland, some of whom I played with when I was there, so you couldn't let them in."

Ryan paid a price for his toughness, as he has one terrible knee, and shoulder problems impair his gardening. In the mid-70s, he had a cervical disk operation which stemmed from an injury with the Browns. Ryan endured because he had Jim Ninowski and later Bill Nelsen hungry for the job. Also, Ninowski had surrendered the job to Ryan because of an injury. So Ryan played hurt, and his toughness was noticed.

Frank Ryan

"Frank took some terrible shots, and he would never let anyone help him off the field," defensive tackle Jim Kanicki said. "People appreciated that."

And they appreciated his play. In his five seasons as the primary starter, Ryan averaged 23.4 touchdown passes and fifteen interceptions a season. His 2,974 yards, in 1966, remained a Browns record until 1979.

Ryan was smart enough to use his weapons: Hall of Fame receiver Paul Warfield and two Hall of Fame running backs in Jim Brown and Leroy Kelly. Not to mention receiver Gary Collins. Ryan wasn't accurate—he never completed more than 52 percent of his passes in his five full seasons as starter—but he could hit the big play. And he improved after coach Blanton Collier tutored him, helping him to focus on his target.

"He was highly intelligent and a good passer," receiver Paul Warfield said. "He had the ability to throw the long ball and liked to throw it. Of all the passers I played with, he threw it the best. He was just bigger and stronger than others I played with."

How far? Ryan said he once won a bet with a college friend by throwing the ball 100 yards.

But Ryan also was known for his off-field pursuits, particularly mathematics. Five months after winning the world championship, Ryan earned a Ph.D. in math from Rice University. He studied during the season, staying up late after watching game films with his shoulder wrapped in tape. His thesis, titled "Characterization of the Set of Asymptomatic Values of a Function Holomorphic in the Unit Disc," made for numerous cracks in the media.

"Jim Murray, the [late Los Angeles] columnist, wrote the funniest line I've ever seen," said broadcaster Gib Shanley. "He wrote, 'The Browns have a quarterback who understands Einstein's theory of relativity and 10 other guys who didn't know there was one.'"

Writers labeled him as a "kook," among other things, which angered Ryan.

"I didn't see anything with it," said Ryan, who was living in Vermont and on leave from his professor duties at Rice in 1998. "Many people played football and were very successful doing other things. There were doctors, lawyers. . . . It was an easy angle, and it was different, so they could exploit it. People clearly missed the mark of trying to hit those two drums simultaneously. They were totally disconnected as far as I was concerned."

Sort of.

"I enjoyed the intellectual pursuit of the degree very much," Ryan said. "That was as much an accomplishment for me as playing football."

19 Offensive Resurgence
1968 vs. Dallas

Browns 31, Cowboys 20
December 21, 1968

The decision came at 3:00 A.M., deep into a sleepless night for Browns coach Blanton Collier, kept awake by an offense that had fallen asleep. A change needed to be made. And Collier knew where he must turn: to a veteran quarterback whose passes wobbled and whose knees ached so bad they hurt his teammates.

So, three games into the 1968 season, Collier benched Frank Ryan, he of the 1964 championship ring and three Pro Bowl appearances. In came Bill Nelsen, he of the two knee surgeries in three years. The change was necessary. In the past two games, the offense had scored just thirteen points as the Browns dropped to 1–2. A lingering shoulder injury and age had caught up to Ryan.

"When I got there [in 1963], he was strong-armed and he could throw a sixty-yard pass, and it's on the money and thrown before the guy broke," Browns defensive tackle Jim Kanicki said. "In the end, he was just slingshotting it out there."

Collier noticed, as did the players. With stars such as receivers Paul Warfield and Gary Collins and running back Leroy Kelly, an offense must produce more than this one had. But all this offense had produced were headaches.

After losing to the Los Angeles Rams, 24–6, in Cleveland, Collier had seen enough. He called Ryan into his office the next day and informed him of the change, later saying, "he was hurt, but understood." Those who knew Collier said the change must have hurt him, too, given his feelings of loyalty. Ryan had delivered to Collier his only NFL title four seasons earlier.

This was not what Nelsen expected when Pittsburgh traded him to Cleveland in the off-season. The Browns shipped their backup quarterback, Dick Shiner, and veteran tackle Frank Parker to the Steelers for Nelsen and defensive back Jim Bradshaw. To Nelsen, it was an exchange of backups. The Browns' staff, however, had witnessed a decline in Ryan's health and play. They needed insurance.

Yet who would figure the gimpy-kneed Nelsen, twenty-seven, would be the answer? He had missed parts of the past three seasons with various knee injuries, including the first two of an eventual twelve surgeries—seven on his right and five more on his left. In a roundabout way, the injuries helped Cleveland.

Safety Mike Howell returns a first-quarter interception, one of four on the day by the Browns, in this 31–20 play-off win over Dallas.

"We never would have had Bill Nelsen if he had been in good health," guard Gene Hickerson said. "He could barely walk when he came to the Browns. And if we broke down in pass protection? Oh Lord, I felt bad about that."

Nelsen, in later seasons, wore large metal braces on both knees, but he rarely complained.

"They weren't real good," Nelsen said of his knees. "But I could walk."

He didn't plan on sticking around. Nelsen had bought a home in Los Angeles, expecting to last a couple seasons with the Browns then return to the west coast. After all, Nelsen said, "Frank was the quarterback." But four games into his first season in Cleveland, Nelsen started and led the Browns to a win over his old team. After losing the next week to St. Louis, Cleveland ripped off eight straight wins, scoring thirty or more points in seven of them and forty or more in three. The Browns' 394 points were the third most scored in franchise history. It's no wonder they clinched the Century Division with one week to play, their fourth division title in five seasons.

To punctuate the success, five offensive starters—Kelly, Warfield, Hickerson, tight end Milt Morin, and tackle Dick Schafrath—made the Pro Bowl. Warfield certainly enjoyed Nelsen. Though the Browns used more short passes, which were Nelsen's strength, Warfield had his best season since his rookie year of 1964, catching fifty passes for twelve touchdowns and a 21.3 yards-per-catch average—best ever by a Brown.

"Bill was a very smart quarterback," Warfield said. "He didn't have the talent Frank did. As a matter of fact, Bill was pressed to throw a spiral, and secondly, he was pressed to throw it fifty yards in the air. But what he could do, he did very well. He knew exactly how to get the football to me. He knew when I wanted it, where I wanted it, how I wanted it. Whenever I said something to him, he listened intently, and he would come back to me and get it to me how I wanted it."

Nelsen, with nineteen touchdown passes and only ten interceptions, had saved the offense and, perhaps, the Browns. He provided guidance to the NFL's second-youngest team, one that had bid farewell to longtime starters Paul Wiggin, Galen Fiss, and Lou Groza. Also, Ben Davis and Mike Howell became full-time starters in the secondary, and second-year receiver Eppie Barney had to fill in for Collins, injured in week four.

"A lot of players had lost confidence in Frank," linebacker Dale Lindsey recalled. "But Bill had tremendous leadership skills. You watch the guy each week get his knee drained and get his injections to play, and you know he's going to show up.

"He'd be after the defense if we weren't playing well. He added a spark because we were a young team and we didn't have the great leadership we did when I first got here [in '65]. Back then, we were more afraid of the veterans than we were of the coaches, and they told you what the deal was. We had lost that in the transition of Galen retiring and Paul's retirement. Nelsen filled that role as well as anyone. He'd get on everybody."

But Nelsen knew when to chew out a player or when to buy him a beer. Before this Eastern Conference championship, Nelsen treated his offensive line to lunch. Nelsen told his line: "Just give me three seconds to throw the football Saturday and forget about the bill."

"He was the type of guy who hung out with the boys," remembered Dan Coughlin, then a backup Browns writer for the *Cleveland Plain Dealer*. "That wasn't Frank's style, but it was Nelsen's. And the guys responded to Nelsen. It's not that they didn't like Frank, but it was night and day how they responded to this guy."

Nelsen said, "I had a little fire in my ass, and I enjoyed playing. I could get on people and say, 'Come on!' Fortunately, I could do some things on the field, too. I threw a lot of bad passes. Gary Collins used to kick the ball after I threw it at his feet and say, 'Jesus Christ!' But I wanted to play and win.

"Frank had been at a point where he didn't have the fire left in him. He did a great job there, but this was an opportunity for me to play with these great players. Maybe I got some breaks, and things moved along well. Sometimes the personality of the quarterback and the team makes the difference."

So, even though the Cowboys had defeated the Browns four straight times and crushed them by thirty-eight points in last year's play-offs and whipped them by twenty-one in the season's second week, Cleveland was confident—thanks to Nelsen.

Before Cleveland (10–4) took the field for its divisional play-off game against favored Dallas (12–2), with 81,497 fans awaiting the contest, one man rose to speak, walking to the middle of the locker room as his teammates sat on their stools. Receiver Tommy McDonald, a former great with Philadelphia now in the sunset of his career and acquired when Collins was injured, sensed his last chance for a second championship.

"I didn't earn my way here," McDonald told his teammates. "I'm here because Gary Collins got hurt. I'm proud to be wearing this uniform. I'm proud to be a Brown."

On he went, the intensity and volume increasing with each sentence until he began screaming. His teammates started screaming, too. Collins later said it was "like Knute Rockne."

"That was the only time all season that he said anything," Kanicki said. "And it was an impassioned plea. It gives you an extra kick because here's a guy who had proven himself as a great player and he's at the end of his career and he's saying things that you know he felt."

After the game, McDonald played down the speech's significance. But tackle Monte Clark told Coughlin, "It was the trigger that turned everyone's switch."

Maybe it was needed. Maybe it wasn't. But it made for good legend. Still, the Browns had to produce for any speech to be deemed inspiring. They did. While

Nelsen and the offense sparked the Browns en route to the play-offs, the defense provided the boost in this game. Not surprisingly, it came via thievery. In 1968, the Browns led the NFL in interceptions with thirty-two, still a franchise record. Against Dallas, Cleveland would pick off four passes.

It began when safety Mike Howell intercepted quarterback Don Meredith early in the first quarter, setting up a thirty-eight-yard Don Cockroft field goal for a 3–0 lead. Then came a big break for the Cowboys and a test of the Browns' mettle. Late in the first quarter, blitzing Dallas linebacker Chuck Howley crashed into Nelsen, jarring the ball loose. Howley scooped it up and raced forty-four yards for a touchdown and 7–3 lead. Would this be like 1967 when Dallas won, 52–14, at the Cotton Bowl? No. This time, the Browns didn't collapse.

"We weren't down at all," Warfield said. "We were at home, and that was the biggest boost. The Cowboys were a better ball club than us at that point, but we hung in there and made things turn around."

Nonetheless, Dallas increased the lead to 10–3 on a sixteen-yard Mike Clark field goal. But the defense kept doing its job, and finally the offense chipped in its share. Late in the first half, Nelsen flipped a forty-five-yard scoring pass to Kelly, tying the score at 10 and giving Cleveland momentum. The Browns had run a similar play on the previous down, but no Cowboy covered Kelly, a defensive lapse that he relayed to Nelsen in the huddle. So they ran it again.

"There wasn't anyone around me," said Kelly, who caught the pass alone at the fifteen. "That was an easy touchdown pass."

It didn't take long to add more momentum, not to mention points, in the second half. On Dallas's first possession, Meredith dropped back, scanned the field, spotted running back Dan Reeves on the left side, and threw the ball.

Apparently, Meredith didn't see Lindsey. He intercepted the pass at the Dallas twenty-seven, bobbled it for a few seconds, and scampered in for a touchdown, where he was mobbed by his teammates, including McDonald, who had raced over from the bench and pulled Lindsey down.

"Meredith underthrew the ball," Lindsey said. "Or he didn't expect me to be where I was. He hit me in the hands with it. It's not like I did anything spectacular. It was a poor play on his part. I would love to say, 'Oh, yes, I knew it was coming all along.' But I'd be lying. A lot of things happen that are pure accident. That's all that really happened. It was one of those deals where I was in the right spot at the right time."

Meredith would throw one more interception in the NFL. Three plays after Lindsey stung Dallas, cornerback Ben Davis picked off a pass intended for receiver Lance Rentzel at the Cowboys' thirty-six.

On second and nine, Nelsen called for a sweep—"old chestnut," he called the play—and Kelly swept around right end, breaking one tackle and getting key blocks by guard Gene Hickerson, tackle Monte Clark, and center Fred Hoaglin, for

Linebacker Dale Lindsey, being pulled down by Tommy McDonald, is a hero after returning this third-quarter interception for a score.

a thirty-five-yard scoring run. All of a sudden, with 2:31 elapsed in the second half, Cleveland took a 24–10 lead.

"You could see the steam go out of them," Lindsey said.

That was enough for Dallas coach Tom Landry, who had called this his "best team in Dallas." Meredith was out; Craig Morton was in. Nothing changed.

With Dallas trailing 24–13 in the fourth quarter, Morton led a drive to the Cleveland thirty. But on third down, cornerback Erich Barnes intercepted his pass for Rentzel. Nelsen took advantage by moving the Browns to midfield, where they faced third and one. Then he fooled everyone. Nelsen faked to Kelly up the middle, dropped back, and hit Warfield for a thirty-nine-yard gain, setting up Ernie Green's two-yard game-clinching touchdown, providing the Browns a 31–13 lead. It was only the fourth rushing touchdown Dallas had allowed all season.

The Cowboys drove for a meaningless late score as thousands of fans—some of whom would swipe fifteen of the Browns' fur-lined parkas—positioned themselves behind the Browns' bench, ready to smother the team.

Cleveland's young defense, which received numerous standing ovations, made this scene possible. This unit had allowed twenty or more points in five of the first seven games, but they squashed one of the NFL's best offenses in the Eastern Conference championship, holding Dallas to 286 total yards and only 86 on the ground. Ends Jack Gregory and Ron Snidow, who had to replace Bill Glass (injured) and Paul Wiggin (retired), respectively, withstood constant runs their way. But it was a shared mind-set that spurred the defense.

"We never feared the Cowboys," Lindsey said. "They were a finesse team so we knew we wouldn't get hit too hard, but they might try to trick you. Our coaching staff was strict: We wanted to be as physical as we could, and if we did that long enough, we would win the game. Damn the coaches were right."

Cowboys fullback Don Perkins said afterward, "This is the toughest time I've ever had against Cleveland. . . . Without a doubt, this is the best I've ever seen the Browns. Even on film, I've never seen them as strong as they were today."

They were so good it was laughable, at least to linebacker Jim Houston.

"They'd run at us, and we'd knock them down," he said later. "We were standing there laughing at them. They had beaten us four times in a row, and we were tired of it."

This win didn't resonate around the country like the '64 championship, because two more wins still were needed for the ultimate title. But *Plain Dealer* writer Chuck Heaton wrote that it was "comparable" to that victory. Many were surprised that the Cowboys, favored by 3½ points, had lost.

"I remember afterward, [announcer] Tom Brookshier interviewing me and I'm saying, 'We did this, we did that,'" Nelsen said. "And he was so awestruck that we actually won the game."

At the beginning of the season, the Browns didn't anticipate greatness. Instead, they found it. But their path to the Super Bowl would be blocked by Baltimore, eager to dish out the same pain it had received four years earlier.

The Colts had no problem accomplishing their goal at Cleveland Stadium, winning 34–0. It was the first time the Browns had been shut out since 1950 and a reversal of the teams' '64 championship meeting. As in that game, Baltimore would lose as heavy favorites to the Joe Namath-led New York Jets. The Browns went home, stung by a loss that still hurts.

"That was my biggest career disappointment," Kanicki said. "In my mind, this was a better team than the one we had in 1964. Leroy was at the top of his game. Paul was at the top of his game. The defensive line was better. I knew Baltimore could not beat the Jets, but we matched up so much better against the Jets."

Nelsen is still convinced about what would have happened.

"We would have won," he said.

They say that because of what they did against Dallas. It was Cleveland's most complete game of the season, one that showed the Browns' potential when everything clicked.

"I've said before, this is the greatest Browns team I've ever played on," said Houston, a starter in 1964. "I guess I'd have to say this is the greatest game."

	1	2	3	4	Total
Cowboys	7	3	3	7	20
Browns	3	7	14	7	31

FIRST QUARTER
C - Cockroft 38 FG. Browns, 3–0
D - Howley 44 fumble recovery (Clark kick). Cowboys, 7–3

SECOND QUARTER
D - Clark 16 FG. Cowboys, 10–3
C - Kelly 45 pass from Nelsen. Tie, 10–10

THIRD QUARTER
C - Lindsey 27 interception return (Cockroft kick). Browns, 17–10
C - Kelly 35 run (Cockroft kick). Browns, 24–10
D - Clark 47 FG. Browns, 24–13

FOURTH QUARTER
C - Green 2 run (Cockroft kick). Browns, 31–13
D - Garrison 2 pass from Morton (Clark kick). Browns, 31–20

20 **Gary Collins**
Receiver/Punter, 1962–1971
Number 86

 A young Gary Collins watched the star end on TV and film, absorbing the moves Baltimore's Raymond Berry used to escape defenders. He wasn't fast, but he was always open. Or so it seemed. This intrigued Collins, never known for his speed.

So, after watching Berry, Collins headed to the University of Maryland field and mimicked this future Hall of Famer's routes. Then Collins nearly copied his career. He never reached the Hall of Fame, but he did do this: catch the ball and score touchdowns. Few Browns ever combined those talents better than Collins.

"He was as fine a big receiver as anyone I've seen in the game," receiver Paul Warfield said. "If [a defensive back] allowed him to get close, he could break off a pattern very sharp and crisp. I saw him take a number of the great cornerbacks and cut them to pieces. He was really a clutch player."

Then there was Collins's punting. Few in the NFL kicked better than Collins, especially in 1965.

But Collins knows his spot in Browns history. So the game everyone wants to talk to him about is the '64 championship. Several days before the game, Collins, never afraid to voice his opinion, told a Cleveland television station that the Browns would win big.

"When you're twenty-four and stupid, you do things like that," he said. "I didn't give a damn who the Colts were."

Apparently not. Collins caught three touchdown passes in the 27–0 rout.

"Everyone thinks that's the only damn game you ever played, which is understandable," Collins said. But, he added, "It's good to be known."

That wasn't all Collins was known for, however. His post move became legendary, and he developed a wicked out-route off that pattern. Collins called the latter his best move, because everyone waited for the post. Everyone knew this: When a big catch was needed, the Browns often went to the six-foot-four Collins. During his six seasons with future Hall of Famer Warfield, Collins led the Browns in catches six times to Warfield's two.

"We had a great receivers' coach in [former Brown] Dub Jones, and he incorpo-

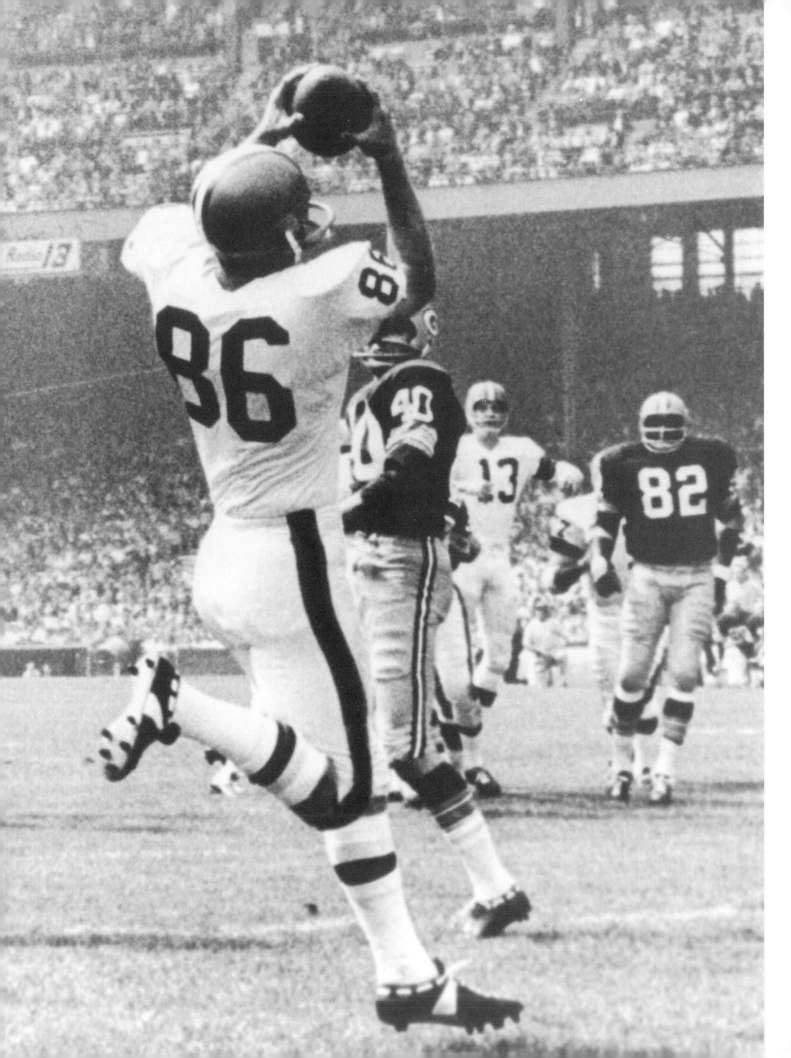

rated the things that fit your style," Collins said. "I couldn't do the stuff Warfield could do, and Warfield couldn't do stuff I could do. I was big. He was small. I could do things great, and he could do things great. That's why it's unfair to compare people."

In ten seasons, Collins caught 331 passes, seventy of which ended in touchdowns, and averaged sixteen yards per catch. Only running backs Jim Brown and Leroy Kelly scored more for Cleveland. No Cleveland receiver can top his mark of one score for every 4.7 receptions. The Browns' receiving tandem of Collins and Warfield was one of the NFL's best.

"Gary had great quickness," quarterback Bill Nelsen said. "People don't realize that. With his size, he could wall off [defensive backs] and overpower them. And he had great hands. He chewed me out many times, saying, 'Throw me the ball!' I had two receivers who were so quick making their breaks, and I was late throwing the ball because I was watching their moves."

Collins reached that point by watching moves of other receivers, notably Berry. First, though, he starred at Williamstown (Pennsylvania) High School and then accepted a scholarship to the University of Maryland where he played receiver and defensive end.

When he went to college, Collins hoped football was his ticket out of the coalmining existence. Collins's father worked twelve-hour shifts in the mines, and Collins once said that, when he was thirteen, he went into the mines for the first time. He never went back. To make sure he didn't have to return, he worked on his receiving by copying his idol Berry.

"I was probably faster than him, but he ran such precise patterns," Collins said. "I took what he was doing and expanded on it. If he went one, two, three, I took it to four, five, six. The best compliment I ever received was when we played an exhibition game against the Colts in the mid-'60s [in Cleveland]. Raymond didn't play, but he watched from the sidelines. After the game, he came over and said what great patterns I had run. That was quite a thrill."

Collins also had keen eyes.

"A lot of times if I broke early and the quarterback was ready to release the ball, I could see it just as it was leaving his hands," Collins said. "It wasn't real clear. But it meant that I could follow it if it was good or bad longer than someone who didn't pick up the ball quite as quick. And if it was a bad pass, I could make a great catch. But my greatest asset was that I could catch."

Still, when he left Maryland, even his coach, Ted Nugent, expressed doubt over his future in the NFL, questioning his work habits. The Browns were convinced otherwise and picked him fourth overall. "Paul Brown made a good choice," Collins said.

He blossomed in his second season, grabbing forty-three passes, thirteen of which ended in touchdowns. Then, in 1965, Collins made his first Pro Bowl after catching a team-high fifty passes, including ten touchdowns, and leading the NFL with an average of 46.7 yards per punt, still a Browns record.

"I go in for negotiations, and [owner Art] Modell was gonna give me a $3,000 raise for receiving," said Collins, who stopped punting upon Don Cockroft's arrival in 1968. "He said nothing about the punting."

Collins followed that up with another Pro Bowl receiving season in '66, catching a team-best fifty-six passes. But various injuries, including a separated shoulder in '68, limited Collins to one more strong season. He led the Browns with fifty-four catches in '69.

He retired two years later. Hard times followed as a flood wiped out his Pennsylvania farm, in 1972, cleaning out his savings. A stint in the World Football League couldn't revive him, and his sporting goods shop closed, in 1979, the same year he divorced. But Collins viewed his situation in football terms, once saying, "There are things in your life you have to cope with. That's like third and twelve. You've got to get thirteen yards, and you do it."

So he did it, and soon his life turned around. He remarried and became an insurance agent and is now semiretired in Hershey, Pennsylvania. He said he's not nearly as opinionated as in his early days—teammates called him an "individual" and "loosey-goosey"—but the strong thoughts remain.

Among them:

• On looking back: "It's gone, like last winter's snow. It's over. It's nice that people remember you, and I still get fan mail. But I was never a big superstar. Who was, except someone in New York or Jim Brown? Now a relief pitcher who saves four games in Cleveland is a hero. It's a little different."

• On Modell's decision to move the team to Baltimore: "I didn't [care]. I cared about my friends that I played with, but the Browns that I knew, there aren't any left. I'm just not nostalgic. It's over, folks. People ask, 'Don't you love the Browns?' No, they stopped paying me in 1972. I loved what *I* did, and I loved my teammates. I liked the bread, too."

• On hard work: "If I had worked harder, I would have been a hell of a lot better. I smoked, but I never took drugs, and since then I don't drink or smoke. If I did what I've been doing the last fifteen years, I would have been a much better player in the fourth quarter. And that's when I shined."

• On the Hall of Fame: "What really tees you off . . . is that people just look at statistics. My stats would never get me in the Hall of Fame. I have nothing against [former Pittsburgh receiver] Lynn Swann, but people consider him for the Hall of Fame and my stats are better. We had an identical number of catches [Swann had five more], and he had only fifty-three touchdowns and I had seventy. He was the MVP of [Super Bowl X], and I was the MVP of the [1964 NFL championship]. I punted and had higher career stats, but if you said, 'Should Lynn Swann or Gary

Collins be in the Hall,' nine out of ten people would say Lynn Swann because they see him on Saturday football games. They measure stats instead of quality, and that irks me. But I told my family, 'Don't ever look for me to get in the Hall of Fame.'"

But his last opinion sums up what he'll truly be remembered for. Not one game, but one quarter.

"I was a son of a bitch in the fourth quarter," Collins said. "I made the big plays. I hear people say, 'Michael Irvin is The Man. He wants it.' I say, 'That's what *I* did.' People would ask Dub Jones, 'Why did you throw the ball to Collins in that crucial situation?' And Jones would say, 'I ain't stupid. I'm throwing the ball to the guy who could catch it.' Guess who was on the other side? An All-Pro receiver who got selected to the Hall of Fame. But everyone knew who was catching the ball."

21 **Paul Warfield**
Receiver, 1964–1969, 1976–1977

Number 42

Paul Warfield, nearing the end of his junior year at Ohio State, sat slumped in front of his locker, frustrated over his role and concerned about his future. At least in football. Nearby sat teammate Joe Spano, his mind heavy with similar thoughts. When Spano announced he would chuck his football career for baseball, Warfield spouted out he'd do the same. A handful of major league teams had expressed interest in Warfield from the time he was fifteen. Now it was time to go. Spano knew better.

"You won't sign," Spano told him. "You'll be back next year."

Spano was right. But not by much. After much haggling, Warfield rejected a contract offer from Pittsburgh before his senior season. The biggest reason: The Pirates wanted to send Warfield, who had played only sandlot ball after high school, to the low minors. Also, they wanted the gap-hitting center fielder to report immediately and spend three weeks to a month at an affiliate in the South. By this time, though, Warfield was committed to returning to Ohio State, and this would have cut into practice. So he turned down the offer. And wondered. He still does.

"Of course, I do," Warfield said. "I really thought at one point that, before I went to Ohio State, I was as good in baseball, or better, than I was in football."

His football career, however, took the sting off any regrets. Making the Hall of Fame has a way of erasing any second-guessing. No Browns receiver played the position with more grace than did Warfield. Yet few were tougher. That combination served him well. One play he was an artist, floating for passes over the middle, a ballet dancer in pads. The next play he sought the head of a linebacker.

"Warfield was one tough dude," linebacker Dale Lindsey said. "He and I used to get into it in practice. People think of Paul as one of those beautiful Bambi reindeers running all over catching the ball. He would knock you right on your ass if you weren't careful. I remember, in 1969, he took out [the Los Angeles Rams' six-foot-eight defensive end] Lamar Lundy. Laid him out like a tree. They beat us, but Paul laid Lamar out."

It pleases Warfield that teammates remember this side of him. It's a side he developed at run-oriented Ohio State.

"That came in handy, and other coaches recognized my value as a blocker in the

Paul Warfield

running attack," Warfield said. "Most receivers are finesse guys. I want people to remember I was a complete player."

When he arrived in Cleveland as a first-round pick, in 1964, he had the skills to become that player. Even former Cleveland coach Paul Brown spotted his talent, which is why he recommended to his old team, for whom he was doing some scouting, that they draft Warfield. But Brown suggested the secondary-thin Browns use him in the defensive backfield, where he had earned accolades in college. However, in a minicamp workout at Lakewood High School, Warfield impressed Blanton Collier and his staff at receiver.

"I was gung ho to do something to let them know I should be a wide receiver," Warfield said. "I ran a pass pattern, and I don't know what I did, it was almost accidental. Sometimes fate comes into the picture. They had Billy Truax, their second-round pick and a tall, gangly linebacker, cover me. I made a move on him, and the combination of the quickness and the burst and the sharpness of the cut . . . Blanton made the decision right there."

They were sold. But doubts remained for Warfield. He recalled driving the sixteen miles from his home in Warren, where he had grown up a Browns fan, to Hiram College for his first training camp with uneasy feelings.

"There were literally a thousand things going on in my mind," Warfield said. "First and foremost, I kept asking myself if I was good enough to play. Today, a lot of these young men think, 'It's the NFL, I'm good enough to be here.' I had doubts, serious doubts because there was no other level. I had passed the test at other levels, but I wasn't sure. But it was good for me to have that little bit of doubt or that anxiety to know that I didn't have it made, even if I was a first-round draft choice."

The Browns quickly eased his transition. On his first day, Collier called Warfield into his office where former Cleveland receivers Dub Jones and Ray Renfro had gathered. Renfro, who had retired after 1963, told Warfield he would be his project and teach him all he knew about playing receiver.

For the next six weeks, Warfield did whatever Renfro suggested. He suggested a lot, teaching Warfield everything from the proper stance to running precise patterns. Renfro also taught him always to think ahead. In an exhibition game against Los Angeles that summer, Warfield ran a post pattern for a touchdown. When he reached the bench, Renfro congratulated him and then asked, "What are you going to do next?" So next time out, Warfield ran a pattern that began like a post but didn't finish that way. He scored again.

"When Ray told me about attacking a defensive back, I understood perfectly, and I could put myself in their perspective and how it would affect them," Warfield said. "Ray was the greatest teacher of pass-pattern execution I had ever been around. I worshipped him because I had known him as a player."

Warfield took Renfro's knowledge and crafted quite a career, one that lasted fourteen seasons. Though other receivers retired with more inflated numbers, few could match his productivity where it mattered most. He averaged one touchdown every 5.2 receptions, second best in club history to Gary Collins, and only Renfro's 19.6 yards per catch topped Warfield's 19.2, making him a perfect threat to keep the defense from keying on the Browns' vaunted running game.

Warfield also retired with three championship rings, but only one came with Cleveland. After the 1969 season, the Browns, desperate for a quarterback, traded Warfield to Miami so it could draft Mike Phipps.

"That was probably the worst thing that ever happened to the Browns," quarterback Bill Nelsen said.

Initially, it was a horrible event for Warfield.

"It came out of nowhere," he said. "I didn't want to play anywhere else. It was a tremendous shock and an emotional jolt."

Yet, in an odd way, the trade allowed Warfield to see what he meant to Cleveland. When he returned for a *Monday Night Football* game, in 1973, with two Super Bowl titles to his credit, the fans thanked him for his service. They stood and cheered. Warfield saluted them back.

"Of all the things that happened, that's one of the greatest moments," said Warfield, who would return for a two-year stint in 1976–77. "They let me know they had not forgotten me."

Nor had Warfield, who still lives part-time in Cleveland and runs a sports apparel business out of South Florida, forgotten the fans or the Browns. That's why he was part of an ownership group which tried to buy the new franchise.

"I enjoy revisiting that period," Warfield said. "I have to admit, my heart belongs to the Cleveland Browns."

22 **Prime Time Hit**
1970 vs. New York

Browns 31, Jets 21
September 21, 1970

Howard Cosell blew into town, carried, it seemed, by his own hot air. Yet no one appeared to notice. It was *Monday Night Football.* It was ABC-TV. It was Cosell and Don Meredith and Keith Jackson. It was prime time.

But it was also ABC's first Monday night game. Until now, Cosell was just a—take your pick—arrogant, opinionated, loudmouthed boxing announcer. And Mondays were saved for second-guessing the quarterback or the coach, not for playing a game. Besides, there was a bigger attraction. Much bigger. One that quickened even the heartbeat of some Browns.

"All I knew was, Joe Willie Namath was coming to town," said Cleveland defensive end Joe Jones, a rookie soon to be nicknamed "Turkey." "We didn't get into the hoopla of the TV."

The fans knew Namath was coming, too, which is why 85,703 turned out for this season opener, the largest crowd in Browns history and the thirteenth straight home crowd of more than eighty thousand fans. Another two thousand were turned away at the gates. Had the game been televised in Cleveland, that wouldn't have been a problem. But it was blacked out. The only option was to watch it live. Many came to see the New York Jets panty-hose-wearing, night-life-loving, Super Bowl-winning quarterback nicknamed "Broadway Joe."

The Browns would try to swarm him later. The fans got to him first. As Cleveland quarterback Bill Nelsen walked out of the Hollenden House, a downtown hotel where both teams had stayed, he spotted Namath surrounded by autograph hounds.

"What's going on here?" Nelsen recalled thinking. "This is our home city."

Namath, though, was one of football's biggest stars, if not its biggest. Less than two years earlier, he sat poolside at the Super Bowl and predicted his upstart American Football League Jets would beat the heavily favored Baltimore Colts of the more established NFL. They did. Namath, goatee and all, became a legend.

That's why ABC, and Roone Arledge in particular, wanted the Jets on its first Monday night telecast. Browns owner Art Modell, chairman of the NFL's televi-

Browns receiver Gary Collins is about to grab the first TD pass in a *Monday Night Football* game, hauling in this eight-yard toss from Bill Nelsen.

sion committee as well as the league's president, offered his team as the first opponent.

The league agreed, perhaps because of Modell's TV influence during the previous decade. Also, Modell had helped orchestrate a merger between the AFL and NFL that same year, convincing Baltimore and Pittsburgh to join the Browns to play in the new American Football Conference, a move that angered Cleveland fans by a two-to-one margin, according to a *Plain Dealer* poll. Of course, the $3 million each of the three teams received made the decision easier. So the league rewarded Modell, giving him the game. And Namath.

But Namath wasn't the only draw. The Browns had reached the NFL championship game the past two years and were coming off a 10–3–1 season. In twenty years, the Browns had played in eleven championship games, a mark no other team could match in that span.

The Jets had their Super Bowl win, but they still wanted to prove they weren't some novelty act from a supposed inferior league. Sound familiar? It did to Cleveland coach Blanton Collier, who had embarked on a similar quest as an assistant coach on the Browns' 1950 team, their first year in the NFL. Cleveland's dominance in the old All-America Football Conference drew snickers and sneers from the NFL, until the Browns repeated their success in their new league. That's why Collier understood the Jets' mind-set.

"I remember Blanton talking in training camp about the old AFL teams coming up against the NFL teams," Browns defensive tackle Jerry Sherk said. "And he was scared to death about what would happen. He said, 'These teams are hungry and innovative. We can't stand pat and think we're going to walk all over these teams.' He recited what Namath had done to the Colts.

"It wasn't only about the Jets' game. It was about the hunger the AFL had. Blanton was correct. The AFL really brought some things into the game offensively and defensively, not that they dominated, that the NFL teams did not know how to handle."

Dale Lindsey said, "They were still a great team, and we were new in that conference, and we had our noses stuck in the air, which were soon to be bloodied and put on the ground. There were a lot better players there than we thought."

The Browns had some hunger, too. In their minds, they, not Baltimore, should have played New York in the Super Bowl in January 1969. But the Colts beat them, 34–0, in the NFL championship, earning a spot in the Super Bowl where they were favored by eighteen points.

"We should have played them in the Super Bowl," Nelsen said. "Then poor Baltimore wouldn't have lost to them. We would have won."

Other factors merged to heighten the meaning of this game: Jets coach Weeb Ewbank and Collier once lived together when both were Browns assistants, and New York defensive coordinator Walt Michaels was a four-time Pro Bowl linebacker in Cleveland. So playing in the first *Monday Night Football* game was not a dominant thought on the players' minds.

"We could have played the Jets on a Tuesday afternoon," Lindsey said.

The Browns didn't hide what their early game plan was. They wanted to pick on the Jets' rookie cornerback tandem of Steve Tannen and Earlie Thomas, and they wanted to do it early. They did. After the Cleveland defense held, Nelsen led a fifty-five-yard, nine-play march that ended in an eight-yard pass to receiver Gary Collins for the first touchdown in a *Monday Night Football* game. Big deal? Not to Nelsen.

"Fifteen years after the game, someone said, 'You were the first one to throw a *Monday Night* touchdown pass,'" Nelsen said. "I didn't know that. I just went out and did what I did, and we won the game."

And don't ask Collins about the play.

"I was the first to get knocked out on *Monday Night Football* [in the third quarter]," he said. "So I don't remember the day of, the day before, or the day after."

He doesn't remember the Browns' second possession, which also resulted in a touchdown. Consecutive pass interference calls keyed an eighty-four-yard drive, one that ended when running back Bo Scott ran around left end for a two-yard touchdown and 14–0 lead.

But no lead was big enough against Namath. New York had a plan, too. Namath told Cosell in a pregame interview that the Jets would test Sherk, a rookie second-round pick from Oklahoma State, who would be facing veteran left guard Randy Rasmussen.

Sherk's day already had been long and grueling. He enlisted in the National Guard, rather than go to Vietnam, and that weekend he was stationed at Camp Perry, near Sandusky and about two hours from Cleveland. On Monday morning, Sherk was awakened at 4:00 A.M. to peel potatoes.

"Had I been in the league one more year," Sherk said, "and had my wits about me, I would have said, 'Go to hell, I've got a Monday night game to play. You peel the darn potatoes.' I was very tired [at game time] and at the same time very excited. Then it was Namath. I was stepping into the arena, and I was in awe. I was lost that first game."

How lost?

"All I remember was chaos," Sherk said. "And people hitting me from all directions."

Or running over him. All night, Cosell picked on Sherk, seemingly blaming him whenever the Jets gained any yardage. Later in the game, Sherk split his chin open when Rasmussen's helmet banged him. Sherk needed eight stitches after the game.

This, along with Cosell's harping on his play, is what Sherk wrote about in a 1980s article for *Sports Illustrated for Kids,* titled, "My Worst Day." And it's a lesson he delivers to at-risk kids, telling them things can get better.

For Sherk, that would be true. But not on this night. New York took advantage of his inexperience, driving sixty-one yards with halfback Emerson Boozer crashing in from the two for a touchdown. The Jets' offense was clicking, even against the Browns' blitzing defense, which rarely touched Namath.

"I'd be [a couple of feet away], and he would just get the ball off," Lindsey said. "The Jets were the first team that could throw the ball against a blitz without picking everybody up, because they had a great quarterback who could get the ball off."

Cleveland, though, could do something once the ball was in the air. With New York at the Browns' seventeen, cornerback Walt Sumner jumped high and intercepted a pass intended for receiver George Sauer.

Linebacker Jim Houston followed with an interception deep in Cleveland territory as the Browns led 14–7 at halftime. A new member, obtained in a controversial trade, was about to thrill his new fans.

With Nelsen's knees ailing and no solid backup, the Browns needed a quarterback of the future. They found a willing suitor in Miami, which owned the third pick overall. It would only cost Leroy Kelly or Paul Warfield, two all-Pro players in 1969 en route to the Hall of Fame. The Browns traded Warfield. All the Warren, Ohio, native had done in six seasons with Cleveland was catch 215 passes for 4,346 yards and forty-four touchdowns.

Then the Browns shipped seven-year defensive tackle Jim Kanicki as well as reserve linebacker Wayne Meylan and rookie fullback Ron Johnson to the Giants for receiver Homer Jones. With the third pick, Cleveland chose Purdue's all-American quarterback Mike Phipps.

Jones, though, was supposed to replace Warfield. He already had posted similar numbers to Warfield in New York: 215 catches, 22.6 yards per catch, thirty-five touchdowns. But Giant fans often booed his numerous drops. Clevelanders didn't have that chance—Jones was gone after one year.

In his first game, though, Jones thrilled his new fans. Jones took the second-half kickoff ninety-four yards for a touchdown, which, Cosell said, justified the trade. Instead, as Sherk said, "It was probably the only play he made for the Browns." It was enough to give Cleveland a 21–7 lead. Namath wasn't done. He spent the second half piling up yardage and moving New York into scoring range. Boozer scored from ten yards out, cutting the Jets' deficit to 21–14 in the third quarter.

Cleveland's Don Cockroft kicked a twenty-seven-yard field goal, hiking the lead to ten points, but missed an eighteen-yarder early in the fourth. Four plays later, Namath hit Sauer, who slipped past defensive back Freddie Summers, playing man coverage while the linebackers blitzed, for a thirty-three-yard score. If fullback Matt Snell, who gained 108 yards, had not fumbled at the Cleveland seven yard line early in the fourth quarter, the Jets might be leading.

Cleveland linebacker Jim Houston returns a second-quarter interception off Jets quarterback Joe Namath.

But, with 1:30 remaining, New York would get another chance after it forced Cleveland to punt. The Jets' Mike Battle called for a fair catch at the New York thirty, but he let the ball bounce. Bad move. The ball rolled to the Jets' four.

After a pass moved the ball to the eighteen, Namath dropped back again, looking for tight end Pete Lammons. But reserve linebacker Billy Andrews, who had replaced a tired and ineffective Lindsey earlier in the quarter, intercepted. Collier, ever the gentlemen, said Lindsey was fatigued. Andrews returned the interception for a game-clinching twenty-five-yard touchdown, giving the Browns a 31–21 victory.

New York had dominated the yardage—455 to 221, with Namath throwing for 299 yards—but the Jets finished with four turnovers and a club-record 161 yards in penalties.

In the booth, Cosell did his shtick. He raved about Namath. He bad-mouthed Sherk, which the rookie read about the next day, and he ticked off at least one parent.

"My mother sent Cosell a letter after the game," Nelsen said. "She said, 'Who won this game? All you talked about was Joe Namath.'"

Eventually, though, Cosell's style attracted viewers. His ego might have forced out Keith Jackson, the play-by-play man who left after one season. But others tuned in to hear him hype the story lines before the game and deliver Sunday's highlights at halftime. And maybe he'd say something outrageous. Or maybe they'd hear Meredith say something like this, "Fair Hooker. I've never met one." Which is what Meredith said about the Browns' receiver by that name in the opener. Now *Monday Night Football* is steeped in tradition. Who knew?

"No one had any idea it was such a great night to have a game," Sherk said. "But Monday is a dreary back-to-work day, so it's great to come home and zone out one more day. For the players, it became a day where they could sit around and turn on football, and you became a fan by watching other teams. That was another reason to play hard. And no one knew. It all started with Cosell and the drama he infused."

	1	*2*	*3*	*4*	*Total*
Jets	0	7	7	7	21
Browns	14	0	10	7	31

FIRST QUARTER
C - Collins 8 pass from Nelsen (Cockroft kick). Browns, 7–0
C - Scott 2 run (Cockroft kick). Browns, 14–0

SECOND QUARTER
N - Boozer 2 run (Turner kick). Browns, 14–7

THIRD QUARTER
C - Jones 94 kickoff return (Cockroft kick). Browns, 21–7
N - Boozer 10 run (Turner kick). Browns, 21–14
C - Cockroft 27 FG. Browns, 24–14

FOURTH QUARTER
N - Sauer 33 pass from Namath (Turner kick). Browns, 24–21
C - Andrews 25 interception return (Cockroft kick). Browns, 31–21

23 **Blanton Collier**
Head Coach, 1963–1970
Assistant, 1946–1953, 1962, 1975–1976

He tamed men with his smile or a kind word, reminding them, perhaps, of their father. Or grandfather. Those zingers that stung their souls vanished when Paul Brown left. Now Blanton Collier was in charge. And he was nice. They liked that.

"He was a sweetheart of a human being," fullback Jim Brown once said.

"He treated us like we were his sons," linebacker Dale Lindsey said.

None of that would have mattered, however, if Collier couldn't coach. Fortunately for the Browns, and owner Art Modell, he could. Otherwise, Modell's firing of Paul Brown could have ruined the franchise he had bought only two years earlier.

The players responded to Collier's soothing touch. Collier opened up the offense, restored Jim Brown's enthusiasm, and the Browns rolled to a 10–4 record his first season, followed by the NFL championship in his second when Cleveland stunned heavily favored Baltimore, 27–0. In Collier's eight seasons, the Browns never finished below .500. His career record was 76–34–2, and Cleveland advanced to the championship four times under Collier.

His influence continued after he left. When Forrest Gregg was hired, in 1975, he coaxed Collier out of retirement to be his quarterback coach. One year, Collier put in two plays in training camp.

"I remember those two plays more than any plays we ever ran," tackle Doug Dieken said, "because Blanton broke them down and said, 'This is what you're supposed to do, why you're supposed to do it, and how.' He was unbelievable in that respect."

After he retired following the '76 season, Collier remained a part of the organization despite living in Houston. Whenever the Browns played the Oilers, Dieken said he would get a scouting report on Houston defensive end Elvin Bethea from Collier, who had watched film of him. Another time, Collier noticed a flaw in Dieken's footwork and offered tips. A year later, Dieken made his only Pro Bowl.

Dieken never played for Collier, yet he says: "Everyone asks me who was the best coach I ever played for, and it was a guy who never coached me, and that was Blanton. I wish I had the opportunity to play for him."

Blanton Collier

Those who did relished the moments. Certainly, Collier benefited from Paul Brown's influence, not to mention the players he had assembled. Collier latched onto Brown when he was in the navy and Brown was coaching at the Great Lakes Naval Training Station near Chicago.

Collier, whose coaching career began at Paris (Kentucky) High School, in 1928, returned day after day to Brown's practices, leaning on a fence and absorbing the action. Eventually, Brown and Collier chatted, and soon he joined Brown's staff. Collier followed Brown to Cleveland, in 1946, and quickly made a deep impact, helping teach Otto Graham how to play quarterback in the wing-T.

After that inaugural season, Collier, on Brown's orders, analyzed every play the offense ran. Collier wrote down the reasons why a play worked or failed. "I'd have settled for something half as comprehensive," Brown later said. "But Collier doesn't do things by halves."

This effort led to the annual grading of players and began Collier's rise in coaching. Then, in 1954, Collier replaced his first legend, taking the job Bear Bryant had vacated at Kentucky. But eight years later, Collier was fired and returned for Brown's final season in Cleveland, which ended with a 7–6–1 record. In 1963, he replaced his mentor, a promotion the players supported, especially Jim Brown. In 1962, Brown rushed for 996 yards. The next season, under Collier, he gained 1,863.

"Jim and Paul didn't get along at all," said guard John Wooten, a former roommate of Jim Brown's. "He and Blanton were like father and son. You've never seen such a relationship. It was like Michael Jordan and Phil Jackson. Jim and Blanton always got along. Jim saw in him a gentle, great teacher who just knew football. I remember standing at Fleming Field watching those two walk off the field arm in arm or sitting and talking in meetings. Blanton had that hearing problem so Jim would always sit where he could talk to him without having to talk loud. And they would talk about plays."

Collier solicited ideas from his players, something Paul Brown, right or wrong, never did. In meetings, Collier would list twenty to twenty-five running plays that might work against that week's opponents. Then he would open the floor for suggestions.

"He'd say, 'Jim, which plays do you like best,'" receiver Paul Warfield recalled. "And Jim would select no more than four or five out of twenty that he wanted to work on. Blanton respected his ability and insight as to how people tried to stop him."

"Blanton knew his football," running back Leroy Kelly said. "He was The Man. We had some good assistant coaches, but he was the brains behind what we did offensively." Collier helped develop the concept of "option blocking" which, in short, gave linemen the option of taking their man one way or another, depending on how they were aligned. Collier also returned to using Brown on sweeps and having him throw a pass or two.

But Collier wasn't limited to offense, as he once was a defensive assistant under Brown. Also, Collier enjoyed nothing more than a quart of ice cream and game film. He loved digesting both.

"Where he gained respect was on the practice field," said Dan Coughlin, a backup beat writer for the *Cleveland Plain Dealer* in the '60s. "He went from position to position and taught them. The defensive tackles, the cornerbacks. He was an expert on technique at every position. Players told me he knew more about the technique of every position than any other coach, even the coach who coached that position."

Jim Brown, left, and Blanton Collier discuss strategy.

Defensive tackle Dick Modzelewski joined the Browns in '64, then coached under Collier for three seasons. Before Modzelewski started coaching, Collier asked him if he wanted to be a coach or a teacher.

"I said, 'I hope to be a teacher,'" Modzelewski said. "He said, 'You're absolutely right. There are too many coaches that line up dummies and have their players hit those dummies for twenty to thirty minutes. You take the film and you study and you become a teacher.' On my last day of coaching, in February 1990, I finished watching tape and writing stuff down. I got into that habit and couldn't get out of it because I still heard his words. That was the only way to be a good coach."

Collier wanted everyone to understand what was going on and in meetings, if a player looked confused, Collier would start over. Even if it added an hour or two.

"You got to where you paid attention and knew what the hell was going on," safety Ken Konz said.

But Collier found other ways, mostly through a gentle approach. Kelly learned that on his first day of training camp. Kelly missed his bus from Cleveland to Hiram, and then, on the next bus, neither he nor the driver knew where Hiram was. Kelly was dropped off beyond Hiram and had to wait until the same bus made its way back. By the time he reached Hiram, it was 5:30 P.M. He was supposed to arrive by 2:00.

"He said, 'At least you know what time to get here, it's time to eat,'" Kelly said.

But he never barked at Kelly. Another time, broadcaster Gib Shanley recalled bumping into Collier in the lobby of a St. Louis hotel room the night before a game.

"He has a handkerchief and is wiping the tears away from his eyes," Shanley said. "I said, 'What's the matter?' I thought Frank Ryan had broken his leg or something. He said, 'Mike Howell fell asleep in the meeting.' I asked why he was so upset about that. He said, 'It's my fault.'"

Receiver Gary Collins said, "Blanton [rarely] said anything to me for nine years, and when he did, it was before a big game. He would say, 'I need a big one from you.' And that's it. He never got on me. My entire career, I was used to coaches riding my ass, and now they found out that wasn't the only way to do things."

Players liked this side of Collier. It's what Dale Lindsey saw when he was selecting a college and chose Kentucky because of Collier. When Collier was fired, Lindsey transferred to Western Kentucky. And when he was drafted by both the Jets of the AFL and the Browns, in 1965, Lindsey chose Cleveland.

"I felt I would get an honest shot," said Lindsey, who named his first child after Blanton. "I felt I could trust Blanton. He had principles and philosophy, and he didn't change them because the situation changed. That's a rarity, especially when money and egos are involved. If you were a great player and did something wrong, you were punished. If you were a bad player and did something wrong, you were punished too.

"If we didn't play well, he'd tell us in a nice manner, but strong and firm. And if he had to bench a player, he had no problem with that. He did it with Frank Ryan [for Bill Nelsen in 1968]. That was a pretty damn tough decision, and it may not have been a popular one."

Collier, in his first camp, set the tone when he addressed the team and said, in part: "I'm not a tough person and I don't try to be. But I do get fired up about things, especially a lack of effort and a lack of attention to detail."

Only linebacker Vince Costello rapped Collier, saying, "He didn't have the people skills of Paul Brown. Sometimes he said the wrong thing at the wrong time. Paul couldn't say the wrong thing at the wrong time."

Part of the problem, Costello said, was Collier's deafness. Others, however, saw it as a strength and, in some cases, a ruse. Coughlin is convinced Collier's hearing problems helped his coaching.

"He told me people thought he was stupid or retarded because he never said much as a kid," Coughlin said. "No one knew he had this hearing problem. He had to read lips. My theory is that he used his eyes and studied everything. He read and, on the practice field, he studied. He learned more football because he watched it differently than anyone else."

Players sometimes believed Collier pretended not to hear, forcing them to repeat their assignments to him, deepening their understanding. But they didn't take advantage of him. Besides, they never knew when he could hear.

"I learned that my rookie year [in '63]," said defensive tackle Jim Kanicki. "One Friday, we were going over the game plan, and I was talking to a teammate while Blanton said something to the team. Blanton walked up to me and said, 'Don't you ever talk while I'm talking to the team.' I was whispering to this guy, but he heard me."

Modzelewski, told by his teammates that Collier was deaf, learned, too.

"I came out of the game once after the other team had a twelve- or fifteen-yard gain, and he said, 'They ran a trap on you,'" Modzelewski recalled. "I said they didn't and tried to explain. He told me he saw where I was trapped. So I walked away, and his back was to mine, and I swore. Next thing I know, someone grabbed me and said, 'Don't you ever talk to me like that again.' And I said, 'Those lying bastards told me he couldn't hear.' I remember the coaches used to yell when they talked to him, and he called me aside one time and said, 'I don't know what they're yelling for. I can hear, and I can read lips real good.'"

But, by the end of 1969, Collier realized his hearing would force him to retire. In a 6–2 loss at home to Dallas, the crowd noise drowned out his hearing aid, preventing him from hearing his assistants on the phone. He left coaching for good after '76 then retired to a life of golf in Texas. But he never considered himself anything but a coach.

"If it weren't for these darn ears, they probably would have had to tear my coaching clothes off me," Collier told Coughlin in 1982. "You can take the man out of football, but you can't take football out of the man."

24 Dick Schafrath
Tackle, 1959–1971
Number 77

 A canoe trip across Lake Erie appealed to him, even though he couldn't swim and boats made him seasick. Somehow, Dick Schafrath completed the journey. A sixty-six-mile run from Cleveland to Wooster sounded just as good. Until he ran it. But at least he finished. And all-you-can-eat buffets tweaked his competitive juices as well.

"Everything was a challenge to me," Schafrath said.

Especially when it came to playing left tackle for the Browns. That provided Schafrath his biggest challenge, one he accepted for thirteen seasons, including eleven as the starter. All he had to do was replace Lou Groza, but that wasn't Schafrath's biggest obstacle. Gaining weight, and learning a new position, were.

Schafrath joined the Browns as a second-round draft pick, in 1959, out of Ohio State, where he played a variety of line spots. But he wasn't skilled at any in particular and wasn't sure what his future held. Coach Paul Brown told Schafrath he needed linemen for the future. So Schafrath asked which position was the toughest.

"Left tackle," Brown replied.

Brown, without realizing it, had issued a challenge. So Schafrath embarked on becoming a left tackle. First, though, the 220-pound Schafrath had to add weight, which turned out to be a surprising problem for someone who loved to eat as much as he did. He was a self-described "eating machine." No one would argue.

"I saw that man eat so much food I got sick watching him," guard Gene Hickerson said. "You can't believe how much he ate every day. He'd eat four or five square meals, and his meals consisted of five pounds of prime rib. I used to tell Dick, 'You won't have teeth very long because you're going to wear them out.' But he had trouble keeping that weight on."

Others tried to help him. Before training camp, Schafrath worked at a construction company in Wooster. He dug holes to build muscles and devoured all the food that coworkers, and their wives, brought to him. It didn't work.

With time running out, they made a thirty-pound iron jockstrap for his weigh-in. That bumped his weight to 255, which pleased Brown. Then he discovered the extra weight. Brown appreciated Schafrath's attempt to make the team.

"I'll give you a chance for a year," Schafrath recalled Brown saying.

Another rookie, defensive tackle Floyd Peters, sold Schafrath on lifting weights at a time when few believed in it. The two secretly worked out at a Cleveland club, and by next camp, Schafrath said he had gained forty-five pounds. Naturally, his appetite increased, particularly after games. He routinely lost twenty to twenty-five pounds during a game and poured everything from wine to beer to soda and water down his throat to recoup the loss. Then he headed to dinner.

"He tried everything to keep that weight on," Hickerson said. "There were restaurants in Cleveland that asked him to leave. They didn't want to see him at a clambake because he ate enough for forty people."

"I was a garbage machine," Schafrath said proudly. "I was in every all-you-can-eat contest all over the state. At one place, I ate twenty-four lobster tails and fifteen halves of chicken. In one sitting."

What he did best, however, was block opposing ends. Schafrath became the starter, in 1960, after Groza retired. Schafrath held onto that position in '61 and '62, despite being on active duty in the Ohio National Guard, which forced him to miss most practices because he was stationed in Mansfield.

Coaches would send copies of his blocking assignments as well as the game plan. But Schafrath never missed a game, for which the Browns are thankful. Schafrath earned six Pro Bowl berths and was named all-Pro three times. Yet he's not in the Hall of Fame—though one who is, fullback Jim Brown, once said Schafrath would be on his all-time team. After all, Schafrath helped spring Brown on Cleveland's trademark sweep.

"Dick had a great desire to get downfield," tackle Mike McCormack said. "He was always out in front trying to knock people down."

During Schafrath's days as a starter, the Browns failed to produce a 1,000-yard rusher only three times. Seven times either Jim Brown or his successor, Leroy Kelly, averaged at least five yards per carry. Four of the Browns' top eight all-time rushers ran behind Schafrath. Three are in the Hall of Fame: Brown, Kelly, and Bobby Mitchell.

"Dick built up to play that position, and that right there tells you something about the man," Kelly said. "He was just determined."

In 1963, Schafrath's teammates voted him their most valuable player, despite Brown rushing for 1,863 yards. Schafrath didn't consider himself the most talented player, yet he survived a long time, holding his starting job until Doug Dieken replaced him in week ten of 1971. Reading was the key for Schafrath. He zipped through books on athletes, seeking tips on what made them successful.

"Most of them had good hand-eye coordination," Schafrath said. "So I worked on mine. And keep your eyes open. Boxers, tennis players, basketball players, and baseball players do this. If I wanted to be a good player, I had to keep my eyes open until the last second [and not blink]. Another thing they had was quickness, so I worked on my quickness off the ball. You can always improve that. And hustle, hustle, hustle. That makes up for a lot of your faults."

The hand-eye coordination, and the ability to keep your eyes open as long as possible on contact, were important in this era of head slaps.

"Lou really helped me with that," Schafrath said. "It was vicious. One of my first games was against [Pittsburgh's Hall of Fame defensive tackle] Ernie Stautner, and he was the premier head slapper. He hit me five or six times in a row, and I went back about twenty yards. You couldn't use your hands [as an offensive lineman].

"We had water in the helmets [to cushion the blows], but my helmet would break and it would flood. I had to come to the sidelines to get another helmet all the time. Then we had helmets with air pockets, and the air would go out all the time. I never played a game without a bad helmet."

That's why it's important to have a thirst for competition and to win those challenges. His father, Norman, instilled this in him while they worked on their farm. Schafrath said they farmed the "old-fashioned way, like the Amish did." They'd shock wheat, cut wood, and pitch manure by hand. And competed while doing it.

A love for competing spilled into other areas, some of them silly. Sometimes, rather than ride the bus five miles to school, Schafrath said he would race it. He read that Jim Thorpe used to do the same thing. Schafrath's search for new challenges never ceased. Schafrath used to wrestle Victor the Bear, who stood eleven feet tall and weighed 650 pounds.

"That was a fun thing," Schafrath said.

This wasn't as much fun: in 1971, a Cleveland car dealer told Schafrath he would give him a free car if he ran from Cleveland to Wooster. Schafrath, who was thirty-six and weighed 260 pounds, agreed.

"I thought I would cheat and jump in a friend's truck and ride, run then ride," Schafrath said. "But this guy hired a police cruiser who followed me the whole way so I had to run the damn thing."

But he did it, in eleven and a half hours.

"I couldn't walk or bend," Schafrath said. "They threw me right in an ambulance and took me to the hospital."

Another time he canoed seventy-eight miles across Lake Erie in 17½ hours, something he began planning while recovering from intestinal cancer. He and his hospital roommate, Sam King, discussed doing it, and when King died, Schafrath made the trek in his memory.

"I was obsessed with going across that lake," said Schafrath, ignoring his inability to swim and susceptibility to seasickness.

Then, in 1985, Schafrath ran for, and won, the senate seat in District 19. The Republican had campaign help from his father, Paul Brown, and Ohio State coach Woody Hayes. Still, Schafrath barely won. But he was reelected twice and, in the fall of '98, was running for the last time.

After that, Schafrath isn't sure what he'll do. But he's looking for a challenge. Perhaps, he jokes, he'll try baseball. That was his first love, and Cincinnati even drafted him in the mid-1950s, but Hayes talked him out of signing.

"I'll see if they'll still honor my contract," he said.

Schafrath was joking. Or was he?

It would be another chance to conquer something new. That's what drove him in football and became his signature in life.

"It wasn't about the money," Schafrath said. "I would have signed for anything. It was just the chance to compete."

Coaches Blanton Collier, left, and Paul Brown shook hands forty-five minutes before the game, but this scene would not be repeated afterward, which stung Collier and angered fans.

25 Shaky Homecoming
1970 vs. Cincinnati

Browns 30, Bengals 27
October 11, 1970

 The man in the felt hat, the one with the franchise named after him, raced off the field, snubbing an old friend and igniting a rivalry. His old team noticed this act. So did his former city. It didn't matter that it happened in an exhibition game. Paul Brown wouldn't shake Blanton Collier's hand. And no one in Cleveland liked it. For seventeen years, Brown owned Cleveland. Not anymore.

"We kept [the handshake] in mind when we played them after that," said Browns linebacker Dale Lindsey. "We had no grudges, no bones to bear. But we kept that as a reminder because guys felt really good about Blanton and we wanted to make sure that any chance to pay it back, we did. And it was strictly because of the handshake. There wasn't any need for that.

"We thought the grudge match was more between [Browns owner Art] Modell and Paul Brown than Blanton and Paul. But Paul had to stiff Blanton to keep his own image up."

Then it got worse. When Cleveland rallied to beat Cincinnati in the season's fourth game—and the first regular-season meeting between the teams—all eyes pointed to midfield, expecting Brown to extend a hand to Collier. Instead, Brown repeated his postgame act, hustling to the locker room. The fans, 83,520 of them, again noticed, and this time they assaulted with boos the man who had delivered Cleveland seven titles.

What most hadn't seen was the two men shaking hands in pregame warm-ups. Collier called him over, and the two men smiled and chatted briefly. Then Brown said he told Collier this would serve as any postgame congratulations. He also told Collier that he didn't shake hands after games and had not done so for years, stemming from an American Football League directive aimed at curbing incidents by fans.

The problem: Collier, who was deaf, didn't hear him. Thus, when this game ended, he again took off for midfield. And Brown again headed for the locker room.

"I'll never forget that," Browns running back Leroy Kelly said. "I walked up in back of Blanton, he was down by the end zone, and I shook his hand. I lost a lot of respect for Paul."

Brown later said, "I was undeservedly criticized for something that was clearly not my fault."

Brown and Collier once had been close, from the time they met, in 1943, during World War II. Collier joined Brown's staff at the Great Lakes Naval Training Station and followed him to Cleveland in 1946. Then Collier replaced Bear Bryant at Kentucky, in 1954, but the families remained tight. Sometimes, as a show of support when Collier was struggling, Brown would drive to Kentucky. When Collier was fired, after the 1961 season, Brown quickly rehired him.

Then Brown was fired.

Then Collier was named coach.

Then a friendship crumbled.

The splinter was caused, in part, when Collier took the job. The oft-told story is that Collier asked for Brown's blessing, and Brown replied: "You must do this for the good of your family."

"I never talked to him about the job," Brown said years later.

Collier's friends begged to differ. "Blanton said it happened," former Browns broadcaster Gib Shanley said. "I happen to believe Blanton."

Brown's allies: "Paul gave him a job, and when he got fired, Blanton took the job, and I don't think Paul liked it," said Costello, who coached with Brown in Cincinnati from 1969 to 1973. "I know Paul didn't like it. And Paul told me he never asked him. I believe Paul. Blanton used whatever he could to make himself look good."

Dick Modzelewski, who played for Collier and coached with Brown, from 1979 to 1983, said, "My understanding was Paul didn't want one of his assistants to take the job. Let's put it this way: I was an assistant for twenty-two years. If someone offers me the job, I'm gonna take it."

Nonetheless, the relationship changed. *Cleveland Plain Dealer* writer Dan Coughlin remembers Collier's daughter, Kay Collier-Slone, telling him of family get-togethers, pre-1963, when she would play her violin for Brown, who would praise her. After the firing, when the families got together, Coughlin said Collier-Slone told him, "Brown was very cold." By the time Brown faced his former team, a once strong friendship had dissolved.

"They were no longer on speaking terms," Costello said.

The first meeting between the teams, at Cincinnati's Riverfront Stadium, was just an exhibition game. But it didn't seem that way, at least in Cincinnati. At the Browns' hotel, the lobby rug resembled a football playing surface, the waitresses wore numbered jerseys, and the assistant managers were dressed like officials.

Brown said the team was "flooded with ticket orders ever since the game was announced in 1968." And, he added, it was "no secret how intense I was about this game."

His players presented him a game ball after the come-from-behind 31–24 victory.

Before the rematch, a *Cleveland Press* headline blared: "Can the Browns Atone for 31–24 Lacing?" One story even called the loss "embarrassing." All this for an exhibition game. But it set the tone in Cleveland.

"That [exhibition game] was like a championship game for the media and for Paul and the Bengals," Lindsey said. "It wasn't for us. We weren't fired up at all. Most of us had never played for Paul. He didn't mean anything to us, but we were concerned about defending Blanton's dignity more than anything."

Much was made of Brown's return to Cleveland, but seven seasons had passed since he had coached there. Brown spent five of those seasons in exile in California before heading the expansion Bengals of the AFL, soon to be absorbed into the NFL—and placed in the Browns' division.

Only four players—tackle Dick Schafrath, receiver Gary Collins, guard Gene Hickerson, and linebacker Jim Houston—and two coaches, Collier and Howard Brinker, remained from Brown's tenure. Schafrath had maintained contact with Brown, albeit minimal.

"It was very eerie to see him back again and not be with the Browns," Schafrath said. "It was a funny feeling, and it brought back a lot of memories. It was very odd to see Paul on the other side with a different team, but he had the same competitive, fiery eyes. He wanted to win."

Modell was still around, which surely was enough to rile Brown. Still, the week of the game, Brown said, "All has turned out happily. I'm satisfied with my lot in life."

He would have been more satisfied to win in Cleveland (which wouldn't happen until 1974). Had quarterback Bill Nelsen (knees), running back Leroy Kelly (ankle), and fullback Bo Scott (knee) not played, as feared, maybe the Bengals would have won. But those three did play and led the ten-point favorite Browns to the comeback victory. Nelsen completed seventeen of twenty-six passes for 226 yards and two touchdowns; Kelly ran for eighty-four yards on twenty-nine carries and caught five passes for seventy-nine more; and Scott rushed for forty-four yards on ten carries.

Cincinnati took a 10–0 lead behind quarterback Virgil Carter, making his first start for the Bengals. Horst Muhlmann's fifty-yard field goal and running back Jess Phillips's two-yard touchdown run provided the lead.

But the Browns slowly rallied, starting when defensive tackle Walter Johnson, with Houston blitzing, sacked Carter for a safety near the end of the first quarter. Then Kelly scored on a three-yard pass, making the score 10–9.

Just as the Browns harassed Carter, though he still would complete twenty of twenty-eight passes, the Bengals pounded Nelsen, who sat at his locker after the game with a wrapped knee and bloodied elbow. In the second quarter, Nelsen fumbled after one collision, and defensive end Royce Berry recovered and ran fifty-eight yards for the touchdown.

Again Cleveland answered. Again Kelly, who barely practiced that week and needed cortisone injections to ease the pain, set up a touchdown, turning a screen pass into a fifty-five-yard gain. Nelsen then found tight end Milt Morin for a four-yard touchdown pass on third down, cutting the score to 17–16 at halftime.

Cincinnati added to its lead in the third quarter, thanks to a twenty-three-yard Muhlmann field goal set up by a fumbled punt return, for the only scoring in that fifteen minutes. But when the third quarter ended, Cleveland was beginning to take control as it was in the midst of an eighty-yard drive, aided when Schafrath, a fullback in high school, ran twenty-seven yards with a Kelly fumble.

"I saw the ball laying in front of me and said, 'Go, Schaf, go,'" said Schafrath, who had never touched the ball in eleven previous seasons. "I'm not in shape to run over forty yards. I'm glad I was run out of bounds."

When Kelly scored on a one-yard sweep at the start of the fourth, the Browns had their first lead of the game. Then defensive end Ron Snidow hit Carter's arm as he threw, forcing the ball to pop in the air. Cornerback Erich Barnes, covering tight end Bruce Coslet, gambled by tipping the ball in the air. It worked. Barnes returned the interception, the forty-second of his career, twenty yards to the six yard line, setting up a one-yard plunge by Scott for a 30–20 lead.

But Carter, who started for an ineffective Sam Wyche, rallied the Bengals, directing a nine-play, seventy-five-yard drive which ended with a sixteen-yard pass to receiver Speedy Thomas. The last big play, three downs after a banged-up Scott had run for twelve yards, came with 1:50 remaining and the Browns facing third and five from their own thirty-eight. During a time-out, Collier, Nelsen, and offensive coordinator Nick Skorich agreed: They needed to pass. Otherwise, as Collier said later, "if we had punted, it was almost like playing for a tie the way [the strong-legged Muhlmann] was kicking."

Also, the Bengals were daring the Browns to throw, using an eight-man front with blitzing linebackers. So Nelsen dropped back to pass, ignoring a hard-charging end, and threw to Collins near the sideline. Then Nelsen was leveled. But when he stood up, Cleveland had a first down after Collins's eight-yard catch. The Bengals finally forced a punt with ten seconds left, and they lined up for one last desperation heave eight seconds later. But they couldn't even manage that as end Jack Gregory dumped Carter for a twelve-yard loss as time expired.

Then Collier headed to midfield and Brown to the locker room, escorted by the shouts of angry fans. Collier shrugged it off after the game, saying, "It has to do with the way he, or anyone, deals with defeat." But those close to Collier said it bothered him.

"That was something he shared with me long after [Collier retired]," Coughlin said. "And he was hurt by Paul's reaction after he took the job."

Browns tight end Milt Morin drives forward for extra yardage against the Bengals' Ken Avery, completing a twenty-yard gain.

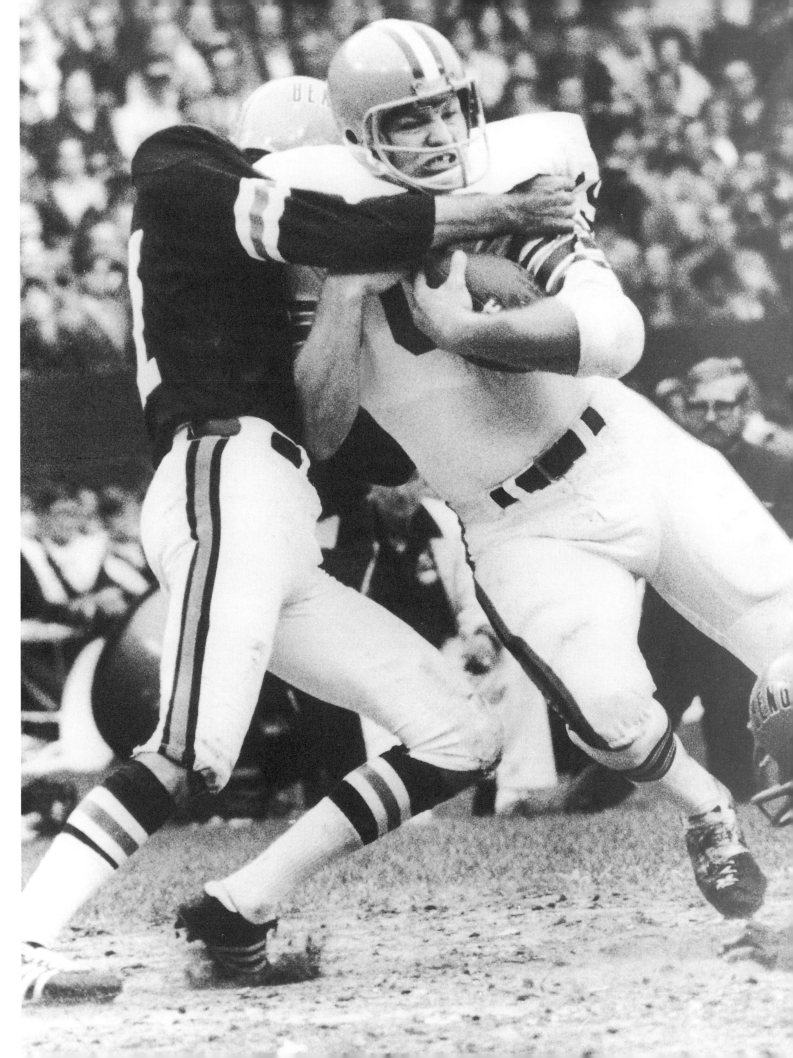

"Blanton was strictly a Kentucky gentleman," Modzelewski said. "I know he was hurt. Paul Brown was very unprofessional at that time, and he was wrong. I enjoyed working for Paul, but I never brought the subject up, and he never did either."

Besides, Brown had more immediate, and important, matters to ponder, like how to improve his third-year squad. He quickly found answers as the Bengals won seven of their next ten games to finish 8–6 and win the Central Division title, edging the Browns by one game. The difference: a 14–10 Cincinnati win over Cleveland in November, a victory that caused Brown to tear up when his players again handed him the game ball.

Once more, he ran off the field, waving his hat to the crowd and eschewing the handshake.

"That's what makes people mad at the press," Costello said. "You run off the field, you run on, no one thinks about that. Then someone picks it up and writes an article and makes an issue of it. Who gives a damn whether the guy goes across the field and shakes his hand or not?"

Apparently, an entire team. And city.

	1	2	3	4	Total
Bengals	10	7	3	7	27
Browns	2	14	0	14	30

FIRST QUARTER
Cin - Muhlmann 50 FG. Bengals, 3–0
Cin - Phillips 2 run (Muhlmann kick). Bengals, 10–0
Cle - Johnson sack of Carter for safety. Bengals, 10–2

SECOND QUARTER
Cle - Kelly 3 pass from Nelsen (Cockroft kick). Bengals, 10–9
Cin - Berry 58 run of fumble recovery (Muhlmann kick). Bengals, 17–9
Cle - Morin 4 pass from Nelsen (Cockroft kick). Bengals, 17–16

THIRD QUARTER
Cin - Muhlmann 23 FG. Bengals, 20–16

FOURTH QUARTER
Cle - Kelly 1 run (Cockroft kick). Browns, 23–20
Cle - Scott 1 run (Cockroft kick). Browns, 30–20
Cin - Thomas 16 pass from Carter (Muhlmann kick). Browns, 30–27

26 **Gene Hickerson**
Guard, 1958–1973

Number 66

 He hung up on Paul Brown. Sort of. When the Cleveland coach called Gene Hickerson's college dormitory, Hickerson figured it was a prank. So he shouted a smart-alecky response to the person who answered the phone—and the student hung up. Then Hickerson, convinced Brown had never heard of him, had a good laugh. The next day, his line coach at Mississippi delivered the news.

"You know, Paul Brown tried to reach you last night," Bruiser Kinard told Hickerson.

"It *was* him?" Hickerson replied.

Fortunately for Hickerson—and the Browns—the legendary coach called back the next night. This time, Hickerson talked to him. Then, for sixteen years, Hickerson answered the call for Cleveland, etching his name among the best offensive linemen in Browns history. When highlight films of running back Jim Brown are shown, chances are Hickerson is out front clearing the path. Same goes for Leroy Kelly. And Bobby Mitchell. Even Greg Pruitt, at least for one year. No other Browns lineman blocked for all four.

"He's the reason I'm in the Hall of Fame," Kelly said. "He should be in the Hall right now. I don't know why he's not. He put three running backs in there."

Only Pruitt is not in the Hall of Fame. And when the Browns lost a back, the running game never suffered. After Brown retired in 1966, Kelly ran for 1,141 yards and then led the NFL in rushing the next two seasons. Even fullback Ernie Green, a premier blocker, racked up 3,102 yards in the 1960s. All of these players averaged at least 4.2 yards per carry for their careers.

Yet the only Browns lineman from the 1960s in the Hall of Fame is tackle Mike McCormack, who retired in '62. Hickerson and tackle Dick Schafrath are the two most prominently mentioned as being snubbed. When Hickerson is discussed, many remember him leading the sweeps. But he did more than that.

"Gene was an all-around player," defensive tackle Dick Modzelewski said. "A guard can run block, that's one thing. But when you have to pass protect, especially against a defensive tackle . . . and don't forget the rules didn't favor the offensive line. Hell, now they can hold you, grab you, bite you, and get away with it.

Before, we could head slap a guy and everything. But Gene was a great pass protector. He should be in the Hall."

Hickerson isn't waiting for that call.

"I probably never will get in," he said. "There are a lot of players in the Hall that I know damn well I have a better track record than. I don't kiss asses with the [voters] and I never will. I'm in Burger King's Hall of Fame, and that's enough. . . . I always tried to earn the respect of my teammates. Hell, I had a good career."

Good? Hickerson made six Pro Bowls and was named all-Pro seven times. Doug Dieken is the only Browns offensive lineman to appear in more games than Hickerson (Lou Groza only kicked in his last seven seasons). And Hickerson closed his career by starting 165 straight games, playing every down in his last two seasons.

For three years, Hickerson warned the Browns to draft his replacement, telling them he'd had a "bellyful of [football]." Instead, they kept convincing him to return.

"I'd tell the coaches to announce my retirement, and they wouldn't do it," Hickerson said. "When I finally retired, I had to announce it."

In 1975, first-year coach Forrest Gregg tried to coax Hickerson, already a year removed from football, into playing another season.

"I thought it was a joke," Hickerson said. "I didn't even answer him. A week later, he said, 'Would you consider coming back?' And I said, 'I wouldn't come back if they gave me the franchise.'"

Besides, Hickerson was making more money as a manufacturer's representative, a job he started while playing. Every Monday and Tuesday during the season, the players' off days, Hickerson awoke at 5:00 A.M. and headed to work, calling on shops that opened by 6:00 and laying the groundwork for a successful career.

Working never was a problem for Hickerson. These days he wakes up at 5:00 A.M. to get to his office at the Anchor Tool and Die in suburban Cleveland two hours later, so he can do crossword puzzles, read the papers, and call clients. Lots of work can get done by 9:00 A.M. That work ethic derives from his parents and Hickerson's own background.

As an eighth grader, Hickerson convinced a construction firm that he was several years older than he actually was. Given his size—he was well on his way to the 230 pounds he would weigh four years later—they didn't question him. But his job was taxing. Hickerson pushed a wheelbarrow of bricks up plank bridges, at times zigzagging up five floors in ninety-five-degree heat with 90 percent humidity.

"You'd go home at night and be so damn tired you couldn't even walk," Hickerson said. "I said, 'Boy, it's got to get better than this.'"

Hickerson, a highly-recruited 235-pound fullback, used football to find a better life. He ran the forty-yard dash in 4.7 seconds, prompting several schools to talk to him about switching to end. But the six-foot-four Hickerson wanted no part of

Gene Hickerson

that position in college. Nor did he want to remain at fullback. Hickerson wanted to play guard. The reason: heat. Those ninety degree, high humidity days would torture a player forced to run a lot during practice. Running twenty fifty-yard sprints after practice was bad enough.

"They would have killed me running pass patterns in that weather," Hickerson said. "In those days, they didn't give a person a drink of water in two-hour practices. I lost so much liquid, I cramped all over."

His speed helped make him one of the NFL's top pulling guards. It also helped make him an effective messenger guard with the Browns. Many times Hickerson waited and waited while Paul Brown pondered the next play. By the time he settled on one, Hickerson had to sprint to the huddle, sometimes racing fifty yards.

Hickerson filled this role for one season with Chuck Noll. Then the Browns stuck him in there full time. Hickerson could plow forward with the best, too, due to his quickness. Before defenders could punch into him, Hickerson already was in their chest, shoving them back. But pulling is how he made his name. What better way to get on TV than to lead Jim Brown or Leroy Kelly around end? Soon, everyone in Cleveland knew who wore number 66.

"That was one way for offensive linemen to get exposure," said Hickerson, who also owns a restaurant in Cleveland that bears his last name. "So I tried to take advantage of it, to be honest. No one in the world doesn't want publicity and a little pat on the back. TV brought it out about pulling linemen. But most of [the linemen] were so damn slow, they couldn't pull."

Hickerson had a ready answer for anyone who wondered how he developed the agility to lead runners.

"I used to tell everyone I took polka and cha-cha lessons," Hickerson said.

No one believed him. Since he never took those lessons, they were smart. But Hickerson does think his days as a fullback and those fifty-yard sprints in college increased his quickness.

Ironically, Hickerson's work ethic riled coach Blanton Collier, who used to tell his guard that he was the "laziest practice player he'd ever had." Hickerson said that was a bad rap. But in the next sentence, Hickerson said he didn't believe in practice or warm-ups. Teammates knew this. Quarterback Bill Nelsen remembered a one-mile run at practice in the early 1970s.

"He ran two laps, ran under a tree, and said, 'Piss on this,'" Nelsen said. "But when he had to run, he ran like hell."

And when Hickerson ran, a Hall of Famer usually followed. Maybe Hickerson isn't in Canton, but, without him, maybe some others wouldn't be there either.

27 Walter Johnson
Defensive Tackle, 1965–1976

Number 71

Frostbitten fingers couldn't force him from the field. Nor could pneumonia. Or a brutal shot to the knee. Through it all, defensive tackle Walter Johnson just kept playing. And playing. For twelve seasons, Johnson never missed a game, ignoring his ailments and his opponents' constant double-teaming. When Johnson retired, he owned the Browns' record for consecutive games played (168). Few Browns faced the all-day pounding that Johnson endured.

"Of all the players I've known, Walter is probably the most durable," his line coach Dick Modzelewski once said. "He's unbelievable. The man can stand pain, no question."

Examples of his toughness, and pain threshold, are easy to find.

• Pneumonia forced Johnson to spend a week in the hospital before a 1967 regular-season game against Minnesota. Johnson started.

• In a 1968 game against Dallas, Modzelewski saw Johnson get drilled in the knee, with enough force to knock out most players. So Modzelewski sent in reserve Bill Sabatino. Johnson waved him off. When he returned to the bench, Sabatino said, "The only way I'll play is if he breaks his leg."

• That toughness paled next to the 1969 December play-off loss at Minnesota, where the wind chill was eighteen below zero. Johnson had jammed three fingers on his right hand and took a shot of Novocain to help him play. By the end of the first quarter, his hand ached, and the pain increased. His right hand, which he planted on the iced ground every play, was freezing. Chunks of ice clung to his paw. But Johnson played the entire game. When it ended, ice covered his hand. The Novocain helped him play, but it wore off in the Minnesota airport.

"Suddenly, he falls down on the floor and is writhing in pain and screaming," *Cleveland Plain Dealer* writer Dan Coughlin said. "His hand was defrosting."

Doctors in Cleveland considered amputating three of his fingers. But after twenty-four hours in the hospital, Johnson had improved. Within a month, he played in the Pro Bowl.

"If they had amputated the fingers, I don't think I would have been able to continue playing," Johnson once said. "You have to do too much grabbing with your fingers."

161

Walter Johnson

Johnson not only played with pain, but he also inflicted it, which is why he started every game from 1966 to 1976 and made three Pro Bowls. That's not bad, considering he didn't even play defensive line until he reached Cleveland.

At Taft High School in Cincinnati, Johnson played fullback, and, in his first season at California State in Los Angeles, he gained seven hundred yards. But blocking was his primary job, and the coaches switched this six-foot-four, 230-pound man to guard and, later, linebacker. When the Browns drafted him in the second round, in 1965, they moved him to left defensive tackle. He was lost as a rookie.

"My first year, I used to sit there at the line reading plays," Johnson said. "I always had the instinct for reading plays, so the main thing I had to work on was the technique of pass rushing. It was the only thing that didn't come naturally."

But he bulked up to 275 pounds and caused havoc. Johnson's forte was plugging the run, but he still managed fifty-eight career sacks, third highest by a Brown. That despite the double-teaming, which opened lanes for linemates. Johnson appeared in three straight Pro Bowls, between 1968 and 1970, but others say he should have gone more.

"He hasn't been recognized for being as good as he was," said right defensive tackle Jim Kanicki, who played next to Johnson from 1965 to 1969. "Some good players, because of the Merlin Olsens [with Los Angeles] and Bob Lillys [with Dallas], never get the recognition. But I would take him any time. He was the best lineman I played with. He could go left and right, and he had a low center of gravity. He was just a good athlete."

"I would love to play alongside Walter again," said end Joe Jones, who played next to Johnson for four years in the '70s. "He took me under his wing and taught me the work ethic that they had built in Cleveland and how to keep your nose clean. He taught me how to keep the linemen off the linebackers. He was smart, super strong, and very encouraging. He was a quiet man, but if you asked him a question, he'd tell you the truth. He was the MVP of my era."

Johnson teamed with Jerry Sherk, from 1970 to 1976, to form the Browns' best-ever tackle combination. When Sherk joined Cleveland, in 1970, Johnson's play improved. Finally, someone could take the offensive line's attention away from Johnson. They played off each other's strengths as Sherk rushed the passer better, but Johnson was more stout against the run. Sherk parlayed his college wrestling into effective techniques. Johnson combined muscle and speed—he once ran the 100-yard dash in ten seconds—to dominate.

"I'd put them on top with the rest of the guys I've coached," Modzelewski said. "Those guys were consistent workers who never died on me. Walter was so quick and strong and powerful. When he would lift weights, everyone would go gaga because of how much he lifted."

Another time he drew a crowd when he tried to lift something else: a bear. In 1969, teammate Dick Schafrath opened a camping and recreation area in

Loudonville, Ohio. Schafrath wanted the place to draw attention. So he talked Johnson, a pro wrestler in the off-season, into wrestling a 650-pound bear. For an hour, with only an occasional rest, Johnson tangled with the bear and once nearly lifted him off the ground. But the bear proved tougher than Johnson's human opponents. Call it a draw.

"I still don't know why I let Schafrath talk me into that," Johnson said two years later. "At one point, I had a headlock on the bear, looked down and saw the muzzle on the floor. I let go and beat a hasty retreat for the door."

"The fact that Walter would do it is scary enough," safety Thom Darden said.

Turns out, it was as tough to get the bear off his feet as it was to get Johnson out of the lineup. Perhaps the bear's philosophy was as simple as the one Johnson used in his twelve seasons.

"You just have to get your mind together," Johnson said, "and go out and do it."

28 **Leroy Kelly**
Running Back, 1964–1973
Number 44

He showed up three hours late for his first camp; pulled a hamstring four days later; fumbled two punts in the last exhibition game; and sweated out the final cuts, convinced he would be squeezed out of a crowded backfield.

Then running back Leroy Kelly embarked on a Hall of Fame career. All he had to do to reach Canton was replace the NFL's all-time leading rusher at the time, Jim Brown, who retired to make movies. Maybe no one forgot Brown, but Kelly made sure they remembered his name, too.

When he retired, Kelly was second to Brown on Cleveland's all-time rushing list with 7,274 yards, and he's second only to Brown on the combined yardage list (12,329 yards) and touchdowns (ninety). Then the question became "How do you replace Kelly?"

"Maybe I was dumb or ignorant, but I just didn't feel the pressure of [replacing Brown]," Kelly said. "We had great coaches, a great offensive line, and a great team. I had enough confidence to know I could do it, barring injury."

Kelly immediately showed what he could do, taking the sting off Brown's surprising retirement during the 1966 training camp. By season's end, Kelly had rushed for 1,141 yards and an NFL-high fifteen touchdowns.

"I don't think any of us realized he was *that* good," linebacker Dale Lindsey said. "It was a great shock. But here's a guy who had the ability and some surrounding players to help him."

"The signs were there that he could play," receiver Paul Warfield said. "No one really knew, however. He not only played well, he instantly became, along with [Chicago's] Gale Sayers, one of the top two running backs in the league."

Not bad for an eighth-round pick out of Morgan State. Kelly had a decent career but went undrafted by the rival American Football League, prompting him to reconsider his future plans. But the Browns shocked Kelly by drafting him in 1964. At his first minicamp, the 188-pound Kelly worked as a defensive back, a position he had also played in college. Afterward, coach Blanton Collier told him to gain ten pounds and forget defense.

"I didn't think I was that terrific as a running back," he said. "I was young, nervous, and scared."

Leroy Kelly

Not to mention three hours late for his first day. But Collier excused his tardiness, and Kelly began to impress. Then came the hamstring injury, suffered when he tried to block defensive tackle Jim Kanicki in a drill. Brown saw Kelly wince his way through drills, so he asked Collier to let him rest the leg. Collier obliged.

Compounding matters was a crowded crop of veteran running backs. The Browns would keep five, and Kelly figured he was destined for the taxi squad. But when one of those veterans, Kenny Webb, had contract problems and left camp on the last day of cuts, Kelly knew he had made the team. This came less than a week after he had fumbled twice in an exhibition game.

"But Jim Brown came up to me and said, 'Don't worry, we all fumble the ball,'" Kelly said. "That made me feel real good, but I thought I was a goner. But I'll never forget seeing Kenny walk out [of camp]. He came walking out of League Park with his shoes saying, 'Good luck.' And I said, 'I've made this team.'"

First Kelly teamed with Walter "The Flea" Roberts to form one of the NFL's top return games. This allowed Kelly to flash his potential while awaiting an opportunity. In his first two seasons, Kelly averaged 16.8 yards on twenty-six punt returns and scored three touchdowns. He averaged 25.9 yards on his first twenty-four kick returns.

Also, in his second season, with starting back Ernie Green injured, Kelly teamed with Brown in the backfield in a 24–19 win over Pittsburgh in the rain. Still, Kelly carried the ball only forty-three times for 151 yards in two years.

He then used his slashing, long-striding style to accumulate huge yards offensively. From 1966 to 1968, only ten players in the NFL rushed for one thousand yards or more. Kelly did it three times. In '67 and '68, Kelly led the NFL in rushing and touchdown runs. Also, he averaged more than 5.0 yards per carry each of his first three seasons as a starter. The offensive line helped, but so did Kelly's quickness.

"Leroy had the fastest start I've ever seen in my life," former Browns broadcaster Gib Shanley said. "[Officials] used to call backfield in motion a lot, and finally the Browns sent a film to league headquarters to the director of officials telling them to just watch this guy. He was so quick on that first step. They finally got away from calling [a penalty]."

Quarterback Bill Nelsen sometimes had to change his delivery to Kelly.

"There were many times I almost had to pitch the ball to Leroy rather than hand it off," Nelsen said. "Did he have great speed? No, but he had the quickness. We ran a play, a wide sweep where I'm supposed to hand the ball to Leroy off the end. Many a time I had to reach as far as I could to get him the ball."

Then Kelly's talent took over, and he reverted to his childhood days in Philadelphia, when he and his friends played all day in a local park. They would play football, run around, and do all sorts of kid things. Kelly became accustomed to avoiding pursuers and used that to become an all-city quarterback for Simon Gratz High School.

For Kelly, those days helped create an elusive running style. This made him dangerous in the open field, which is why the Browns also liked to throw to him. Kelly caught thirty-two passes for 366 yards in his first season as a starter.

"It was just instinct," he said. "Some runners have good peripheral vision and just sense guys on you. I wasn't the type of guy to run over you. I was a Gale Sayers type. We tried to avoid the guys."

Kelly's career slowly wound down, in the 1970s, as nagging knee injuries decreased his effectiveness. He retired in 1974, ending a surprising run of success that started when Brown, who could have played at least three more years, provided him an opportunity.

"Who would have thought Jim Brown would retire after '65?" Kelly said. "I didn't even know he was making movies. I was shocked. We're in camp, and [Collier] said, 'We're going to give you a shot.' The rest is history."

29 **A-Mays-Ing**
1976 vs. Pittsburgh

Browns 18, Steelers 16
October 10, 1976

He planted the quarterback on his head, nearly drilling him into the ground. One move earned him a lifetime pass into the hearts of Browns fans. And a lifetime of scorn in Pittsburgh. In Cleveland, they called him "Turkey." In Pittsburgh, they called him all sorts of things—none of them nice.

With 10:46 remaining in the game, Cleveland defensive end Joe "Turkey" Jones burst through from the left side, wrapped his arms around quarterback Terry Bradshaw, hoisted him, and dumped him on his noggin as if he were tossing a sack of garbage into a dumpster. Flags flew, tempers flared, and Bradshaw squirmed. Jones owned the moment.

But a teammate owned the day. And the city. Ironically, Dave Mays got his chance when starting Browns quarterback Brian Sipe departed with a concussion in the second quarter. Sipe's backup, Mike Phipps, was sidelined with a shoulder separation. Enter Mays, better known as Dr. Dave Mays, dentist and third-string quarterback wrapped in one. To this point, he was best known for drilling teeth, not passes. Soon that would change.

Mays's statistics weren't eye-popping in this win: he completed five of nine passes for seventy yards and ran three times for fourteen more. But in Cleveland, beating Pittsburgh meant conquering the world. That's what Mays did.

"Dave Mays had a career in one Sunday afternoon," said Browns offensive tackle Doug Dieken. "For the people of Cleveland, when you beat Pittsburgh, it was almost like, 'Screw the rest of the season.' You can make or break your season just by beating them."

You can also etch your name forever into the minds of Cleveland fans. That's what Mays and Jones accomplished on the same day.

Once upon a time, a win over Pittsburgh was greeted with a yawn. It was almost a guaranteed occurrence, like snow in January. From 1950 to 1973, the Browns won thirty-five of the forty-eight meetings. Pittsburgh swept Cleveland only once.

But the reversal started, in 1969, when the Steelers drafted defensive tackle Joe

Browns defensive end Joe "Turkey" Jones slams Steelers quarterback Terry Bradshaw into the ground, ending his day, in the fourth quarter.

Greene. The next year they plucked Bradshaw with the first pick in the draft and defensive back Mel Blount in the third round. They followed that with linebacker Jack Ham, in 1971, and running back Franco Harris a year later. Here were their first three picks in '74: receiver Lynn Swann, linebacker Jack Lambert, and receiver John Stallworth. Center Mike Webster was the fifth choice.

All but Swann and Stallworth are in the Hall of Fame. They still might make it. That's why the Steelers were a feared team in 1974. The Browns weren't. So the rivalry turned, with Pittsburgh winning five straight, including a 31–14 triumph in the first meeting in 1976.

Each victory stoked the rivalry's fire in Cleveland and heightened the fans' hatred. Then the Steelers won back-to-back Super Bowls starting in 1974. The Browns hadn't even reached the postseason since '72 and had lost twenty-one games in the Steelers two championship seasons. Suddenly, Browns fans loathed the Steelers, and their black-and-gold-dressed faithful who flocked to the stadium, sometimes numbering more than ten thousand. More than a few would leave with bloodied, but smiling, lips after a Steeler win.

"All of a sudden, they were the king of the mountain, and they stuffed it down the Cleveland fans' throats," Dieken recalled. "And that regurgitated to us, and we got tired of hearing it. When we'd go [to Pittsburgh], we'd take the bus, and beer cans would be bouncing off the bus, and you'd be saluted that you were number one.

"It was like a play-off game. You don't want to think you cranked it up to a higher level, but you did. There was a lot of pride and honor on the line. And it was always physical. We got Lambert thrown out of two or three games, which was probably the best part of our game plan. One time he hit someone in front of our sidelines, and [offensive lineman] Henry Sheppard, who wasn't in the game, walked a foot onto the field and said, 'Nice hit, Jackie.' Jack turned around, took a swing, and got a personal foul.

"In the last game of the 1983 season, Jack hit Brian in front of our bench, and I went over to get Jack. Jack went down, and a couple guys came off our bench, [tight end Harry] Holt and [nose tackle Dave] Puzzuoli, and decided to do a tap dance on Jack. It was not uncommon to end up with a minor rhubarb."

A rivalry had always existed between these similar Rust Belt cities, produced by a shared mind-set. Both cities were filled with hard-working blue-collar citizens, many of whom punched a clock in steel mills. Football provided their release. So they filled the stadiums and unleashed their emotion, saving it most for their turnpike rivals, who were only two and a half hours away.

"Pittsburgh was way beyond the Cincinnati game," said Cleveland defensive tackle Jerry Sherk. "The townspeople identified with it more than any other game, so when we played Pittsburgh, it was an unbelievable week. You could sense the mood of the town before and after the game. If we won the game, the town would be on fire and people would go to work for a couple weeks in a positive mood. And if we lost the game, it would be the exact opposite."

Beating the Steelers, or at least the notion of it, unified Browns fans.

"You'd have some blue-collar guy talking in a bar downtown with a high-powered attorney," Sherk said, "and they'd both have the same point of view: 'We have to kill those guys.'"

Both teams wanted to kill anyone in this game. Each side was 1–3, with their seasons slipping away.

Sipe, who was in his first season as the full-time starter and had yet to capture the city, was having a bad day, thanks to the Pittsburgh pass rush. The Steelers repeatedly knocked him woozy, causing Sipe at one point to forget the formations. Finally, in the second quarter, he left the game with the Browns trailing, 10–6.

Enter Mays, the unlikely hero. He was a twenty-seven-year-old rookie making his NFL debut, one year after completing dental school at the University of Southern California. Mays's only professional experience came, in 1974, when he played for Houston and Shreveport in the World Football League. But the former Texas Southern quarterback had showed enough in training camp to beat out Will Cureton for the third-string job.

"I was surprised I made the team," said Mays, who answered to "Doc," and who later became known as "Dr. Bomb."

His lack of confidence was evident to some.

"He was the most insecure guy I've ever known," said Dan Coughlin, then a backup Browns writer for the *Cleveland Plain Dealer.* "All the time he'd come up to me and say, 'What are the coaches saying about me? What are the coaches saying?' He had a rifle arm and could throw it far, but the team did not have any great confidence in him. He was a nice guy and I liked him, but he didn't have the emotional makeup to be a quarterback. It was also tough being a black quarterback [the Browns' first and only]. I'm not sure the Browns players were ready for that."

Black quarterbacks were a rarity. Add to it Mays's small-school background, and he had twice as much to prove and overcome.

"It had to weigh on him," safety Thom Darden said. "There's no doubt in my mind that you can't place a guy in that position, which is The Position, and with the turmoil of the times, and in Cleveland where there's a significant black population, and not have him feel pressure to succeed. He really never had a chance to command the team, and that's why he wasn't as confident as he could have been, because the team was never his. But he always came in and made something happen because of his strong arm."

Whether or not some of his teammates, or the city, were ready for a black quarterback is debatable. But both were ready to win. Mays helped them do that. When he entered the game, quarterbacks' coach Blanton Collier delivered a simple mes-

Reserve quarterback Dave Mays, aka Dr. Bomb, completed five of nine passes to help the Browns upset the two-time Super Bowl champion Steelers.

sage: Block out the crowd, block out everything. The Browns eased Mays's mind by calling the plays in the second quarter, but the offense didn't move and Pittsburgh maintained its 10–6 lead at halftime.

Two Don Cockroft field goals, from forty-one and twenty-eight yards, sandwiched Harris's one-yard run. Cleveland's second kick was set up by a forty-five-yard Sipe to Reggie Rucker completion. Pittsburgh's Roy Gerela booted a thirty-yard field in the second quarter. Mays gained control in the second half, in part because the coaches allowed him to call his own plays.

"He was on his own in the second half and did better," Browns coach Forrest Gregg said.

One of the biggest calls came after cornerback Clarence Scott blocked a forty-four-yard field-goal attempt by Gerela. Mays soon called for an option pass, giving the ball to running back Greg Pruitt who floated a twenty-nine-yard pass to receiver Paul Warfield, in his first year back in Cleveland since he was traded after the 1969 season.

Dieken also contributed on this drive. Cockroft's fifty-one-yard field goal was blocked by Steve Furness, and Pittsburgh's L. C. Greenwood recovered—then fumbled. Dieken picked up the ball, ran for a first down, and was smothered by angry Steelers.

Fullback Cleo Miller, who played the entire game with hip, thigh, and foot injuries, punctuated this series with a one-yard touchdown run, plunging through a path created by guard Robert Jackson. Cockroft missed the extra point, but the Browns led, 12–10.

"When we got the lead, it pepped everything up," Mays said. "The offensive line gave me all the time in the world."

Mays bought himself time, too. That was needed against the Steelers, whose line included Greenwood and Greene, who had combined for ten Pro Bowls.

"I don't know if Doc had a real grasp of football, compared to Brian," Dieken said. "He was just a guy who probably would be better off in a street game, but when you play Pittsburgh, that's what it turns out to be. That worked to Doc's favor. He made a lot of good plays. But by the same token, I remember him calling his own plays and calling the same play two or three times in a row, and the running back is looking at him like, 'Hey, they've figured this one out.'"

Still, Cleveland marched downfield, getting itself in position for another Cockroft field goal. He booted a fifty-one-yarder for a 15–10 lead after three quarters. Meanwhile, Turkey Jones and the defense had shut down the Steelers, harassing Bradshaw all day. They limited Harris to thirty-nine yards rushing, which was more than any other Steeler managed. Pittsburgh gained 196 total yards. Jones was the catalyst—*Plain Dealer* columnist Hal Lebovitz wrote afterward that it was his best game. But it wasn't memorable. Until just under eleven minutes remained.

Jones was big (six-foot-six, 250 pounds) and athletic, which is why the Browns picked him in the second round of the '72 draft out of Tennessee State. His half brother was Washington's Hall of Fame receiver Charley Taylor. At Dalworth High School in Grand Prairie, Texas, Jones was a star basketball player. In track, Jones ran the high and low hurdles, threw the shot put and discus, and high-jumped.

He was also gullible. The Browns' veterans played an annual joke on the rookies at Thanksgiving, handing them directions to a nonexistent, out-of-the-way farm where they would receive free turkeys. Cleveland tackle Dick Schafrath remembered getting two or three calls from a lost Jones. Each time Schafrath told him to keep driving. Finally, Jones abandoned his efforts. But he never caught on to the joke. Jones fell for it again the next year, prompting Schafrath to nickname him "Turkey."

Jones performed better on the field, working his way into the starting lineup his first season. But Jones missed the 1972 season with a knee injury and, two years later, was dealt to Philadelphia, which cut him during the '75 season. The Browns quickly claimed him.

By 1976, Jones again was starting and making an impact. So when he dug in against right tackle Larry Brown, a converted tight end, Jones felt confident. Then Bradshaw dropped back to pass.

"No tackle could back up faster than I could run forward," Jones said. "I took Brown upfield and turned his shoulders and came on the inside and grabbed Bradshaw and did my thing."

A whistle blew when Jones wrapped his arms around Bradshaw. But Jones said after the game he never heard it. Then he spiked Bradshaw.

"It wasn't like it was totally innocent," Sherk remembered. "But it was probably a bad decision by Joe and not preordained. Joe didn't have a malicious bone in his body. He never cheap-shotted anybody. It was more that Joe did not know his own strength. He was such a powerful man, especially from the hips down. It was almost like he used his legs and leverage to do a wild flip. They both landed on their heads."

"Terry was a big strong guy, and he would keep struggling," Darden said. "The next thing I know, Joe picked him up and dumped him on his head. He looked like a chicken with his head cut off, and his body flinched two or three times. It was something."

Harris ran over to Jones and bumped him. The officials flagged Jones for an unsportsmanlike conduct penalty, marching off fifteen yards. Bradshaw was carried off on a stretcher, headed to the Browns' locker room for X rays, and replaced by rookie Mike Kruczek.

He didn't have Mays's success. When Cockroft kicked a forty-one-yarder with less than two minutes remaining, the Browns led 18–10. Then Kruczek finally connected with Lynn Swann for a big play, completing a forty-five-yard pass.

Kruczek then scored on a twenty-two-yard run late in the game. Mack Mitchell blocked the extra point, and Cockroft eventually punted the ball on the game's final play.

Afterward, Jones approached Bradshaw, still lying on the trainer's table in the Browns' locker room. First, though, he had to get past Bradshaw's wife, Jo Jo Starbuck, who was flanked by two bodyguards.

"She wasn't too happy," Jones recalled. "I can't say the words she used. But she swore at me, very much so. I talked to Bradshaw, told him I was sorry and that it was just in the heat of play. He said, 'I understand, Joe.'"

Lambert didn't understand. While his teammates defended the play, Lambert snapped: "You take somebody and smash them upside down on the ground as hard as you can—that's not trying to hurt anybody?"

The league didn't understand, and Jones said he was fined approximately $3,000, which the commissioner's office returned to him after the season.

Pittsburgh fans didn't understand, either. They shipped angry letters by the dozen, which Jones sent to the NFL. On the Browns' next trip to Pittsburgh, in 1977, Jones said the league placed him in a separate hotel from the team for security reasons.

"I kept my mouth shut and my helmet on when I went to Pittsburgh," Jones said.

The 1976 game spurred a turnaround for both teams. Cleveland won seven of its next eight games, but missed the play-offs when lowly Kansas City whipped the Browns 39–14 on the final day. Pittsburgh won its next ten games and lost in the AFC championship game to Oakland.

Mays didn't have many more heroic moments in a Browns uniform, though in 1977, his last year with Cleveland, he rallied the team with three fourth-quarter touchdown passes at Pittsburgh. Too bad the Browns trailed 35–10 at the time and lost, 35–31. With Sipe hurt again, Mays led Cleveland to a win the next week but then lost three straight and played poorly. It was his last season with the Browns.

In 1994, he was sentenced to five to fifteen years in prison after being found guilty of welfare fraud. Two years earlier, he had been acquitted of trying to kill a fellow dentist. His is a sad story.

But Jones still relishes his role in Browns history. Even now, Jones, a free-service clerk for American Airlines in Florida, is asked about the play, particularly in Cleveland. Coworkers will hear Bradshaw talk about the dunking once in a while on pregame shows, and they'll say to Jones, in wonderment, "You're the guy that did that."

Jones just chuckles, secure that he's remembered for something.

"That," Jones said, "is the play that everyone talks about."

	1	2	3	4	Total
Steelers	7	3	0	6	16
Browns	3	3	9	3	18

FIRST QUARTER

C - Cockroft 43 FG. Browns, 3–0

P - Harris 1 run (Gerela kick). Steelers, 7–3

SECOND QUARTER

C - Cockroft 28 FG. Steelers, 7–6

P - Gerela 30 FG. Steelers, 10–6

THIRD QUARTER

C - Miller 1 run (kick failed). Browns, 12–10

C - Cockroft 50 FG. Browns, 15–10

FOURTH QUARTER

C - Cockroft 40 FG. Browns, 18–10

P - Kruczek 22 run (kick blocked). Browns, 18–16

30 **Jerry Sherk**
Defensive Tackle, 1970–1981

Number 72

Jerry Sherk opened the paper, an excited rookie anxious to relive his first game. A win over Joe Namath and the Jets; national TV; and 85,703 fans at Cleveland Stadium. Sherk remained on a cloud—until he read the stories.

"There was a subhead on one of the stories that said, 'Nightmare ends for Sherk,'" he recalled. "And I was like, 'What are they talking about?'"

Everyone had picked on Sherk. The New York Jets ran his way for most of their 169 yards rushing; broadcaster Howard Cosell constantly pointed out his errors to the nation, blaming him even when the run went the other way. And a cut chin required eight stitches.

Today, it's a teaching lesson, one that he delivers to at-risk kids in California. The lesson is in how Sherk responded. For most of the 1970s, he was not only one of Cleveland's best defensive linemen, but also one of the NFL's. Sherk made his mark in his third season, earning the Cleveland Touchdown Club's award as the Browns' defensive player of the year.

His play blossomed and more honors followed. For two straight years, 1974–1975, Sherk's teammates voted him the Browns' most valuable player. In a '74 game against San Diego, Sherk recorded eight solo tackles, recovered two fumbles, and blocked a field-goal attempt. Defensive line coach Dick Modzelewski remembered another game when Sherk was knocked to the ground, got up, ran forty yards downfield, and made the tackle.

After Sherk's 1975 season, in which offensive linemen voted him the NFL's defensive lineman of the year, coach Forrest Gregg said, "I don't see how he can play any better."

He did. In 1976, Sherk, who had a four-sack game versus Philadelphia that season, was named the league's top defensive lineman, the same year the Browns finished 9–5 but out of the play-offs. If not for their poor records that decade, Sherk, who made four straight Pro Bowls, from 1974 to 1977, might have received more acclaim. If not for knee injuries later in his career, Sherk's bust might be in the Hall of Fame.

Jerry Sherk

Wrestling helped create this success. As a senior at Oklahoma State, where he transferred from junior college, Sherk was the Big Eight heavyweight wrestling champion. That sport did more than just provide Sherk with balance and teach him about conditioning and hard work.

"It gave me the psychological edge," Sherk said. "When you walked onto the wrestling mat at Oklahoma State, you had six or seven thousand people in the stands screaming, and your match was the one that would determine the dual meet between two national powers. That taught me about how to bring that one-to-one mental focus to football so I could line up with someone and it was only him and me. That was a very big part of it."

Sherk attacked football systematically, setting goals and watching film. He watched Dallas's Bob Lilly and tried to mirror his moves. Lilly sometimes would break into the backfield, and, instead of trying for the ballcarrier, he would disrupt the play by tackling the backside pulling guard. Sherk did the same.

He also watched Minnesota's Alan Page use his quickness to bury opponents. That helped trigger a weight change. In 1970, Sherk's first year, he weighed 260 pounds. After that, he played at 245 pounds and capitalized on his quickness.

"He was slower than smoke off manure," Modzelewski said. "But for ten yards he was very quick. He had that great extension, and he had great hip explosion. And he was a very smart player. I remember one time, he came out of the huddle real quick and leaned his ear toward the opponents' huddle. I remember talking to him later, and he said, 'The quarterback usually says the play is, '32 on TWO!' And he'd catch the count. That's how smart the guy was."

Modzelewski also was a big influence on Sherk. The former Browns' tackle would leave Sherk in situations that might have called for him to be removed. But Sherk gained experience, and his confidence soared. By his third season, Sherk made the Pro Bowl.

"I remember games where I could flick my head an inch as the ball was snapped, and the guard would have to react because of my speed," Sherk said. "Then I'd be in the backfield tackling the ballcarrier, and it would seem like I was ten years old back in Oregon playing in the park with my friends with no one hitting me. I remember bringing down ballcarriers thinking, 'Oh, geez, this is a lot of fun. No one touched me on this play, or that play, or the play before that. This is great.'"

But everything changed in the final preseason game of 1977. Sherk tore nearly 75 percent of the medial collateral ligament in his left knee. Surgery wasn't required, but Sherk missed the first seven games of the season.

Sherk wore a brace similar to Namath's, but, by season's end, he was a wreck. His right knee, compensating for his left, bothered him, and Sherk probably should have stopped playing for the season. But when Modzelewski replaced fired head coach Forrest Gregg for the final game, Sherk wanted to play. He hurt his weakened right knee, and this time needed surgery.

But Sherk recovered and, by 1979, was again playing well. Another injury ruined his career and nearly his life. In the season's tenth game, at Philadelphia, Sherk played with a boil on his elbow. On one play, he scraped the elbow and a staph infection entered his bloodstream, eventually settling in his left knee. Sherk was rushed to the Cleveland Clinic, where he stayed for thirty days. Surgery and antibiotics cured the infection in his knee. But his liver had an allergic reaction, causing doctors to fear the infection was alive elsewhere in Sherk's body.

"If it shows up in a second area, you're a goner unless they amputate," Sherk said. "I had teams of doctors trying to figure it out. One older doctor came in, late at night, and he tried to say the right words to me, but they were exactly the wrong words. He said, 'My son, God has put a terrible burden on you.' My thought was, 'What does this guy know that I don't know?'"

Sherk, who lost almost forty-five pounds in the ordeal, tried to play in 1980, but his knee was still too weak. He did play the next season but then retired. He does not look back and wonder, "What if?"

"The injury was a message to me that football wasn't my whole life," Sherk said. "In the middle of my career, I was apprehensive about maybe making the Hall of Fame. I couldn't refuse it, and I would be loving it, but I would be stuck. I didn't want to just be remembered for football. Injuries were my ticket out, strange as that sounds."

Before he left, however, Sherk gained some redemption. In a 26–7 *Monday Night Football* win over Dallas, in 1979, he recorded four sacks and recovered a fumble. And Cosell changed his tune. After that game, Sherk remembers watching a tape and hearing Cosell say: "He's one of the best in the league, and he has been for a decade."

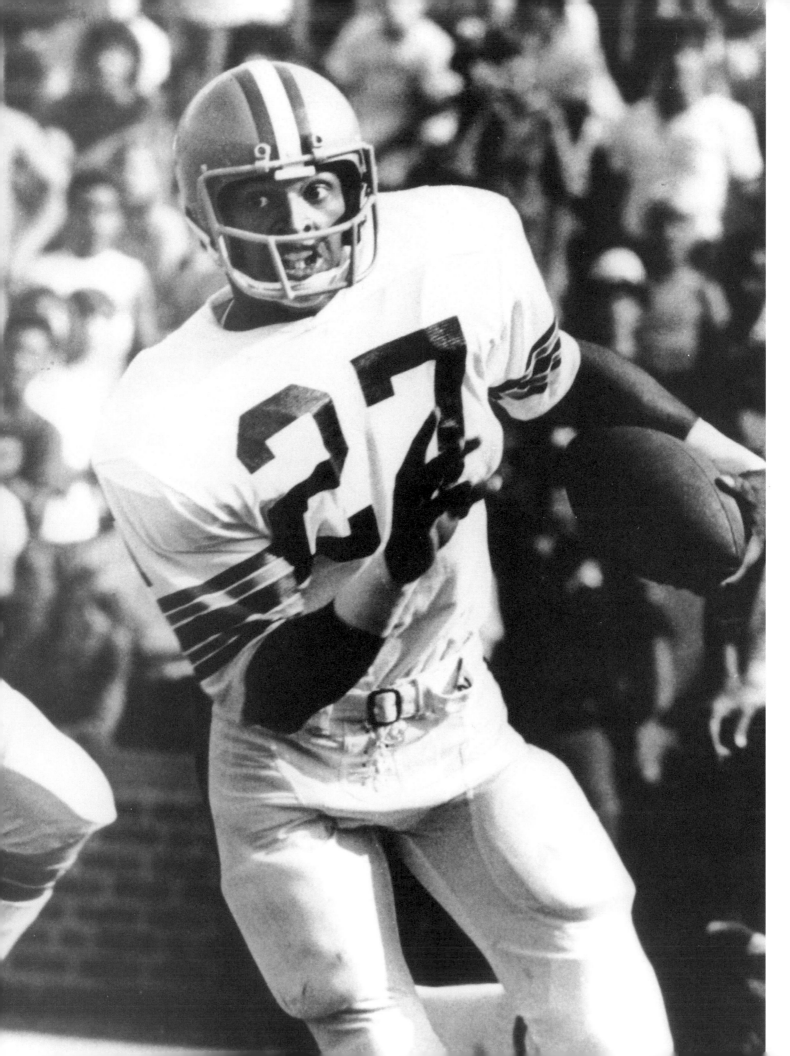

31 **Thom Darden**
Safety, 1972–1981

Number 27

One play haunts him, sometimes replaying itself in his mind. Thom Darden can't shut it off. He has plenty to combat it with: in ten seasons, Darden intercepted more passes than anyone else in Browns history. He picked off ten one season and, in the next, intercepted two in a *Monday Night Football* game, returning one for a score.

But the glory doesn't always erase the heartache. In 1980, with the Browns needing one more win to clinch the AFC Central title, they led Minnesota 23–22 with four seconds to play. A miracle was needed. A miracle occurred.

Quarterback Tommy Kramer, from the Browns' forty-six, dropped back deep and heaved a Hail Mary pass into the right part of the end zone. Darden, running up at an angle from the left, leaped and, as a teammate bumped him, tipped the ball. Straight into the arms of Minnesota's Ahmad Rashad for the game-winning score. Eighteen years later, Darden hesitates to relive the play.

"I don't even want to talk about that because I still have nightmares," Darden said. "I was so distraught, I couldn't come back with the team."

Instead, he headed to Detroit, where he stayed with family on Monday, a day off for the players. Then he focused on Cincinnati, where the Browns could still win the division. There, another pass caused a furor. Darden likes to relive this one.

It happened in the first quarter, when Cincinnati tight end Pat McInally made a leaping catch over the middle on third and six. This was Darden territory, and the free safety flew up and nailed McInally as he grabbed the ball. Darden's blow knocked McInally backward onto the artificial turf where he lay unconscious for ten minutes. Officials marched off fifteen yards, saying Darden, who claimed the hit was unintentional, had been "unnecessarily rough."

The league later fined him $1,000. Not only did Darden dislike that, but he also was miffed that the Browns didn't pick up the tab. Still, Darden, sometimes chided by the press for his arm tackles, doesn't mind the memory of this play. He'll occasionally watch a tape of the hit and often is reminded by fans of the collision.

"I had to make the choice to go for the interception or the hit," Darden said. "I chose to make the hit because the timing wasn't right for me to cut inside and try

Thom Darden

and get the ball. I knew I had a good shot at him, and I took my shot and hit him right in the chest. As we're going down, my arm rises up to his head. That's what I was fined for."

"It wasn't a cheap shot," coach Sam Rutigliano said.

Darden also picked off a pass in that game, the forty-second of his career en route to his club-record forty-five. He broke Warren Lahr's mark earlier in 1980 with a theft versus Green Bay in Cleveland, after which he received a congratulatory call from Lahr's widow.

Two other picks came in a 1979 *Monday Night* win over visiting Dallas, breaking Roger Staubach's streak of 149 passes without an interception. Darden had predicted the interceptions to ABC broadcaster Howard Cosell the night before.

A knee injury sidelined Darden, in 1975, preventing his record from being even higher. The ensuing knee surgery occurred just as Darden was becoming one of the premier safeties in the game, intercepting eight passes the previous year. After he returned, Darden intercepted seven passes in '76, six in '77, and a franchise-record ten the next season.

"He was a consummate free safety," Rutigliano said. "He could play center field like Duke Snider and Willie Mays. Thom roamed all over and supported people. He made the big plays, the big tackle. He did all the things he needed to do. He was a great player."

The interceptions didn't come by accident.

"There was an art to it," Darden said. "You have to have soft hands and good hands, but you have to have a keen understanding of your own defense, the offensive scheme, and the ability to read the quarterback and to try and get the quarterback to believe you're doing something different than what you're doing."

Darden studied quarterbacks and their tendencies, checking out how they took the center snap and how they retreated. Does he back out or run out? Quarterbacks will show where they're throwing the ball based on how they take the snap, Darden said. For instance, Darden still remembers his scouting report on Pittsburgh's Terry Bradshaw.

"When he would run out, he would throw to his right," Darden recalled. "And when he would back out, he would throw to his left. When he was at the forty yard line and in, he was more inclined to throw the ball deep, and when he was in his own territory, they would run more inside plays."

A little edge can allow the safety to cheat a few steps, which could result in another interception. But Darden also had help up front with tackles Jerry Sherk and Walter Johnson. The defensive scheme freed Darden of responsibility for an area and allowed him to roam and anticipate where the pass was headed. Some years, Darden felt he couldn't be fooled and was locked in a zone, as when he set the club record for interceptions.

"That's exactly how I felt," Darden said. "I don't know what that is. You hear guys talk about a zone. I was in that all year. I *dropped* six interceptions that year—I could have broken the league record."

That's not what some scouts expected, in 1972, when the Browns drafted Darden in the first round out of Michigan. Darden remembers hearing whispers that he was too small and too slow to play in the NFL. He had played a combination strong safety/linebacker in college—Michigan's first "Wolfman"—and, at 195 pounds, he would be too small to continue that role in the pros. With a 4.6 seconds forty-yard dash time, he didn't have great speed for a safety.

So he relied on fundamentals, which stemmed from his days at Sandusky High School where he made all-state in basketball and football. There, his football coaches, three of whom later coached at powerhouse Massillon, stressed the basics, and the team benefited. The Blue Streaks won a state title and finished in the top five two other times during Darden's career. By the time he reached the NFL, he knew how to play. Even a switch midway through his rookie year from strong to free safety didn't bother him.

"It was incumbent upon me to learn the reads," Darden said, "and to be in position so that, if I'm supposed to stay on the inside of a receiver and I had help on the outside, I would always stay on the inside. In the pros, more important than having one-on-one capabilities is you need to know where your help is."

Darden also prepared himself for life after football, working a variety of off-season jobs, from a sales rep to the radio host of a Sunday night jazz show. He's now a stockbroker in Cedar Rapids, Iowa.

But it was his football career that provided him countless memories. As a boy, Darden attended Browns games several times a year with his father, and they would buy $2 bleacher tickets.

"I couldn't have scripted it better for me," Darden said. "My family got a chance to see me play, and I was comfortable in Cleveland because of the way the fans took to the players and because I knew the city. To come there on a Sunday morning before the game, especially in September and October, it was exhilirating because that was the only place in my working life where I was totally in control. It was based on my abilities against the other guy's abilities and what I had been taught. And only I could execute them. That was the greatest thing of all."

32 **Kardiac Kids**
1979–1980

 Comedians shredded Cleveland on a nightly basis, poking fun at a city that constantly fed them new material. A river burned one day; a loan defaulted the next. Then came bankruptcy and more jokes. All the world took jabs at this punching bag of a city in the 1970s.

Citizens rushed to its defense, but they were armed with squirt guns. Race split the city, thousands fled to the suburbs, and jobs became scarce. The baseball Indians provided no help, holding ten-cent Beer Night in 1974. Drunken fans poured onto the field in the ninth inning, and the Indians forfeited the game. And comedians thanked them. By 1980, the Cavaliers, under Ted Stepien, became an NBA laughingstock. But, hey, how 'bout that polka fight song? More thank-yous.

The Cavs' and Tribe's losing ways became magnified, however, because of the Browns. Once a perennial play-off contender, they struggled to crack .500. When 1980 rolled around, they hadn't been in the postseason since 1972. From 1974 to 1977, the Browns finished 25–34, their worst stretch ever. They needed a comeback. Just like the city.

Enter the Kardiac Kids, who made an art out of coming back. In 1979 and 1980, the Browns made a habit out of playing close games as twenty-six of thirty-three games were decided by seven points or less. Sixteen of those games ended in Cleveland victories. Hence the nickname.

"All of a sudden, the town turned itself around, and the team turned itself around," said tackle Doug Dieken. "It was two different groups, but they were on the same mission, and that was to do something you could be proud of. There were three or four years where we weren't very good, and that made it even greater because it went from such an extreme. We went from Pete Franklin having funeral services for us on his radio show to being the toast of the town."

And, in many ways, the nation. An exciting team from an underdog city made for great copy around the country. The Browns had the charming quarterback with the big numbers and the pleasant coach with the witty lines.

Quarterback Brian Sipe had hung around on the Browns' roster since 1972, spending two years on the cab squad as he wondered if football was his calling. He decided it was. Cleveland was thankful. Just as the Browns were thankful for Sam

Browns coach Sam Rutigliano and the Kardiac Kids
won over the city with their thrilling finishes.

Rutigliano, who seemed more like everyone's favorite uncle than a football coach. Those who played under hard-nosed Forrest Gregg cherished the new regime.

Rutigliano was a former high school coach who held firm to his teaching roots. He didn't treat football as the only thing that mattered, and he implored others to do the same. What he taught was a passing-first offense. In 1978, Rutigliano's first year, Sipe threw for 2,906 yards, second most in Browns history, and set club records for completions (222) and pass attempts (399). Against Baltimore that season, Sipe had his first three-hundred-yard game.

"That was when people began to realize he was a legitimate quarterback," Rutigliano said. "Fans realized that this guy would give them probably the most entertaining years in the history of the Browns."

A bend-but-don't-break defense and high-powered offense ensured these teams were entertaining. Comedians persisted with their Cleveland jokes, though not with the fervor of previous years.

"By the time I got in comedy in 1980," Cleveland native and comedian Drew Carey said, "you didn't hear Cleveland jokes. That was so old school."

Besides, Clevelanders had a retort, something to puff out their chests about. The Browns would serve as a bridge to a new era for the city. Sure, 112,000 people had left the city between 1970 and 1975. And yes, in 1978, a *New York Times* article stated: "Cleveland . . . has problems so diverse and deep that agreement on a long-range plan to put the city on a new course is nowhere in sight." But the Browns were back, and that meant more to fans than any long-range government plan.

"We rejuvenated the fans and the city," tight end Ozzie Newsome said. "Now we had an identity. The city had been through some tough times, and now they had an identity, something positive to identify with. It not only did something for us on the football field, but it did something for the city nationally."

Safety Thom Darden said, "The Kardiac Kids gave all those people, whether they were in politics, or business, or manufacturing, or any side of the community, something to hold onto. Guys on the team got together more socially, and more players started doing promotions. It seemed like the entire community thoroughly engulfed the Browns. There was never any separation from the team and the city. Some places you go, the team is just the team. That year, the team and the city were one."

The Browns fever that spread throughout Cleveland, in 1980, could be traced to the previous season, when thirteen of the team's sixteen games were decided by a touchdown or less. But it was a rout that most energized the fans. Cleveland entered a September 24, 1979, *Monday Night Football* game against defending NFC champion Dallas with a 3–0 record, winning each game by three points. The city was ready for Dallas. Too bad the visiting Cowboys weren't ready for the city, or the Browns.

"I was at home getting ready to leave, and friends of mine are calling saying, 'Man, the downtown is already packed,'" Darden said. "This is at 2:00 or 3:00 in the afternoon. So when I get downtown, the whole city is fired up."

"I'll never forget that game," radio play-by-play man Gib Shanley said. "I got there at 7:30 [for the 9:00 P.M. game], and the place was packed, and everyone was cheering. I thought I was late. They just wouldn't stop. I don't think Dallas had a chance."

They didn't, thanks in part to Darden. On his Sunday night jazz show on WMMS-FM, Darden's guest was ABC's Howard Cosell, the voice of *Monday Night Football*. Darden told Cosell he would intercept Dallas quarterback Roger Staubach. No small feat, considering Staubach had not thrown an interception since the previous season.

It didn't take Darden long. In the first quarter, his theft snapped Staubach's streak of passes without an interception at 149. Darden returned the pass for a touchdown, giving the Browns a 7–0 lead as 80,123 fans cheered wildly. Darden added a second interception later in the game as the Browns rolled to a 26–7 win and 4–0 record.

"That was just awesome," Darden said. "If I could put time in a capsule, that would be the one night I would put in there."

He's not alone.

"That was a defining moment," Rutigliano said. "That night, people began to realize that, 'These guys are going to give us some good years.'"

Never mind that the Browns finished the season 9–7. They had revived the city's football pulse and would shatter it one year later.

The 1980 season started poorly. First New England, then Houston on a Monday night game in Cleveland, won easily as the Browns' defense faltered. Expectations dropped with each loss.

Then the Browns started to roll. They beat Kansas City by a touchdown and did the same to Tampa Bay a week later, though the Bucs reached the Cleveland twenty as time expired. A week later, Denver nipped the Browns by three, followed by a 27–3 win in Seattle. The roller-coaster ride had begun. The Browns needed a forty-six-yard touchdown pass from Sipe to receiver Dave Logan with sixteen seconds left to beat Green Bay. That play typified the Browns' chemistry as Logan wasn't the primary receiver. But the Packers came out in man coverage, prompting Logan to look in Sipe's direction.

"We made eye contact, and with his facial expression, he signaled, 'I'm coming to you,'" Logan recalled. "I don't remember what route I was supposed to be running, but I just took off on an up-pattern, and he threw it. That was the kind of year it was. We were always on the same page. I knew from that motion with his eyes that he was coming to me."

It got better one week later as the Browns battled Pittsburgh in Cleveland for first place. The Steelers were playing minus quarterback Terry Bradshaw, receivers Lynn Swann and John Stallworth, running back Franco Harris, and linebacker Jack Lambert. Yet they grabbed a 26–14 lead.

Sipe rallied, finding a new hero on each scoring drive. First he passed seven yards to running back Greg Pruitt for a score and later tossed an eighteen-yard strike to Newsome for the winning touchdown in the 27–26 victory.

"At one point during the year, I remember yelling out, 'Fasten your seat belts! Here they go again!'" Shanley said. "That was the most fun I've ever had."

In the next two weeks, the Browns built leads of 27–7 over Chicago and 28–13 over Baltimore. But they needed to recover a last-minute onside kick in each game to preserve the win.

The city was about to burst. Finally, after the visiting Browns beat Houston, 17–14, to take a one-game lead in the AFC Central, a win preserved by cornerback Clarence Scott's interception with 1:17 to play, Cleveland exploded. Thousands of fans flocked to Cleveland Hopkins Airport to greet the Browns. They poured in from all over, creating human gridlock inside the airport. Travelers missed flights; cars had to be parked a half-mile away on I-71, and the thirty-five Cleveland police officers could do little to contain the throng.

"When we landed, the pilot told us there were a few fans there to greet us," Logan said. "We were given the option of whether we wanted to go through the airport or meet the buses on the tarmac. The players wanted to go through the airport. When we walked off the gate, it was wall-to-wall people. It was just nuts. I had my shirt ripped. It was just a level below being scary."

Fans had begun to treat them like rock stars.

"It was nothing but a sea of bodies," Darden said. "People were grabbing you, pushing you, hugging you. My bag was stolen, but when I got outside, some guy came running up with my bag."

No one could escape the excitement. Signs popped up in downtown buildings. Local musicians churned out Browns songs, including, "The Twelve Days of a Browns Christmas." And fans began talking Super Bowl, or, in some cases, Siper Bowl.

The hysteria mounted. Even after the Browns lost on a Hail Mary pass at Minnesota, one thousand fans turned up at Hopkins to greet the team. That number swelled to fifteen thousand a week later when the Browns returned from Cincinnati with the AFC Central Division title, their first since 1971. This time, the airport was prepared as the fans were ushered to the nearby tank plant where the Browns would board their bus. Cleveland Mayor George Voinovich was among the crowd.

"No [players] knew who he was," Dieken said. "But I happened to know him, and I took him on the bus, introduced him to the players, and asked him if he

Fans packed Cleveland Hopkins Airport to welcome home the victorious Kardiac Kids.

wanted a drink. It was a good party. That year and a half there, it was like one big party week after week." One that Voinovich liked to host.

"This is the best thing to happen to the city since I've been mayor, next to getting out of default," Voinovich told the crowd that night. "But maybe this is more important."

Maybe?

But the ride ended in a cruel, yet predictable manner: a last-second play-off defeat to Oakland. The Browns lost the same way they had been winning, as Sipe tossed an end-zone interception.

What made the year special for the fans were weekly finishes that challenged the heart, most of them resulting in wins. For the players, the abundance of heroes also made it enjoyable.

One week, rookie running back Charles White was beating Kansas City. Then it was Logan against Green Bay, or Pruitt and Newsome against Pittsburgh. Fullback Mike Pruitt had the game-winner against Chicago, Scott's interception sealed the win at Houston, and, against Cincinnati, receiver Ricky Feacher caught two touchdown passes and kicker Don Cockroft booted the winning field goal. All along, Sipe led them with his calm demeanor en route to being named the NFL's MVP. Five players caught at least fifty passes: Mike Pruitt (sixty-three), receiver Reggie Rucker (fifty-two), Logan (fifty-one), Newsome (fifty-one), and Greg Pruitt (fifty). Two lineman, offensive guard Joe DeLamielleure and defensive end Lyle Alzado, obtained in trades, added toughness. No wonder the Browns never doubted themselves.

"Week after week, we dug ourselves a hole," Greg Pruitt said. "But it was like, 'OK, who's going to do whatever we need to do to win the game?' We didn't know how it was going to happen or when it was going to happen. But it was going to happen. And it happened. It was a magical year."

"It had been so many years since the fans had anything to hang their hat on," Logan said. "And then add to the fact the way we won our games. They were jazzed the whole year. It was one of those times you may never have again."

This group never saw it again, dropping to 5–11 the next season. But those players accomplished something few figured possible: they hoisted a city on their back and altered its image.

"When I think back now, it scares me a little bit," Rutigliano said. "We'd have two or three minutes to go and man, anything can happen. We rode it and had a lot of fun. Sometimes I say to myself, 'Was I really there? Was I really part of it?' It was just a great group of guys with a real resourceful quarterback. We were truly entertaining. I want you to know, as much as I had to pinch myself sometimes, I really savored and enjoyed it."

Just like everyone else.

33 **Silent Night**
1981 vs. Oakland

Raiders 14, Browns 12
January 4, 1981

 They drove into the noise as the fans hopped to their frozen feet and ignored the frigid weather, warmed by visions of yet another last-second victory. Yard by yard, the momentum built, convincing fans and players, on both sides, of the likely outcome. Each yard raised the volume. Each first down left Cleveland Stadium shaking. Then the Browns called time. Then coach Sam Rutigliano suggested a pass play. Then quarterback Brian Sipe dropped back to pass. Then he threw into the end zone. And then . . .

Silence.

"It was like someone pulled the power on the generator," tackle Doug Dieken said. "There was no sound."

"It was like someone turned off the sound on the TV," said former *Cleveland Plain Dealer* reporter Russ Schneider.

"Like an atomic bomb had been dropped over that whole place," tight end Ozzie Newsome said. "That silence is something you never forget."

Mike Davis pulled the plug, on the game and the season. The Oakland Raiders' strong safety, beaten off the line of scrimmage, scrambled back into position and blocked Sipe's path to Newsome. But it was too late for Sipe to do anything. Davis intercepted the pass.

The Kardiac Kids were finished, toppled by a play called Red Right 88, the most infamous play in Browns history, and one that has followed Rutigliano to this day. In 1989, his Liberty University team played at Eastern Michigan University. There, on a banner that Rutigliano said seemed as big as the stadium, were the words, "Red Right 88." Another time, while vacationing in Auckland, New Zealand, Rutigliano was asked about the play. At least, he says, he's remembered.

To Rutigliano, the call was, and still is, a no-brainer. Cleveland had driven to the Oakland thirteen yard line and faced second and nine, trailing 14–12. A field goal was no certainty, not with Don Cockroft already having missed two field goals at the open end where the Browns now stood.

Just before Sipe, who initially balked at the call, left the sideline huddle,

Oakland safety Mike Davis intercepts Brian Sipe's pass, ending one of the Browns' most exciting seasons.

Rutigliano issued the now famous line: "If you get in trouble and the receivers are covered, throw the ball into Lake Erie."

In the huddle, Dieken doesn't remember much squawking about the call. Yes, they were in field-goal range. But this was how the Browns had won all season. Besides, Sipe was the NFL's most valuable player that season. Why not take a shot?

"There was no way we were going to sit on the ball and kick a field goal," Rutigliano said. "Cockroft had already missed three, and we're kicking into the open end in minus-thirty-nine degree wind chill late in the day. I felt, here we've got the MVP of the NFL, and, as I said to the press after the game, 'My mother told me a long time ago, the girl you take to the dance is the one you take home.' And all our guys agreed. We just didn't make the play."

Here is how it was to unfold: The Raiders would play man coverage, and the two receivers to the right side, Ozzie Newsome and Reggie Rucker, would run slants, and the primary receiver Dave Logan would run a crossing pattern from the left side, prying free of defensive back Dwayne O'Steen, and catch the touchdown pass in the right corner.

"It was a great play," Newsome said. "We knew the coverage they would be in and felt that it was the proper call at that point. It was going to be a pass that would be easily completed because it wasn't a long throw. Plus we were a highly confident offensive team at that point."

Maybe too confident. When the play unfolded, Newsome quickly escaped Davis's coverage.

"I had beat Mike so cleanly off the line of scrimmage that Sipe did what he was supposed to do," Newsome said. "He was going to me. Mike made a great recovery, running for his life, and he looks up and there the ball is."

Sipe was slammed to the ground on the play. Meanwhile, Logan, a college teammate of Davis, fell backwards onto the frozen turf in frustration. He was open. Wide open.

"Absolutely," Logan said. "But I'm not pointing the finger at Brian. I loved that guy, and I wouldn't have played with any other quarterback."

The next day, Rutigliano watched the game film. There he saw Logan. By himself.

"He could have handed him the ball," Rutigliano said. "It was sickening. Brian was a great player and saw Ozzie open and, bang!, threw him the ball. But the ball hung inside. On a good day, it would have been a great play."

This was a bad day.

"He tried to force the ball into Ozzie," Rutigliano said.

The second-guessing began immediately, and defensive end Lyle Alzado led the naysayers. Offensive tackle Henry Sheppard also was peeved. Then *Plain Dealer* reporter Dan Coughlin recalled seeing Sheppard, "out of his mind with rage about that play," in the locker room afterward. Naturally, Cockroft was disappointed, though Rutigliano said the veteran kicker had forgotten about his misses.

But Rutigliano has remained firm in believing the right call was made. If Sipe had thrown to Logan . . . if Sipe had thrown the ball away . . . if conditions had been better.

Then Rutigliano knows what would have happened.

"There would have been a monument to me in center field," Rutigliano said. "Instead, it's just Red Right 88."

Long before the ending numbed the 77,655 in attendance, the weather did. A heavy midweek snow buried the tarpaulin and froze the field. Kerosene blowers and hot air were used to thaw the field. They failed.

Not much can be done when the temperature is one degree with a minus thirty-five wind chill, courtesy of a sixteen mph wind blowing off Lake Erie from the northwest. Heated benches were trucked in from Philadelphia to warm the players. Snow was plowed off the field, leaving the field surrounded by white mounds.

The Browns practiced in the cold that week. The Raiders didn't. They arrived in Cleveland late Friday night, barely beating the NFL rule of getting into town thirty-six hours before game time. They didn't want to deal with the weather any more than was necessary. The Browns, too, could have done without it.

"That was the coldest game I've ever played in," running back Greg Pruitt said. "At thirty degrees, even eighteen, you could function because when you're playing, your body could generate heat. The cold was such a factor and it was a distraction, especially when you're playing a skill position. Your hands have to be warm; if not, you don't feel them. And if you don't feel them, you can't grip the ball. That day, I had to cut the fingers off my gloves. I *had* to touch the ball with my fingers. It was brutal."

The first time Cleveland's defense was on the field, a TV time-out was called, angering the players.

"Everyone on the team was yelling, 'Come on, let's play!'" linebacker Clay Matthews recalled. "Now that was cold. That field was frozen solid, so not only was it hard to stand up, when you fell it was like falling on concrete."

In pregame warm-ups, Logan, as well as most players, wore AstroTurf cleats. But he couldn't stand up.

"It was like an ice rink," he said.

So he and his teammates switched to something called broom ball shoes that had little suction cups on the bottoms. It worked enough to help them stand. That was about it. Dieken, though, found a positive in the extreme cold.

"It was a great day for an offensive lineman because no one could move," he said. "You didn't have to worry about chasing someone all around the field because it was in such bad shape that no one could make a cut or plant your feet. You didn't move real quick, and you didn't try to do anything fancy because you were going to lose your balance and be down on the ground.

"But everyone talked about the cold. Hell, the players didn't always notice the cold because they were moving. It was the poor people in the stands who had to be freezing their rear ends off."

The media in the auxiliary press box, the one behind home plate, had it rough, too. They had no heat.

"Our breath steamed up the inside of the window, and it froze to ice," Coughlin

Hot seats were a necessity on this day as the temperature dropped to one degree with a minus thirty-five wind chill.

said. "You couldn't see out. We were taking credit cards and scraping a peephole through it to see the game."

One banner summed it up: "God, it's cold."

Like Cleveland, Oakland ignored gloomy preseason predictions. The Raiders had been picked last in the AFC West, yet they finished with the same record as the Browns (11–5) and entered the play-offs as a wild card. Quarterback Jim Plunkett resurrected his career, after starter Dan Pastorini broke his leg in October, and was the key to Oakland's success, which included a 27–7 win over Houston in the wild-card game and, eventually, a Super Bowl win over Philadelphia.

But Plunkett couldn't do much early against the Browns. Nor could they do much against the Raiders as the first quarter evolved into a field position and punting battle. Browns cornerback Ron Bolton intercepted a pass. The offense couldn't do anything. Oakland cornerback Lester Hayes picked off Sipe. And the Raiders managed nothing.

It appeared Cleveland might end the quarter with points when Sipe, from the Raiders' twenty-nine, threw to an open Rucker in the end zone. He dropped it. Three plays later, Cockroft was short on a forty-seven-yard field-goal attempt.

Fortunately for the Browns, the defense had dominated, allowing only fifteen yards all quarter. They kept hammering the Raiders and, after Cockroft's miss, got the ball back by forcing Plunkett to fumble on a sack. End Marshall Harris recovered at the twenty-three. But Cockroft missed again, this time from twenty-seven yards.

Finally, the defense did what the offense couldn't do: score. Bolton stepped in front of a Plunkett pass to receiver Bob Chandler at the Browns' forty-two. He scored easily. Again, the kicking game hurt Cleveland as Ted Hendricks blocked the extra point, leaving the Browns with a 6–0 lead with 6:01 to play before halftime. But Oakland took a 7–6 halftime lead when fullback Mark Van Eeghan smashed over for a one-yard touchdown, capping a sixty-six-yard drive.

The Browns' offense generated points in the third quarter but still couldn't reach the end zone. Cockroft, kicking into the closed end, drilled a thirty-yarder for a 9–7 edge. He had another chance when Cleveland reached the Oakland eighteen. But rookie holder Paul McDonald fumbled the snap and was dropped for an eleven-yard loss.

Still, Cockroft came through once more in the third with a twenty-nine-yard field goal and 12–7 lead. The lead lasted only six minutes as the Raiders' offense, which stumbled in the third, drove for a touchdown in the fourth. Plunkett completed passes of nineteen yards to receiver Cliff Branch and twenty-seven to tight end Raymond Chester. But Van Eeghan again punctuated the series with a one-yard run for a 14–12 lead.

The Browns appeared doomed when Sipe fumbled at his own twenty-five with 4:39 remaining; defensive back Odis McKinney recovered. Three Van Eeghan runs gained nine yards, setting up a Raiders' gamble. Rather than have Chris Bahr attempt a thirty-two-yard field goal, coach Tom Flores ordered another Van Eeghan run.

"He never failed in a situation like that," Rutigliano said.

He did this time, thanks to linebackers Robert L. Jackson and Dick Ambrose, who stuffed Van Eeghan at the fifteen for no gain. With 2:22 remaining, Cleveland readied for another Kardiac Kids finish. Sipe to Newsome gained twenty-nine yards, though it could have been more had Newsome not been tripped up at the last second.

A third-and-eleven pass interference call on O'Steen gave Cleveland a first down on the Raiders' forty-nine. Greg Pruitt then caught a twenty-one-yard pass.

Browns players celebrate cornerback Ron Bolton's second-quarter interception return for a touchdown.

"You expected it was going to happen again," Dieken said. "It was all going to fall into place."

In 1981, Pruitt was traded to the Raiders. Player after player told him this: "We thought we were going to lose."

Matthews recalled reading an article about former Raider tight end Todd Christensen, then a special teams player, who said, "I knew we were going to lose." Those thoughts heightened after Mike Pruitt's fourteen-yard run on a draw play to the fourteen was followed by a one-yard gain on first down. Then came the timeout.

"We were on the sidelines saying, 'Man, we think this town has been rocking, now it's *really* going to rock,'" said Greg Pruitt, who came out of the game on second down and was warming his hands on the bench. "I looked back just in time to see Sipe going back for a pass, and I'm saying, 'He's not . . . gonna . . . throw . . . the football.' I have to say this, you live by the sword, you die by the sword. So many times he lifted us from the jaws of defeat. I can't fault them for calling the play."

After the interception, Sipe retreated to the sidelines, yanking his helmet off just before reaching the bench. There, Rutigliano delivered another famous line: "I love you, Brian."

Love didn't ease the sorrow.

"You could see the anguish on his face," Logan said of Sipe. "The locker room was totally silent, and I remember just sitting there for the longest time and not even moving. Not taking my tape off, not cutting anything off. Just sitting because it couldn't have ended that way. There had to be something next week where we would go back out. The finality didn't hit me until we got to the locker room."

And the ride ended.

In the video *The Cleveland Browns: Fifty Years of Memories,* Sipe said, "It breaks my heart that I didn't come through. I made a bad throw. But that's exactly what we did that whole year and the year before. That's what made us the Kardiac Kids."

Greg Pruitt recalled his first training camp with the Raiders. On a sunny, eighty-plus-degree day, the Raiders were practicing eight-on-eight passing drills. Time and again, a defensive back dropped easy interceptions. It was Davis.

"I stopped practice and said, 'Wait a minute, is this the same guy that intercepted the pass?'" Pruitt said. "They said, 'Yeah.' And I said, 'Well, it just wasn't meant to be.'"

	1	2	3	4	Total
Raiders	0	7	0	7	14
Browns	0	6	6	0	12

SECOND QUARTER
C - Bolton 42 interception return (kick failed). Browns, 6–0
O - Van Eeghan 1 run (Bahr kick). Raiders, 7–6

THIRD QUARTER
C - Cockroft 30 FG. Browns, 9–7
C - Cockroft 29 FG. Browns, 12–7

FOURTH QUARTER
O - Van Eeghan 1 run (Bahr kick). Raiders, 14–12

34 **Brian Sipe**
Quarterback, 1972–1983
Number 17

 The noise would pound their ears as one by one the players sprinted from the dugout, forcing their heartbeats to quicken. This was the time to throw a fist in the air or to bounce up and down like a pogo stick. Time to get swallowed up in the excitement. Except for quarterback Brian Sipe. He would sit in the dugout, waiting to be introduced, engrossed in a conversation about his family or another personal matter—maybe laughing, minutes before game time.

"He would talk about anything but football," coach Sam Rutigliano said.

Sipe remained calm while madness circled all around. He transferred that trait to the field as well, directing the Browns to numerous last-minute wins or furious rallies during his eight seasons as the starter.

A few fans might never shake the memory of his last-second interception against Oakland in the 1980 play-offs. But fewer still can forget who led Cleveland to one of its most exciting seasons in history. Sipe did it by thriving in moments that caused others to tremble. He was like that as a kid when he was the starting catcher for his victorious California team in the Little League World Series. He was like that in the pros.

"Sometimes he would come to the sidelines on a critical third down," Rutigliano said, "and just laugh. Brian was always calm, and he just relished those moments. His father told me, in 1979, that Brian had been like that his whole life. He was just a guy who was tremendous under pressure."

That's when he was at his best. The six-foot-one Sipe waited until nearly the last minute to get serious about his NFL career after being drafted in the thirteenth round, in 1972, out of San Diego State. He spent the first year on the taxi squad, enjoying life in the NFL without the hassles of stardom.

"I was more interested in having a good time than I was in impressing the coaches," Sipe said in *Sam, Sipe, and Company.* "That's a tough thing to explain, but I was not 100 percent committed to making a career out of professional football. I more or less figured it was an opportunity, that if somebody wanted to pay me to stick around, it would be a break from Southern California and certainly an interesting way to kill a fall."

Sipe pondered his future in the off-season and knew he couldn't continue with this mind-set, one that worried the Browns. But he received a jolt, in 1973, when Cleveland drafted a quarterback in the fourth round and traded for another. Sipe spent another year on the taxi squad. Still, a transformation was taking place.

"He would sit in the film rooms," said defensive tackle Jerry Sherk, a close friend, who lives a few miles from Sipe in suburban San Diego, "and see things happen and think, 'Why didn't the quarterback do this?' or, 'Gee, all he had to was flip the ball to this guy.' He finally began to realize he could play ball."

Sipe landed a spot on the regular roster, in 1974, but it was Mike Phipps's shoulder injury in the season opener two years later that provided Sipe his first extended playing time. It would be Phipps's last season in Cleveland after Sipe threw for seventeen touchdowns. Injuries caused a brief career roadblock the next season, but, in 1978, Rutigliano was hired, and Sipe blossomed under this offensive-minded coach, throwing for 2,906 yards and twenty-one touchdowns.

He threw for three hundred or more yards four times the next season en route to twenty-eight touchdown passes. By this time, Sipe's mind had slowed the game to a crawl, giving him time to analyze every situation. Sipe could nag a defense with his short throws, then zip one past them for a big gain. If they gave it to him, Sipe took it.

"Brian saw things so clearly," Rutigliano said. "He didn't complete every pass he threw, but very rarely did he throw a ball in a bad place. He used to tell me, 'Listen, Sam. I don't have the strongest arm in the world, but you give me a scheme and the protection and surround me with the people I need to have and my arm is sufficient.' He was exactly right. His mind was like a reservoir, and he was never without an idea."

"Not only did Brian have the intelligence," Sherk said, "but he was probably one of the most instinctive guys I've ever seen play. He was the type of guy who could know if someone's coming from a totally blind side, duck, and get rid of the ball. It was a pleasure watching him develop."

But some concerns remained as running back Greg Pruitt, before the 1980 season, questioned whether or not Sipe could lead the Browns to the Super Bowl. The comment angered Sipe who used it as motivation. Cleveland didn't reach the Super Bowl that season, but it wasn't Sipe's fault, as he was named the NFL's most valuable player after throwing for 4,132 yards and thirty touchdowns and finishing with a league-high 91.4 quarterback rating.

Nowadays, Pruitt says, "If I could have played above the ability God gave me on a consistent basis as much as Brian played above his, man, I would have broken all the records. He was slow, not very big, and his arm wasn't very strong. But he knew what his abilities were, and he perfected that."

But in 1980, Pruitt's words stung Sipe.

"I thought I was on a honeymoon for a long time because I don't think anybody expected much from me," Sipe told the *Cleveland Plain Dealer*'s Tony Grossi in 1994. "In order for me to get through it, I internalized it as kind of my crusade. I always felt I had to prove myself. I never wanted anybody to take snaps in practice. I was real possessive of the position because I didn't feel I was going to be given much slack."

Six times he surpassed three hundred yards, and each time the Browns won. He threw a last-minute pass to beat Green Bay for forty-six of his 391 yards, and later tossed four touchdowns in wins over Pittsburgh and Cincinnati.

Sipe enjoyed the wild finishes, telling Grossi he was most effective in two-minute situations. Then, he said, he could get a defense on its heels and keep it there. His teammates witnessed this joy.

"If we were down by a couple touchdowns at halftime," Dieken said, "he'd tell [quarterbacks coach Jim] Shofner, 'Hey, we've got them right where we want them.' The success of that team was based around Brian and the year he had. He came through every time we needed him."

Tight end Ozzie Newsome called him an unflappable leader.

"He would say, 'Hey, I'm calling the play, and you're the man this time,'" Newsome said. "He had a good way of seeing what was about to happen so you were going to be the man."

Sipe still owns eleven franchise passing records, including most touchdown passes (154) and most career yards passing (23,713). Not bad for a guy who would be a long-shot free agent if he had come out of college today. Sipe was also someone Rutigliano called a "'60s guy; a California guy a little to the left."

He liked music, politics, history, geography, travel, reading, and architecture (he's now an architect in San Diego). Sipe had a handle on life, which might explain why he kept a tight grip on himself during games.

"Brian would sit in the locker room before the game and read his ying and yang books on karma while everyone else is trying to get their game face on," Dieken said. "He was on a different wavelength than me. But Brian was a salesman, and when he called the plays, he made you believe that the play would work. There was an air of confidence around him."

35 **Greg Pruitt**
Running Back, 1973–1981
Number 34

Hello: When Greg Pruitt came to Cleveland, he battled his coach for playing time, convinced that his five-foot-ten body could vault the Browns to stardom. Nick Skorich begged to differ. So Pruitt sat, sometimes venting in the media, waiting for his chance.

Goodbye: By the time Pruitt left, in 1981, he was third on Cleveland's all-time list for rushing and combined yardage.

In between, he confounded defenders, marketed T-shirts with "Hello" on the front and "Goodbye" on the back, and razzed his teammates.

"He might have been only 195 pounds, but he thought he was 215," Browns tackle Doug Dieken said. "We called him, 'King.' He was the king. He was the guy. Greg was an unbelievable competitor. He was one of the first generation of the little scatbacks and he was out to prove he could play in the league."

Pruitt did just that. No one ever questioned his speed—Pruitt ran the forty-yard dash in 4.3 seconds and, at B. C. Elmore High School in Houston, he was second in Texas in the high hurdles. Nor his athleticism—Pruitt was an all-state baseball and basketball player. Even now, Pruitt regrets he didn't pursue baseball while at Oklahoma. His dimensions were another matter. But that proved to be both a demon and a blessing. While his size, and, for one season, Leroy Kelly, kept Pruitt on the bench, it also drove him.

"It was incentive," Pruitt said. "My grandfather used to tell me, 'You can always find good in tragedy; you just have to look for it.' The tragedy to me was that God shorted me by two inches. I despised that, but it was the motivation that I needed to help me play. I had to learn how to use size as an advantage. When guys would ask me how I play, I'd say, 'You can only get hurt by a train if you stand on the tracks. If you get the train off the tracks, it's ineffective.'"

Pruitt occasionally vented his frustrations in the press, telling reporters he didn't want to hear about his height from an even shorter coach like Skorich.

But even Pruitt succumbed to the size question at times. During pregame warm-ups in a 1973 game at Kansas City, Pruitt looked across the field where the Chiefs stretched. Their size, even without shoulder pads, stunned Pruitt, who began to wonder if Skorich was right. Then Kelly got hurt, and Pruitt entered the game.

Greg Pruitt

First play: 22 trap, a handoff to Pruitt. He broke the huddle, looked up, and saw all-Pro linebacker Willie Lanier staring at him. Pruitt remembered the scouting reports raving about Lanier reading his keys. Pruitt was his key.

"I'm the one getting the ball, and now I think he knows it, too," Pruitt recalled. "So I started leaning to the left to make him think I'm going outside. I looked back at him and he gave me a smirk and shook his head like, 'Uh-uh.' We run the play, and I get a three-yard loss."

But a couple plays later, Pruitt broke through the line for a sixty-five-yard touchdown.

When Forrest Gregg became coach, in 1975, he removed the shackles on Pruitt. By this time, Pruitt had developed a running strategy.

"When linemen led me on a sweep, I couldn't see the defender because of the linemen," Pruitt said. "That was the first problem I had in adjusting to my size. Then it dawned on me, 'If I can't see him, he can't see me.' So I positioned myself to where the defender had to make a commitment one way or another. If I wanted to go inside, I would press outside to make him appear, then dip back inside. That would put him out of position."

From 1975 through 1978, the first year of the sixteen-game schedule, Pruitt surpassed one thousand yards three times and fell short by forty yards in another. He finished with 5,496 yards rushing, which was third when he retired and is now fourth. Pruitt still is third in combined yardage with 10,700 total yards. He did it with flair, as his Hello-Goodbye T-shirts, which traced back to his junior year at Oklahoma and were meant to tease chasing defenders, became a hot seller in Cleveland.

Then there were his hands. After tearing the medial collateral ligament in his right knee, in 1979, Pruitt became a third-down back, catching passes out of the backfield. His hands were good enough that coach Sam Rutigliano, who took over in Pruitt's sixth season, now says he wishes he had moved Pruitt to receiver rather than trade him to the Raiders. After all, in high school, Pruitt had been switched from quarterback to receiver and caught 108 passes, so this was nothing new. Besides, Pruitt said he had the best hands on the team, a belief he shared with his teammates. He would often participate in receiving drills, catching passes shot from a machine while reminding the receivers how good his hands were. They dished it right back.

"We would tell him, 'You've got great hands. For a running back,'" receiver Dave Logan said.

Pruitt also was a team prankster. After defensive end Joe Jones dumped Pittsburgh quarterback Terry Bradshaw on his head in a 1976 win, Pruitt pulled his friend aside and quietly told him:

"They could put you in jail if Bradshaw dies. I know it's just a football game, but it would be involuntary manslaughter. You need to make sure he's OK."

Linebacker Robert L. Jackson was another frequent target. Jackson had grown up in Pruitt's Houston neighborhood and was often shooed away from pickup football games by the older Pruitt and his pals. Jackson caught up physically and was drafted by Cleveland in 1978.

Jackson spent the first week of his rookie training camp nailing ballcarriers and wowing coaches. Then the veterans reported. When Pruitt witnessed Jackson's smashes, he cringed. The next day, Pruitt approached Jackson, knowing the rookie soon would target him. He reminded Jackson of his Houston nickname, "Poochie."

"I said, 'You're having a good day, Poochie,'" Pruitt said. "He said, 'My name's not Poochie; they're calling me Stonewall.' I said, 'If you hit me like you've been hitting those other guys in camp, I'm going to the TV and letting everybody know that your nickname, before it was Stonewall, was Poochie. The next practice, I hit the hole as fast as I can, and he can't quite get to me. All the coaches are saying [to the other backs], 'Run up there like Pruitt!' They didn't know we had our little secret."

Pruitt was the Browns' little secret to success.

"I got off on having a big part in winning games," Pruitt said, "so that afterward, when I was walking off, I'd hear these big ol' guys, with their heads down after losing, say, 'The little guy just kicked our butts.'"

36 **Doug Dieken**
Left Tackle, 1971–1984
Broadcaster, 1985–1995

Number 73

The bags stayed packed throughout training camp as Doug Dieken, a rookie playing a new position, expected bad news at any time. It never came. Dieken never left.

Fans teased him about his holding penalties, but what Dieken had the best grasp on was his job. He made the first team ten games into his rookie season. Thirteen and a half years later, he finally gave it up. He played through two knee operations, two broken hands, a dislocated elbow, a sprained knee, and countless chipped teeth. Still, Dieken started a franchise-best 194 consecutive games and appeared in 203 games, third most in Browns history.

Dieken also added fourteen years to the left tackle legacy started by Lou Groza and followed by Dick Schafrath. For thirty-seven years, only those three played the position. It's no wonder one of Dieken's prized possessions is a 1970s photo of the three tackles at a banquet.

"Lou is my grandpa, Schaf's my dad," Dieken said. "But I didn't think about [the legacy] because at that time it wasn't that unique to have a team with only two tackles. I was more concerned with surviving. When I tacked on fourteen years and all of a sudden it's up to thirty-seven years, then it got to be unique."

Groza also happened to be the one who recommended the Browns draft Dieken after scouting him, in 1970, at Illinois. Dieken was a tight end and would finish as the Illini's second all-time leading receiver, but Groza figured his future was elsewhere on the line. But it was a future Browns coach who let Dieken know his days at tight end were numbered. When Dieken played in the Senior Bowl, the receivers' coach kept removing him in passing situations.

"I was always upset with that coach," Dieken said, "until 1978, and then I had to change my mind because he became the head coach of the Browns."

The receivers' coach was Sam Rutigliano. By the time Rutigliano got to Cleveland, Dieken was well established at tackle. But even after that Senior Bowl experience, Dieken, a sixth-round pick, persisted with his tight end dreams. However, he knew his days at that position were numbered in his first minicamp when they

handed him a jersey with number 73 on it. Still, he convinced another rookie tight end, Tony Blanton, that they had no chance to make the team, so Blanton quit.

Dieken thought this would increase his chances, a hope squashed when starter Milt Morin showed up in camp. That doesn't stop Dieken from saying with a laugh, "If [then coach] Nick Skorich had kept me at tight end, he might still be coaching."

Or maybe Dieken would have been cut. As a lineman, Dieken landed on the cab squad after the last exhibition game, but then moved to the regular squad before the season opener. Seven games into the season, injuries forced Dieken into the lineup. His first opponent: Atlanta's Claude Humphreys, one of the game's best.

"That's when I first started to hold," said Dieken, who had less than two quarters of experience at tackle before this game. "That was survival."

Three games later, Dieken replaced Schafrath in the starting lineup, where he became a fixture. His streak nearly ended, in 1980, when he sprained his knee in a Monday night game against Chicago. Six days later, he played sparingly at Baltimore, though others might have missed several weeks.

"Doug is an amazing guy," Rutigliano said.

In 1975, the Cleveland Touchdown Club named Dieken the Browns' offensive player of the year, and, in 1980, he made the Pro Bowl. That same season, fans voted the civic-minded Dieken to the Browns' all-time team. They also used to ride him about his penchant for holding. He had fun with it, too, as his license plates read: Mehold.

"I would drive down the street, and people would give me the holding signal," said Dieken, known for his wit as well. "I remember one time going four or five games without a holding penalty and then finally getting one, and people in the stands actually applauded. It was like, 'Hey, they really know what's going on here.' They had fun with it. But they knew why you were [holding]: because you wanted to make sure the quarterback didn't get killed."

Dieken didn't rely on his hands as much as his feet. Maybe he was too slow for tight end, but not for tackle. When defensive ends began widening their stance trying to speed-rush past tackles, Dieken's quickness, as well as his long arms, became more important.

That's how he lasted so long, and it's what helped him make his lone Pro Bowl after the 1980 season in which the offensive line blocked well enough to help quarterback Brian Sipe become the NFL's MVP.

Still, every so often, the Browns would take advantage of Dieken's hands by throwing him the ball. His first taste of the end zone came in a 1978 preseason game when he lined up as a tight end in field-goal formation. Holder Mark Miller threw him the ball for a touchdown.

Finally, in 1983, the Browns threw to Dieken again. This time the pass was supposed to go to kicker Matt Bahr. But Dieken, lining up as a tight end, ran past the secondary and grabbed Paul McDonald's fourteen-yard throw in the Browns' 25–19 overtime win against Houston.

"For some reason, the secondary neglected me," Dieken said. "I was so wide open that even Paul McDonald could find me."

Naturally, Dieken bragged about his hands and breakaway speed. He even made a highlight film of the play for a charity dinner with the lyrics, "Oh, Lord it's hard to be humble when you're perfect in so many ways," being sung in the background. There was no dance, but Dieken did save the ball and even had the words, "First career TD" inscribed on it.

"Like there were going to be a lot more," he said.

Then the club's player relations director Dino Lucarelli snapped a picture of Dieken in the end zone with the pictures of the Browns' top ten all-time receivers surrounding him. A sign read: Welcome to the Touchdown Club.

Dieken retired after the 1984 season and became part of the radio broadcast crew the next season, allowing him to show his consistency once again. He held onto that job until the franchise headed to Baltimore after the 1995 season.

"I had twenty-five great years," Dieken said.

And that's something he likes holding on to.

37 **The Comeback**
1987 vs. New York

Browns 23, Jets 20 (2 OT)
January 3, 1987

This bushy-haired kid, two years removed from college, entered the huddle and stared into the sagging faces of his teammates and convinced them they could win. Never mind the ten-point deficit; the consecutive interceptions; the clock running out. The negatives were piled high. Yet quarterback Bernie Kosar made a promise— "We're going to win this game"—then stuck to it.

Too bad his vow couldn't be piped over the Cleveland Stadium loudspeakers. Perhaps that would have stopped thousands from fleeing to the parking lot after Kosar's last interception, a would-be killer that resulted in a New York Jets touchdown and 20–10 lead. Only 4:14 remained. Time to head home. Kosar, though, wanted to right his wrongs. He begged for a shot at redemption.

"He was almost in tears," tight end Ozzie Newsome recalled. "All he wanted was a chance to get back on the field. Bernie had a look in his eyes like I've never seen before. This was a guy who didn't accept losing. You see that in great competitors, and I saw that in him in only his second year. I was in awe of him not being in awe of the league."

Nor was Kosar fazed by the daunting task of stringing together two scoring drives in less than five minutes. First, though, the Browns' psyche needed recharging. Enter Jets end Mark Gastineau, who provided the jumper cables on Cleveland's first scoring drive by slamming into Kosar's chest, leading with his helmet, after an incomplete pass on second and twenty-four.

The fifteen-yard unsportsmanlike conduct penalty, and automatic first down, revived the Browns. After two incompletions, Kosar took over, throwing for four first downs in a row, two each to receivers Reggie Langhorne and Brian Brennan.

On the radio, color commentator Doug Dieken, an ex-Brown, got sucked up in the emotions, sensed a comeback, and issued this warning, "If you left and you're in your car, you might want to turn around and come back because this one isn't over yet."

Suddenly, Cleveland had reached the New York three. Two plays later, fullback

Receiver Webster Slaughter helped the Browns overcome a late ten-point deficit against the Jets, catching a last-minute fourth-quarter pass at the five.

Kevin Mack ripped through a hole courtesy of tackle Cody Risien and guard Dan Fike for a touchdown with 1:57 to play.

A failed onside kick momentarily halted this new life. But the Browns' defense forced a punt, Kosar got the ball back, and the offense continued to roll. A twenty-five-yard pass-interference penalty preceded perhaps the play of the game: an over-the-shoulder snag by receiver Webster Slaughter at the Jets' five with eighteen seconds remaining. Two plays later, kicker Mark Moseley sent the game into overtime.

Kosar, aching to atone for his mistakes, had accomplished the first part. The Browns were alive and in control. Then it was a matter of time.

Kosar had delivered all season, feeding the craving for a winner in a city that had not won a title since 1964. The Browns hadn't won a play-off game in seventeen years. But, in 1986, they won with defense, which pleased this blue-collar city. They also featured a homegrown star in the twenty-three-year-old Kosar, reared sixty miles east in Boardman, a Youngstown suburb. After leaving the University of Miami, Kosar, a former bleacherite, uttered a phrase few had heard in years: "I want to play in Cleveland."

In the 1950s under Paul Brown, Cleveland was a desirable place to play, mainly because the Browns won much more than they lost. The Browns challenged baseball's New York Yankees for sports supremacy, capturing three titles and appearing in four others.

But from 1973 to 1984, the Browns made the play-offs only once in a nonstrike year. They had lost their luster, much like the struggling city. So when a player expressed a strong interest in coming to Cleveland, the fans embraced him. They did that with Kosar, the subject of numerous songs. In 1986, Kosar, in his second season, passed for 3,854 yards and seventeen touchdowns. Twice he passed for more than four hundred yards in the regular season. Best of all, Cleveland envisioned another Otto Graham, who led the Browns to three NFL championships in the '50s. Another golden age surely had begun.

It was hard to envision success at the season's start. First, the Browns had to recover from the cocaine-induced death of popular safety Don Rogers, one of the NFL's top safeties, on June 27. Cornerback Hanford Dixon was with him in California when it happened. For some, the aftershocks lasted a while.

"That whole training camp was a haze," cornerback Frank Minnifield said. "I don't remember anything about that camp. I know the Browns didn't want us to have any type of memories of Don Rogers on our uniforms. We don't know who made that decision, but we assumed it was coming from the top. The only thing we did was put a memorial picture in the lunch room of Don.

"I tell everybody, if Don doesn't die, we win four Super Bowls. A minimum of two. We spent the remainder of my career trying to replace him. The other person we spent the rest of my career trying to replace is [linebacker] Chip Banks. He and Don were real close, and Chip couldn't deal with it. I would stake my life on it that if we don't lose Don, Chip would be able to stay contained within himself."

Others weren't sure of Rogers's lasting emotional trauma. Certainly, Banks and Dixon went on to have good seasons, each earning spots in the Pro Bowl, though personal problems would make this Banks's last season in Cleveland.

"It was so tragic because Don was so talented," linebacker Clay Matthews said. "But I don't think we had to deal with it after that. Once you get into camp, you get caught up in trying to play the season."

That was difficult early on, as Cleveland lost two of its first three games. But the Browns recovered to win twelve regular-season games, the most in club history, including a win in Pittsburgh for the first time since 1969. They clinched the AFC Central with a 34–3 win at Cincinnati in week fifteen followed by a 41–17 stomping of San Diego in the regular-season finale. Eight wins in the last nine games prompted fans to chant in the finale: "Super Bowl! Super Bowl!" The Browns were ready for the postseason.

Newsome remembered taking the field and checking out all the signs hanging around the Stadium. Four or five caught his eye, and each stated a similar sentiment: No more Red Right 88. The play that just wouldn't die was the last pass thrown by Brian Sipe in the 1980 season, an end zone interception. That was also the last play-off game in Cleveland before this one.

Newsome had played on that team and so, too, had Matthews. Most of the faces were new, however, and the Kardiac Kids had long faded into history, replaced by the Dawgs and the infamous Dawg Pound.

Besides, these Jets weren't the Oakland Raiders. They had won ten of their first eleven games, then made the play-offs despite losing their last five. But New York became rejuvenated after beating Kansas City 35–15 in the first round, while the Browns had a bye.

The week off didn't help Cleveland, as New York grabbed a 7–0 lead on quarterback Pat Ryan's forty-two-yard strike to receiver Wesley Walker on a flea-flicker. Kosar retaliated with his own scoring toss, this one a thirty-seven-yarder to running back Herman Fontenot.

The teams matched scores again in the second quarter, as Moseley's thirty-eight-yarder provided the Browns their first lead. But Pat Leahy tied it two seconds before halftime with a forty-six-yard kick. Then he untied it with a thirty-seven-yarder in the third, giving New York a 13–10 lead.

Cleveland's defense had asserted itself despite the field goals. But Kosar struggled through the middle quarters, unable to generate a passing attack against the NFL's worst pass defense. Finally, in the fourth quarter, he began to solve the Jets and moved the Browns to the two yard line.

This set up disaster number one. On third down, Kosar ignored double coverage on Slaughter and gunned the ball toward him. But New York defensive back Russell Carter intercepted. And Newsome had a flashback to the Raiders' game.

"We had a chance to take the lead, and I'll be darned if we don't throw another interception in [the end zone]," Newsome said.

It got worse. On the Browns' next play from scrimmage, at their own seventeen, Kosar tossed another interception. After throwing 133 consecutive passes without an interception, Kosar had tossed them back-to-back. On the next play, running back Freeman McNeil swept right end for a twenty-five-yard touchdown.

"It looked bleak," Kosar said. "I felt terrible."

So did many in the crowd of 78,106, which quickly thinned out. Some Browns filed out with them, at least mentally.

"We had all given up," Minnifield said. "I don't know if anyone else will admit that. But I was already packing my bags mentally. I was thinking about what boxes I would put my things in to go back to Lexington [Kentucky]."

A small change helped ignite the comeback. On the first scoring drive, the Browns switched possession receiver Brennan to their deep man. He caught two passes to set up Mack's touchdown, and, on the next series, the Jets' safeties became preoccupied with Brennan, allowing Slaughter to get man coverage. Which enabled Kosar to connect with him for the thirty-seven-yard gain.

Cleveland's receivers contributed more of the same in overtime. Kosar read a New York blitz, audibilized, and hit Langhorne for thirty-five yards to the Jets' five. Game over?

"I was ready to go home," Langhorne said.

Except . . . Moseley, the only kicker ever named the NFL's MVP, missed a twenty-three-yard attempt into the closed end. Moseley said later he lost his balance and barely hit the ball. But why he missed mattered little.

"I remember the despair that I felt for just an instant," coach Marty Schottenheimer said. "But all of a sudden I realized, 'Marty, if you get that attitude, your players will pick it up from you.' I immediately changed gears. It was a conscious thing, 'You've got to stay positive.'"

Newsome said, "At that point, we not only told Mark, 'We'll get you another chance,' we believed we would. The game had changed at that point."

Mainly because of the Browns' defense, which helped everyone remain upbeat as the Jets, save for a couple of plays, did little, especially in overtime. Cleveland finished with nine sacks—five and a half by the line—and constantly pounded the Jets' quarterback tandem of Ryan and Ken O'Brien, who entered when the former was injured in the second quarter.

With each hit, the confidence soared. And the defense was convinced it wouldn't fold. While end Carl Hairston recorded three sacks, it was another end, Sam Clancy, who had the last. In the second overtime, with New York facing third and five from its own twenty-four, Clancy burst through and sacked O'Brien for a ten-yard loss.

Cleveland end Carl Hairston sacks Jets quarterback Ken O'Brien, one of nine sacks by the Browns in this double-over-time victory.

"We were just determined that they wouldn't move the ball on us in overtime," said Clancy, a former NBA player who had become a decent pass rusher. "We knew that no matter how long it took, we were going to give the offense the chance to have the ball and score."

The offense took care of its end of the deal on the ensuing series, driving from its own thirty-one to the Jets' nine, thanks to a bruising running game that finally showed life. Of the Browns' seventy-five rushing yards, forty-five came on the final series and twenty-six of those came from three Mack carries.

Again Schottenheimer summoned Moseley, who joined Kosar in seeking a second chance. After his miss, Moseley said he prayed for one more opportunity, not wanting his sparkling career to be overshadowed by a missed chip shot for a team he had joined less than two months ago.

Six weeks before this game, the Redskins considered him done and released their thirteen-year kicker. But when Matt Bahr was injured late in the season, the Browns signed Moseley. His years of experience made him attractive to Cleveland, but they couldn't soothe his pain after his huge miss.

"It was like carrying eighty-thousand people on your shoulders, all of them with knives at your back," Moseley said.

But on first down, and after a New York timeout, Moseley kicked the twenty-seven-yarder at the open end for the win, ending the third longest game in NFL history and sending the Browns to the AFC championship game. His heroics provided a moment few will forget. And it caused the fans to stomp in the stands long after the players had cleared the field.

"That ranks as one of the greatest games of all time," Schottenheimer said eleven years later. After the game, he told reporters, "Just before we said our prayer in the locker room, I told the players to listen. You could still hear the people cheering for us. This is a victory, a game, a moment all of us will remember the rest of our lives."

The moment was crafted by their second-year quarterback, who ignored a fate that had befallen the Browns once before. He also displayed coolness, demanding his team not quit. They listened. They believed. Later, Kosar winked at a reporter as he left the locker room and said, "Just another day at the office."

Some day. Kosar finished with remarkable stats, setting two NFL play-off records—most yards (489) and most attempts (sixty-four)—and tied the mark for most completions (thirty-three).

"He had that competitive spirit to be able to lead a team," said Newsome, who finished with six catches for 114 yards. "He just carried us on his back and said, 'Let's go.'"

	1	2	3	4	OT	2OT	Total
Jets	7	3	3	7	0	0	20
Browns	7	3	0	10	0	3	23

FIRST QUARTER
N - Walker 42 pass from Ryan (Leahy kick). Jets, 7–0
C - Fontenot 37 pass from Kosar (Bahr kick). Tie, 7–7

SECOND QUARTER
C - Moseley 38 FG. Browns, 10–7
N - Leahy 46 FG. Tie, 10–10

THIRD QUARTER
N - Leahy 37 FG. Jets, 13–10

FOURTH QUARTER
N - McNeil 25 run (Leahy kick). Jets, 20–10
C - Mack 1 run (Bahr kick). Jets, 20–17
C - Moseley 22 FG. Tie, 20–20

SECOND OVERTIME
C - Moseley 27 FG. Browns, 23–20

38 **Bernie Kosar**
Quarterback, 1985–1993
Number 19

 Numbers defined his career and measured his impact—on the city and the team. When quarterback Bernie Kosar played, the Browns usually won, collecting four division titles in his first five seasons. He ranks near the top of every major franchise passing record. But first he stole the city's heart with six words: "I want to play in Cleveland." And the city swooned.

Again, numbers told the story: in 1985, while the NFL decided who held Kosar's rights, either Cleveland or Minnesota, the fans couldn't wait. More than ten thousand jammed the *Cleveland Plain Dealer*'s phone lines, knocking out the phone system.

Eight years later, when the Browns dumped him and Dallas picked him up, Browns fans immediately swamped the Cowboys pro shop at Texas Stadium with requests for Kosar's new number 18 jersey. His uniform sold more than Troy Aikman, Emmitt Smith, and Michael Irvin.

"They got hundreds of calls," remembered the *Plain Dealer*'s Tony Grossi, who covered Kosar's arrival in Dallas.

Kosar's first game with the Cowboys tested loyalties. Overall, 32 percent of the city watched the Browns lose to Seattle while 29.3 percent saw Kosar, playing for an injured Troy Aikman, lead Dallas to a win. By game's end, twice as many people were tuned in to Kosar than the Browns.

Why? He was Cleveland's favorite son, rising to glory for the team he grew up following as a kid in the Youngstown suburb of Boardman. He was loyal to his family and his church. Kosar's style matched Cleveland's.

"Once I met him and saw his style, he was like the perfect Clevelander," Grossi said. "He was usually awkward and clumsy and all the negatives. He seemed to be the perfect quarterback at a time when Cleveland was ugly. But he got the job done."

That's all he ever did. When he played at Boardman, his style chased away recruiters from Ohio State and Pitt, the two schools he wanted to attend. It didn't matter that he was the Associated Press's player of the year in Ohio as a senior. Nor did it matter that his high school coach, Gene Pushic, gushed about Kosar's ability to "finesse a ball into the flats, or rifle it seventy yards." Too many recruiters saw a gangly quarterback with a three-quarter-arm delivery, and gagged.

Kosar finally chose Miami, where naysayers followed, even those on the coaching staff. One year, Kosar dueled with Vinny Testaverde for the starting job. When coach Howard Schnellenberger polled his coaching staff as to who should start, only two coaches voted for Kosar. Fortunately for Kosar, those coaches were Schnellenberger and offensive coordinator Marc Trestman. All Kosar did was lead the Hurricanes to a national title. He soon proved all he needed to at Miami and opted to turn pro, despite having two years of college eligibility remaining.

But he only wanted to play for one team: Cleveland. After all, Browns and Indians posters covered his walls in Boardman, and he constantly wore a Browns jersey, Brian Sipe's number 17. A Browns wastebasket sat in a corner of his room. Kosar even sat in the bleachers at Browns games and once ran onto the field during an Indians rain delay. His father, Bernie Sr., told tales of another Cleveland quarterback, Otto Graham.

To Kosar, the fit was natural. So he made it work by declaring for the NFL's supplemental draft in June. Houston and Minnesota had worked out a deal for the regular draft, allowing the Vikings to draft him. Cleveland made its own deal with Buffalo for the first pick in the supplemental draft. Commissioner Pete Rozelle ruled that Kosar could opt for the June draft, handing him to the Browns.

"I probably would have gone back to school otherwise," Kosar told the *Browns News/Illustrated*. "I knew the Browns were looking for a quarterback, but the main thing was to get back home and play for the home team."

The Browns were thrilled that he did. To add pressure, Browns vice president of football operations Ernie Accorsi suggested Kosar wear number 19, as Johnny Unitas once did for the Colts, where Accorsi worked in public relations.

Kosar, who fumbled his first-ever snap, replaced an injured Gary Danielson as the starter in week five and guided Cleveland to its first AFC Central title since 1971. Then he nearly led an upset of highly favored Miami in the play-offs.

In his second season, Kosar directed the Browns' most prolific scoring attack since 1968, leading Cleveland to a 12–4 record and AFC Central title. Kosar threw for seventeen touchdowns and 3,854 yards, second most in franchise history. In a play-off win over the New York Jets—the Browns' first since '69—Kosar threw for a NFL-record 489 yards, vaulting Cleveland into the AFC championship game. Kosar was only twenty-two.

"In his second year, all of a sudden he was the remake of Jim Brown," linebacker Clay Matthews said.

In his third season, Kosar nearly was the NFL's most valuable player, tossing twenty-two touchdowns while completing a league-high 62 percent of his passes and finishing with an AFC-best 95.4 quarterback rating.

"He was a great competitor, which is the trademark of every outstanding quarterback," coach Marty Schottenheimer said. "He was very accurate, and he had tremendous anticipation. Bernie would be willing to throw the ball before the guy came open. I remember occasions where he'd throw the ball to someone on a comeback route and I'd say, 'Oh, no!' And as I said that, he [would complete the pass] and I'd say, 'Great throw!'"

Again the Browns reached, and lost, the AFC championship game. But it wasn't Kosar's fault. He rallied the Browns from a 21–3 deficit and put them in position to tie the game, only to lose on an Earnest Byner fumble two yards from the tying score.

Kosar had established himself as one of the smartest quarterbacks in the NFL, compensating for his immobility. Quick decisions coupled with a strong arm made him deadly. But he needed protection, and the Browns barely addressed their line, drafting one lineman in the first four rounds of the 1987–1989 drafts while drafting three linebackers and three defensive linemen.

"When you protected Bernie, he was the best in the game," receiver Brian Brennan told *BNI*. "Bernie was the most cerebral quarterback I ever played with. He threw the softest pass. He had the best ideas of how to beat a defense. He was at his best when calling plays in the huddle and not getting them from the sideline."

Eventually, the pounding Kosar took wore down his body. He missed seven games, in 1988, first with a strained elbow and then a strained knee. Kosar returned strong the following season and once more helped Cleveland win the AFC Central. He once more advanced to the AFC championship, where the Browns again lost to Denver.

"Before the injury, Bernie was one of the best in the game," cornerback Frank Minnifield said. "He could make up the difference of the time allotted by the offensive line. After he got hurt, it was real difficult for him to do that. He needed more help, and it wasn't coming."

Kosar suffered through the horrendous 3–13 season, in 1990, as he threw ten touchdowns and fifteen interceptions. His numbers improved when coach Bill Belichick arrived a year later, but the end was near. By mid-1993, Kosar was gone, taking with him numerous Browns passing records, including the highest completion percentage for a career (58.8) and season (66.5) and most passes thrown without an interception (308).

Kosar also led the Browns to three play-off wins. In his first seven Decembers, when pressure increases to win, Kosar threw for thirty-three touchdowns and only eighteen interceptions. In the play-offs, he threw for fifteen touchdowns and ten interceptions.

"He had a special quality," Grossi said, "more so than Brian Sipe. Sipe was more of a matinee idol and people warmed to him. But he never won a play-off game. Bernie proved some of the smartest men in football wrong."

Those who met him early could see that happening.

"Bernie wasn't some starry-eyed kid," broadcaster Doug Dieken said. "He was twenty-three going on thirty-three. He had a presence to him that exceeded his age."

A presence that allowed him to ignore consecutive interceptions and rally the Browns from a 20–10 deficit against the Jets with four minutes left in a play-off game. And a presence that shouted team-first. As a rookie, Kosar balked when *Sports Illustrated* wanted to place him on the cover, only to relent as a favor to owner Art Modell. When the *SI* reporter suggested a limo ride to Cleveland Stadium for the picture shoot, Kosar agreed, on one condition: the limo must not pick him up at the Browns' facility.

"I didn't want my teammates to see me in that thing," he said.

It was an attitude that captured a city and explains his enduring popularity.

"There is something healthy about Bernie's success," Pushic told the *Pittsburgh Press* in 1987. "He worked hard as an athlete, he worked hard as a student. He is still close to his family, to his old buddies, to his church. And he wanted to come back home to play for the Browns."

When he did, he changed the way a city viewed itself.

As Grossi said, "He did more to lift the spirits of the town than any one athlete."

39 **The Drive**
1987 vs. Denver

Broncos 23, Browns 20 (OT)
January 11, 1987

"Here we go, Brownies, here we go! Super Bowl!"

The chant started softly—this crowd had been burned before—but spread quickly. Like a forest fire. Nearly eighty thousand fans unleashed years of bottled-up frustration, aching for this one moment. Their Cleveland Browns were headed to the Super Bowl. Or so it seemed. Receiver Brian Brennan had just sped forty-eight yards with quarterback Bernie Kosar's pass for the go-ahead score in the AFC championship game. Only 5:32 remained. The touchdown triggered the chant. This raised the volume: the kickoff pinned Denver on its own two yard line.

"Here We Go, Brownies, Here We Go! Super Bowl!"

The skeptics jumped in, tossing aside their fear of a letdown. They had tempted fate before, only to be knocked down time and again. Not this time. Not here.

Quarterback John Elway, his Broncos trailing 20–13, would need to engineer a ninety-eight-yard drive to force overtime. To this point, he had passed for only 116 yards. Cleveland's defense had smothered him.

No Cleveland team, in any sport, had played in the ultimate title game since 1964. That drought appeared over. So the fans, all 79,973 of them, continued their assault on Denver's eardrums.

"HERE WE GO, BROWNIES, HERE WE GO! SUPER BOWL!"

Then it happened. Elway got hot. The Browns, and their fans, got burned. Again.

For two weeks Cleveland was a crazed city, forcing the Browns to escape the insanity and practice in Vero Beach, Florida. The Browns already had caused their fans to go bonkers with their 12–4 regular-season finish. But the excitement escalated after their double-overtime win over the New York Jets in the AFC Divisional play-offs on January 3, sending them to the championship game.

Immediately after the Jets victory, Peter Kolomichuk and some family members drove from suburban Brunswick to Cleveland Stadium. They camped out for two

days, hoping to be first in line for some of the forty thousand tickets available for the AFC championship. Fans snatched up the tickets in two and a half hours.

"We didn't start thinking about the Super Bowl until the city started thinking about it," cornerback Frank Minnifield said. "And they didn't think about it until after the Jets' game. They were sure we were going to the Super Bowl at that point because whoever gets the home field advantage usually wins. That week leading up the Denver game was the only time we were forced to think about the Super Bowl. It got chaotic."

But what else could be expected? This had become the year of the Dawg, the nickname bestowed on the Browns' defense by Minnifield and fellow corner Hanford Dixon the year before. Cleveland embraced the moniker, and the bleachers evolved into the Dawg Pound. Fans, some wearing dog masks and waving bones, barked at players who woofed right back. Milk-Bones became a pregame snack.

Souvenir shirts were purchased nearly as soon as they hit the stands. Occupants spelled out "Go Browns" in downtown buildings; Browns helmets adorned downtown statues.

Even the *Clearwater Sun,* a small afternoon Florida paper, tired of the woeful Tampa Bay Buccaneers, adopted the Browns as their new team to cover. Then there was Browns Original Beer. Never mind that it was a Canadian import and tasted bad—it skyrocketed in popularity.

Of course, it never reached the kind of popularity enjoyed by quarterback Bernie Kosar. But nothing else did, either, as Cleveland embraced the twenty-three-year-old Youngstown native and former bleacherite who helped the Browns win twelve of their last fourteen games. The last of those wins, their first play-off victory in seventeen years, was the mightiest. That's why the fans responded in maniacal fashion. Everything was perfect. Browns nose tackle Bob Golic, raised in Cleveland, certainly thought so.

"Here I am," Golic said the week of the game, "playing in a championship game for the team I followed as a kid. Who could ask for more than that?"

The fans did. They wanted to win the game.

"This is dangerous territory," Dr. Garland Denelsky, a Cleveland Clinic psychologist, told the *Akron Beacon Journal.* "Some people will have an awful lot of their own self-worth riding on how the Browns do. If the team loses, they won't just be disappointed, they'll be devastated."

He would be right.

Elway dodged Milk-Bones en route to the Broncos' huddle in the closed end zone. When he entered the huddle, Elway smiled and said, "Well, we got these guys right where we want them." Sure, ninety-eight yards from the tying score against one of the NFL's best defenses in a hostile stadium on a field that was a mixture of mud, paint, and ice. Elway's teammates didn't believe him.

Just when it appeared Clay Matthews and the Browns had Denver's John Elway under control, he led a game-tying ninety-eight-yard drive to force overtime.

That would change. Elway, then twenty-six, would sting the Browns by doing the great things long predicted of him. He and Kosar entered this game as two of the best young quarterbacks, ready to duel on a national stage for years. Their styles clashed. Elway was the golden boy quarterback, complete with big arm and agile legs. Kosar was smart and slayed defenses with an arm that was good and a mind that was lethal. But he rarely ran. The joke was, if the Browns needed to kill a minute off the clock, they could simply have Kosar run for a few yards. This would be their first showdown.

Before Elway took over this game, he needed help as Denver faced third and two from its own ten. But running back Sammy Winder slammed forward for the necessary yardage, squeaking past the yard marker by inches. Now it was Elway's turn.

One play after scrambling eleven yards for a first down, Elway zipped a twenty-two-yard pass to running back Steve Sewell to the Broncos' forty-eight, putting so much oomph on the throw that Browns safety Chris Rockins had little time to react. The "Here we go" chant had died long ago as fans could barely breathe—their chests swelling and stomachs tightening—let alone speak.

"The drive was like a slow death," said Mike Trivisonno, sports talk show host on Cleveland's WTAM-1100, who attended the game. "Like you were being tortured."

For a moment, the crowd exhaled when fresh-legged tackle Dave Puzzouli sacked Elway, forcing a third and eighteen from the Browns' forty-eight with 1:47 remaining. Barking resumed in the stands. Elway called time and hobbled to the sideline as his tender left ankle had been twisted.

But the sack only delayed Cleveland's pain. Elway, starting in shotgun formation, then rifled a twenty-yard completion to receiver Mark Jackson.

How close was this to a Denver disaster? Receiver Steve Watson had gone in motion too late, because of an Elway mistake, and passed by center Billy Bryan just as he was ready to snap. The ball grazed Watson's butt, causing it to wobble. If Watson had been a half-second earlier, the ball would have bounced off him. Instead, it nicked him, and Elway grabbed the ball and completed the pass.

"I always thought," Browns coach Marty Schottenheimer said, "that if [Watson] had been another three or four inches short on the motion, that thing would have hit him right in the hip. It would have been a fumble, and who knows what would have happened in the game. That's the one play that stands out in my mind."

Some Browns pointed to a philosophical change as well. On the final drive, they rushed three linemen, one less than they had controlled Elway with for much of the game. But now the coaches wanted extra coverage, though a blitz was used occasionally.

Cleveland defensive end Sam Clancy said afterward, "During the game, we used a four-man line several times, and every time we did, we popped him pretty good. I think we made a mistake by not using more four-man during that drive."

Eleven years later, Schottenheimer still disagrees.

"I never looked back on that [decision]," he said. "People always talk about a three-man rush, but no one ever talks about the fact that we've got an extra guy in coverage. We were in man coverage [on third and eighteen]. One guy was beaten."

Four plays, including a quarterback draw for nine yards, moved Denver to the five yard line. One more play tied the score. Jackson started in motion to his left then darted back to his right, fooling defensive back Mark Harper. That gave Elway an opening, and his touchdown pass to Jackson tied the score at 20 with thirty-seven seconds remaining.

"It looked bleak when [the Browns] got the long touchdown pass and you have to start at your own two yard line," said Denver coach Dan Reeves. "But then you start thinking about what they did against the Jets. You have to think you have a chance. Whenever you have a John Elway as your quarterback, you've got a chance."

On paper, the Browns still had a chance. After running out the clock in regulation, they won the toss in overtime. But the crowd sensed doom.

"When it went to overtime, my son said, 'Now what?'" Trivisonno recalled. "I said, 'Now we lose.'"

Cleveland failed to gain a first down as running back Herman Fontenot, who had carried the ball twenty-five times all season, was stopped on third and two. Denver took over on its own twenty-five and, on second down, Elway gunned a twenty-two-yard completion to tight end Orson Mobley at the Cleveland forty-eight. The funeral procession had begun.

Then, on third and twelve from the fifty, Elway escaped Clancy's rush, running toward the sideline. He spotted Watson for a twenty-eight-yard gain. Three running plays gained seven yards, setting up field-goal kicker Rich Karlis with a thirty-three-yard attempt.

Karlis was about to ruin the season for a team he once rooted for, having been raised in nearby Salem. His mother, who attended this game, remained a Browns fan—except for one afternoon. Karlis's kick hooked just inside the left upright—Browns safety Chris Rockins jumped and signaled wide left, thinking it was no good. He was wrong. Denver wins, 23–20.

Elway's heroics—he passed for 128 yards on the final two drives—obscured Cleveland miscues that led to ten Denver points in the first half. Kosar, facing the league's ninth-rated defense, was intercepted by linebacker Jim Ryan, who returned the first-quarter pass twenty-six yards. Karlis soon booted a nineteen-yard field goal, cutting the Browns' lead to 7–3.

Earlier, Fontenot had grabbed a six-yard scoring toss from Kosar, who finished eighteen of thirty-two for 259 yards with two touchdowns and two interceptions.

Cleveland's second mistake cost it the lead as fullback Kevin Mack fumbled at the Browns' thirty-seven where Broncos linebacker Ken Woodard recovered. Den-

Receiver Brian Brennan is congratulated after a late forty-eight-yard touchdown pass, one that many believed would put Cleveland in the Super Bowl.

ver drove to the one yard line where it faced fourth and goal. Reeves wanted the touchdown and the Browns obliged. Only ten players were on the field, thanks to a substitution error involving linebacker Brad Van Pelt. Running back Gerald Willhite scored easily.

Two field goals by Cleveland's Mark Moseley, sandwiched around another Karlis three-pointer, made it 13–13 in the fourth quarter. Then came the pass to Brennan, who caused strong safety Dennis Smith to fall by cutting outside and then inside. He scored without much of a chase.

"I don't think we celebrated too early," Brennan said.

"I was already at the Super Bowl," Minnifield said. "We had shut them down completely."

The fans were there, too. Vince Cellini, now the host of CNN's *NFL Preview Sunday* but then with the Cleveland CBS affiliate, headed down to the field after Brennan's touchdown. He envisioned a Cleveland-New York Giants Super Bowl in two weeks in Pasadena, California. Cellini was half right—New York would be playing.

"I told the cameraman, 'This is unbelievable, they're going to the Super Bowl,'" Cellini said. "He said, 'Hold on, not yet.' Then they kick off and I watched Elway. I walked along the Broncos' sidelines, and he was just magic. That day he was the best I've ever seen. I really believe in my heart that if they win that game, they beat the Giants in the Super Bowl. The Browns were as physical as any NFC team that year. It stays with me today. That one was tough to take. That's why a lot of people in Cleveland today still hate Elway. As much as I disliked him that day, I had to respect him for what he did."

Respect wasn't a common theme as the fans shuffled to their cars, heads down and hearts deflated. Their "drive," like Denver's ninety-eight-yard trip in regulation, would be completed in silence.

The euphoria of the past weeks had been whisked away, replaced by winter's reality. Another season with snow that sticks around long enough to turn gray, matching the color of the sky and the mood of the city. It happened every year. But seasons like this didn't.

"What made it so hard was the camaraderie of the team," Matthews said. "You can have a great team and the team may not get along. And there's so much turnover. A lot of times you don't have the closeness that we had that '86 season. I can genuinely say, without a doubt, that was the funnest and most rewarding team I played on."

But they all know it could have lasted one more game.

"That's the only play-off game I ever look back on," Schottenheimer said. "I don't dwell on it, but I also realize that was the perfect scenario. You're in your own stadium, and a victory enables you to play in the Super Bowl. Then, all of a sudden, the thing got away from us."

	1	2	3	4	OT	Total
Broncos	0	10	3	7	3	23
Browns	7	3	0	10	0	20

FIRST QUARTER
C - Fontenot 6 pass from Kosar (Moseley kick). Browns, 7–0

SECOND QUARTER
D - Karlis 19 FG. Browns, 7–3
D - Willhite 1 run (Karlis kick). Broncos, 10–7
C - Moseley 20 FG. Tie, 10–10

THIRD QUARTER
D - Karlis 26 FG. Broncos, 13–10

FOURTH QUARTER
C - Moseley 24 FG. Tie, 13–13
C - Brennan 48 pass from Kosar (Moseley kick). Browns, 20–13
D - Jackson 5 pass from Elway (Karlis kick). Tie, 20–20

OVERTIME
D - Karlis 33 FG. Broncos, 23–20

40 Ozzie Newsome
Tight End, 1978–1990
Administration, 1990–1995
Number 82

The ball skipped off his hands and fell to the ground. Jaws dropped with it. Sam Rutigliano can't forget the sight: Ozzie Newsome had just dropped a pass, creating a memory as vivid as the 662 catches he would retire with. So Rutigliano turned to running back Calvin Hill, who had seen plenty in his twelve seasons of pro football, but might have just witnessed a first. As well as a last.

"Take a look at that," Rutigliano told Hill, "because you won't see that again."

That was on December 14, 1980, and Rutigliano swears he didn't see him drop another pass over the next four seasons he was coach. Could anyone argue? Certainly, Newsome probably had a few more passes elude his grasp over his next eleven seasons. But not many. He didn't fumble after the fifth game in 1980.

Newsome arrived in Cleveland, in 1978, with the nickname "Wizard of Oz," and he made it stick. He caught passes while falling to the ground, sometimes even when he was parallel with it. Other times he was twisted like a pretzel yet made the catch. His body might have been contorted, but his eyes never left the prize, which is why he snatched so many seemingly uncatchable balls. Each time that happened, the stadium rang with the most popular chant of the 1980s: "Oz-zee! Oz-zee!" But Newsome wasn't as impressed as the fans.

"I always felt the ball was mine," he said. "You can find a way to come up with the catch, and I did that. The most important thing to me was making the catch. [Since retiring after the 1990 season], I've had a chance to look at some of the catches I made. But when I see them, I still see how I made the catch. I just look at where my eyes are and what I'm looking at. It's a great catch, I guess you could say, but the way it's being done is not so great. I was doing all the things I tried to teach the people who came behind me."

But not everyone had Newsome's background. In retrospect, Newsome points to two reasons that helped him make the circus catches. The first is baseball. Through Little League and into high school, Newsome was a catcher. Tipped balls, knucklers, and last-second breaking curves taught him how to react instantly. That

Ozzie Newsome

developed his hand-eye coordination. The second reason came at Alabama, where he played for Bear Bryant, whose picture still adorns his office wall in Baltimore.

"He taught me what catching the ball was," said Newsome, who is the Ravens' general manager after spending five seasons in the Browns' front office. "A lot of people don't realize what catching the ball takes. They think once the ball touches their hands, the catch is there. With [Bryant], until you get the ball completely tucked away—which means you watch it until you get it tucked—that catch is not completed. If I didn't complete a catch that way, he would say something to me."

Bryant also told Newsome something else before he left college. He predicted Newsome would be moved from receiver to tight end in the NFL. The Browns had similar plans in 1978. They were still smarting from not having drafted tight end Kellen Winslow the year before.

So Rutigliano sent receivers' coach Rich Kotite to Alabama to scout Newsome, whom they would later make a first-round pick. Rutigliano wanted to know the size of Newsome's rear end. The bigger the better.

"If he did have a big butt, he could carry 230–235 pounds and not lose speed," Rutigliano said. "Rich came back and said, 'Sam, he's got a big butt.' From the day he came in, it was his job."

First, though, they worked Newsome as a receiver in minicamp. Then came the oft told story of how Rutigliano called Newsome into his office and said, "You could be a good receiver, there's no doubt in our mind. But you could be a great tight end. We're moving you there because we're going to throw the football and you're going to have an impact on our offense."

That's when Newsome relayed what Bryant already had told him.

"I was coming out of a run-oriented wishbone offense," Newsome said. "As long as I was getting my four or five balls, I was happy. They were going to use what I did best, and that was catch the ball. Our passing game started with me and then went out [to the receivers]."

Newsome scored on a reverse in his first game, but he said it took him five years to feel comfortable at his new position, in part because of the blocking chores. But it didn't take him that long to put up big numbers, as Newsome pulled down fifty-five catches in his second season. In his fourth, his catches shot up as he grabbed sixty-nine.

Then from 1983 to 1985, he caught a combined 240 passes, including eighty-nine in back-to-back seasons. He led the AFC with eighty-nine catches in '84, one year after finishing second in the league with the same number of catches. Newsome, who had two one-thousand-yard seasons, made the Pro Bowl in '81, '84, and '85 and is the Browns all-time leading receiver.

"If there's a tight end that could catch the ball better than Ozzie, I haven't seen him," said receiver Dave Logan. "He had the best hands of any tight end I've ever seen."

"He was so skilled," said linebacker Clay Matthews, also drafted in the first round in '78, "that he always made the hard plays look easy. I was jealous of him because he was so talented."

Newsome once caught passes in 150 consecutive games, the NFL's fourth longest streak. It began October 21, 1979, at home against Cincinnati and ended October 29, 1989, at home against Houston. Occasionally, the streak endured thanks to a short catch or one behind the line of scrimmage.

"The streak meant a lot to me, and it was something I really came to be identified with," Newsome said. "We would get into the third quarter, and if I didn't have a catch, the fans would start chanting. And I knew Brian [Sipe] or Bernie [Kosar] would make sure I got that catch. It became something everyone else wanted me to have as much as I wanted to have it. But in the end, I was the one who made the decision for it to end."

By that point, Newsome had reached the end of his starring role, and his catches dwindled from sixty-two in Marty Schottenheimer's first full season of 1985 to thirty-five three years later, Schottenheimer's last.

Newsome created a stir, in 1987, when he, along with seven other veterans, crossed the picket line during the strike, angering numerous teammates. Cornerback Frank Minnifield was among those who verbally lashed out at Newsome, calling for his removal as captain. Newsome said he had peace of mind about the move.

"When I talk to guys now, that's one thing they always bring up," Minnifield said. "That was probably the start of the demise of our team. When Ozzie went across, it left our team without a leader. That's one reason he's still in management [with Baltimore]. But you can't get upset at Ozzie. He's good people."

Eventually, Newsome patched things up. It helped that he could still produce. One day after *Cleveland Plain Dealer* columnist Bill Livingston called for him to retire after 1987, Newsome grabbed six passes for ninety-four yards in a win at Pittsburgh.

Though Newsome didn't catch more than forty passes his last five seasons, he still retired with more catches than any tight end in history. Winslow reached the Hall of Fame first, but Newsome has more catches (Winslow had 541), yards (7,980 to 6,741), and touchdowns (forty-nine to forty-five) than the former San Diego superstar. However, Winslow played four fewer seasons.

"At this point, I appreciate it more than if I had made it on the first ballot," said Newsome, six months before he was voted into the Hall. "I know that getting in the Hall sets you apart. The longer it takes, the more I want it and the more I'll appreciate it."

So will others.

"Without question Ozzie should be in there," Rutigliano said. "He was one of the true great inside receivers, and he was fearless."

41 **Strock 'N' Roll**
1988 vs. Houston

Browns 28, Oilers 23
December 18, 1988

One by one, the quarterbacks dropped to the side, taking the Browns' Super Bowl chances along with them. One week, it was an elbow. The next, an ankle. It started with Bernie Kosar in the opener. Followed by Gary Danielson in week two. Followed by Mike Pagel four weeks later. When Kosar returned, he got hurt again.

For two years, the Drive and the Fumble had wrecked Cleveland's season. Now injuries did the job. Or so it seemed. The defense still ranked among the best; most of the parts remained offensively.

"We had a group of guys who had been in the play-offs three straight years," tight end Ozzie Newsome said. "We knew what it took to get in there."

All the Browns needed was a healthy quarterback. So they turned to a tanned, rested thirty-eight-year-old with a five-handicap. For fourteen years, Don Strock had played for Miami, a backup capable of stirring rallies, as in the 1981 play-offs when Strock led the Dolphins to a near miracle comeback against San Diego. Miami lost, but not because of Strock.

Usually, though, Strock rested, chained to the bench behind players such as Bob Griese and, later, Dan Marino. Strock was loyal and expected the same in return. But in 1988, when the Dolphins offered Strock what he considered a demeaning offer, he said goodbye.

"Everyone talks about loyalty, but it seems to me it was one-sided there," Strock said.

He was thirty-eight, but still wanted to play. The question was, would anyone want him to? Just in case the answer was yes, Strock stayed prepared. He worked out each morning and threw passes to fellow Dolphins holdout, and receiver, Mark Duper. Strock also was the sports director at Doral Park, a Miami golf course where he honed his own game. Then, when Danielson broke his ankle, the Browns called.

"I wanted to go to a contender," Strock said. "I didn't want to go somewhere just to work with the quarterbacks. I still felt I had something left, and Cleveland was a contender."

Quarterback Don Strock went from working at a Miami golf course to becoming an unlikely hero in Cleveland.

Granted, a contender with a cracked foundation because of the injuries. Kosar had led the Browns to consecutive AFC championship game appearances, each one ending with a crushing loss to Denver. But 1988 would be different—if everyone stayed healthy.

"Going into the season, we thought we would walk through the league," cornerback Frank Minnifield said. "We thought we would lose two or three all year."

"The expectations had gotten so high," linebacker Clay Matthews said. "And we were a team that kept saying we've got to go further and further. The community demanded it."

One game changed those expectations. In a 6–3 season-opening win at Kansas City, Kosar was leveled on a blitz and injured his right elbow. Some feared the worst, calling it career-threatening. It wasn't, but he would miss seven weeks.

A week later, Danielson broke his ankle in a 23–3 loss to the New York Jets. Finally, Pagel separated his shoulder, making a touchdown-saving tackle after an interception, in a 16–10 loss to Seattle.

Others went in and out as well, as receiver Webster Slaughter missed nine weeks with a fractured left arm. A usual assortment of injuries—fullback Kevin Mack and corner Hanford Dixon both missed the regular-season finale—made the situation seem worse.

But the bad luck traced back to quarterback.

"When we started losing quarterbacks," Minnifield said, "we knew we were in for a long season."

In came Strock, wearing a wristband with some of the plays written on it, to start against Philadelphia in week seven. But it didn't begin smoothly.

"On one of the early plays in the game," coach Marty Schottenheimer said, "he goes into the huddle and calls the play and says, 'Ready, break.' And as he says break, the guys said, 'We don't have that play.' And he said, 'Run it anyway.' Then he went to the line and audibilized to a play we did have. I'll never forget that. What he had done was call a Miami play."

Strock said, "I had been part of a system for fifteen years. I had *made* part of it, so this was a big change. I got the hang of it, and the wristband gave me a support group of plays. I still have that wristband."

But after leading the Browns to a 19–3 win over the Eagles, Strock wasn't needed. At least for a while. Kosar returned, and so did the lofty expectations when Cleveland won two straight. Kosar proved he was ready to regain his standing among the league's elite when he threw for 308 yards and three touchdowns in a win at Dallas.

Then he got hot against Miami the following week, throwing for 202 yards in a little more than three quarters. But Kosar had been pounded the previous five games, getting sacked twenty times. When he got drilled by Miami linebacker John Offerdahl in the fourth, Kosar's body snapped again. This time, he strained ligaments in a knee. Then he caused a rift with his line when he said, "We've been taking hits like this the past few weeks, so it was really inevitable."

One unnamed lineman told the *Akron Beacon Journal* before the Houston game, "There's dissension on this team, and I'm afraid it's creating a split at the worst possible time. I was standing right next to him in the locker room when he made the comment, and I couldn't believe it. It was like he was some god passing judgment."

But it didn't matter. With one game left in the season, and needing a win to make the playoffs, Kosar was out. Strock was in.

Leading rallies was nothing new to Strock. All he had to do was remember 1981 when he entered a play-off game in place of Dan Woodley against San Diego with Miami trailing 24–0 in the second quarter. That's when Strock nearly did the impossible. He flung passes the rest of the night, completing twenty-nine of forty-three passes for 403 yards and four touchdowns. But when it ended, Miami had lost in overtime, 41–38, in a game rated among the NFL's best ever. Thanks, in large part, to Strock.

Against Houston seven years later, Strock, making only his second start since 1983, didn't need a similar comeback. This time, his team trailed by only sixteen. Unlike the Chargers' game, it was Strock's fault that his team faced a mountainous deficit. On a gray, snowy day—typical Cleveland late-season weather—Houston intercepted three of Strock's first six passes, one of which safety Domingo Bryant returned thirty-six yards for a touchdown and a 10–0 lead.

Strock was losing the battle of the elements as the wind whipped off the lake and swirled inside the stadium. The wind grabbed hold of one pass, moving it off target and into enemy hands. Another time, Strock was hit as he threw, causing a bad throw. But it wasn't just bad luck.

"Maybe I tried to force things early in the game when we were driving into the wind," Strock said. "Some things happened that were unfortunate, but I hung in there. Bernie said, 'What turned it around?' I said, 'The guy throwing it started throwing it straighter.'"

That didn't happen until late in the third quarter and not before another disaster awaited Strock. First came a Cleveland touchdown when linebacker David Grayson nailed quarterback Warren Moon on a blitz, jarring the ball loose. Rookie defensive tackle Michael Dean Perry recovered and ran ten yards for a touchdown, cutting Houston's lead to 10–7. Two Tony Zendejas field goals, from forty-two and thirty-five yards, bumped the lead to nine. Finally, with thirteen seconds left in the half and Cleveland on the Houston six trailing 16–7, Strock fumbled when a teammate bumped into him.

"We tried to hurry and run a play," Strock said.

It backfired, and the lost scoring opportunity stung even more when Moon connected with receiver Haywood Jeffires on a seven-yard touchdown pass with nine minutes remaining in the third. The Oilers led, 23–7, and the Browns appeared ready to end a season that had seemed so promising in August. Except that Strock, with snow sticking to a frozen field as well as the 74,610 fans in attendance, got hot. And three straight drives ended in touchdowns.

First came a two-yard touchdown pass to running back Earnest Byner, capping a sixty-three-yard drive and cutting the lead to 23–14. The defense held again—the Oilers, with the NFL's third-best rushing offense, would gain only thirty-seven yards rushing on twenty-three attempts—and Byner again scored a touchdown, this one coming on a two-yard run to the outside with 13:17 left in the game.

The breaks had turned Cleveland's way. On the latter scoring drive, the Browns had decided to go for a first down on fourth and three at the Houston twenty-nine late in the third. But they didn't even need to run the play as linebacker Johnny Meads jumped offsides.

Then, on third and six from the nine, Strock drilled a pass over the middle that shot off Byner's hands, ricocheted off linebacker John Grimsley, and fell into the hands of diving running back Herman Fontenot, at the two.

"The ball bounced off my shoulder," Grimsley told reporters after the game. "I don't know how the guy made the catch."

On the ensuing kickoff, return man Allen Pinkett broke through a large hole, his eyes fixed on the end zone. He might have made it, too, if not for kicker Matt Bahr who tripped him up—barely. That, Houston coach Jerry Glanville said later, "was the big, big play of the game."

Again the defense held, and once more Strock, starting at his eleven, guided Cleveland. Receiver Reggie Langhorne helped put the Browns in scoring position with three of his six catches for forty-seven yards. One was a thirteen-yard third-down grab and another came on fourth and two at the Houston thirty-one. Langhorne clung to the ball despite being creamed by safety Jeff Donaldson.

But Slaughter, who would finish with six catches for 136 yards, put them on top. With the Browns on the Oilers' twenty-three, Schottenheimer, whose conservative play calling had been criticized all season, called for Slaughter to run a five-yard pattern for a first down. Strock and Slaughter, playing with a brace on his left arm, had other ideas. Strock had watched Slaughter break cleanly off the line most of the game. So he called for a post.

"Houston had a weak safety who was very nosy," Strock said. "He liked to read the quarterback's eyes, so we went to play action. I had [tight end] Ozzie [Newsome] running a corner route. I looked at Ozzie real quick and got the safety to move. I hit Webbie on the break, and he caught it. A lot of people said the play wasn't in the playbook, but it was just a backside route. I knew if I could get the safety to move and, with the footing as bad as it was, if I threw a halfway decent pass, Web would catch it."

Strock's passes and Marty Schottenheimer's coaching helped the Browns rally past the Oilers and make the play-offs.

Amazingly, in little more than a quarter, the Browns went from a sixteen-point deficit to a five-point lead at 28–23. They were done scoring. So, too, were the Oilers. They were slayed by a quarterback who had played two completely different halves.

In the first half, Strock completed nine of nineteen passes for 111 yards and three interceptions. But in the final thirty minutes, Strock was sixteen of twenty-three for 215 yards and three touchdowns.

"The mistakes we made in the first half, they started making in the second half," Strock said. "We took them out of their run-and-shoot offense. The thing I remember is when we finally left the game, my wife and I are driving home and there must have been two feet of snow on the ground and we're only driving five miles per hour and no one else is on the streets. I don't even know if I was on the road or not."

With Kosar still unable to play the following week in the wild card game in Cleveland against Houston, Strock had earned his first start in a play-off game and would become the fourth oldest quarterback to start an NFL postseason contest. Strock also grabbed a spot, albeit temporarily, next to Kosar in the hearts of Browns fans.

The week of the play-off game, Strock was driving with his wife, Debby, when she said, "Listen to this." The radio blared a new hit, at least in Cleveland: "Rock Around the Strock," to the tune of "Rock Around the Clock."

The music died a week later when the visiting Oilers eliminated the Browns, 24–23. In a perfect statement on the season, yet another quarterback got hurt as Strock injured his right wrist on a bungled exchange from center Gregg Rakoczy.

Yet another season that began with Super Bowl hopes ended prematurely. Yet in many ways, it lasted much longer than anyone could have expected. Five times a Cleveland quarterback left the game with an injury, which could have resulted in no play-offs for the first time since 1984. Somehow, they squeaked in.

"That was Marty's best coaching job," linebacker Clay Matthews said.

It also would be his last in Cleveland. On December 27, three days after losing in the play-offs, Schottenheimer resigned rather than succumb to several demands by owner Art Modell, one of which included hiring an offensive coordinator.

"We saw it coming," Dixon said. "We knew what was going on, so we were not surprised by it."

Two hours before Schottenheimer quit, he had met with Strock and told him he'd like him back in '89. That's what Strock wanted to hear. This wasn't: en route to a UPS store, he heard the news about Schottenheimer on the radio. Strock's days in Cleveland had ended, and he would play just one more NFL season, closing his career in Indianapolis. Byner was gone, too, traded to Washington in the off-season for running back Mike Oliphant. An era had ended, but the Browns made sure they punctuated it with one more memorable game.

"We were down to the old man," Byner said. "And he came in and played lights out."

	1	2	3	4	*Total*
Oilers	10	6	7	0	23
Browns	0	7	7	14	28

FIRST QUARTER

H - Zendejas 39 FG. Oilers, 3–0

H - Bryant 36 interception return (Zendejas kick). Oilers, 10–0

SECOND QUARTER

C - Perry 10 fumble return (Bahr kick). Oilers, 10–7

H - Zendejas 42 FG. Oilers, 13–7

H - Zendejas 35 FG. Oilers, 16–7

THIRD QUARTER

H - Jeffires 7 pass from Moon (Zendejas kick). Oilers, 23–7

C - Byner 2 pass from Strock (Bahr kick). Oilers, 23–14

FOURTH QUARTER

C - Byner 2 run (Bahr kick). Oilers, 23–21

C - Slaughter 22 pass from Strock (Bahr kick). Browns, 28–23

42 Hanford Dixon and Frank Minnifield
Cornerbacks 1981–1989; 1984–1992
Number 29; Number 31

 The city loved their bark and the team loved their bite. While nicknames and canine antics drew attention, their play drew raves. For a time, Frank Minnifield and Hanford Dixon were arguably the NFL's best cornerback tandem and together changed the Browns' defense. Coaches turned them loose on receivers, allowing the safeties to help elsewhere. Their tight coverage gave linemen more time to stalk the quarterback.

"You're only as good as your cornerbacks, and they were two of the best in the league," safety Felix Wright said. "They were the main cogs in our defense."

Minnifield, never one to shy away from a bold statement, took their importance a step further.

"We were the best that ever played the game together, for pure numbers and economics and what we had to work with," Minnifield said.

Cleveland drafted Dixon in the first round, in 1981, and, by his second season, he was the full-time starter. But it wasn't until Minnifield arrived via the USFL, in 1984, that Dixon flourished.

When Minnifield came to Cleveland, he recalled hearing stories calling him the defense's missing link. He also came to town with a much heftier contract than Dixon. So one of Minnifield's first moves was to talk with Dixon in the 1984 training camp.

"We decided there would be a lot of people around the country and in Cleveland that would make comparisons between us," Minnifield said, "and I felt that would be very unproductive. It would make Hanford have to defend himself, and there would be someone in the middle egging us on. We decided not to let that happen and be the best of friends, and we would go win us a Super Bowl."

They didn't accomplish the last goal, but they didn't let anyone drive a wedge between them. Maybe that's because both earned respect during their time together. Dixon and Minnifield each made the Pro Bowl, from 1987 to 1989, and Minnifield landed one more berth in '90. In 1987, they became the first cornerback tandem to start in the Pro Bowl, which they repeated the following season. But they

Cornerbacks Frank Minnifield, left, and
Hanford Dixon high-five after a big play.

stood out even before that: in a 1985 play-off game against Miami and pass-happy quarterback Dan Marino, Dixon allowed one reception. Minnifield allowed none.

"Frank and I were a perfect fit," said Dixon, who retired, after the '89 season, and now is a real estate agent in Westlake. "I knew I had someone else who could play bump and run and the aggressive style I liked playing. If you put us out there and gave us two guys [to cover], you didn't have to worry about the wide receivers."

They knew it would be hard to survive without each other. The five-foot-nine Minnifield loved jabbering with receivers, whom he once called the "scoundrels of the earth." He was fast and athletic—his vertical leap of forty-four inches earned him the nickname "Sky," and he ran the forty-yard dash at 4.4 seconds. Another athletic trait was harder to spot but was just as important.

"My greatest attribute was that I could have a collision and keep my balance," said Minnifield, who retired after '92. "The other thing was my acceleration. I knew if I could run into this person and stop him from running, then I could usually accelerate faster than most of these guys. At that point, I could beat him. If I missed them and it turned into a footrace, they had a chance."

But Minnifield also studied the game and kept a laptop on every receiver he had faced over a five-year period; he often spent flights reviewing his information while many teammates slept. Others noticed his preparation. When Eric Allen played corner for Philadelphia, he once said the first thing he did while preparing is to see if his opponent had played Cleveland.

"And I check out what Minnifield's doing," Allen said, "the type of technique and philosophy he's used. And if it's successful, I go into a game and try to apply that technique to the receiver."

By the time the game rolled around, Minnifield knew a receiver's every move. Then he had to stop them, providing a challenge that called for more than physical skills. He also loved the verbal jousting, particularly with the Houston receivers. But Minnifield usually held the advantage, intercepting five career passes off Oilers quarterback Warren Moon, including three in one game at Houston in 1987. Later that season, he returned an interception for a touchdown in the play-offs against Indianapolis.

For the most part, quarterbacks tried to stay away from him. Not that he didn't want them throwing his way.

"When you're playing man to man and everyone in the stadium knows you're playing man to man, at that point it's all about heart," said Minnifield, president of Minnifield Enterprises in Lexington, Kentucky. "You can't let him beat you. I loved that part of it. Am I going to get him or is he going to get me? That's always been there for me, and it's just part of my makeup. It's still with me, even in private business. It's a mainstay of who I am. It's pretty hard to convince me there's a good reason to back down. That sums up why I tried so hard at the line of scrimmage.

"I liked playing against [Pittsburgh's] Louis Lipps more than anybody. That was a personal game that the city looked forward to, and during those years, he was a player we couldn't allow to have a good game. We knew if we beat Pittsburgh, we would be kings for a week in Cleveland. And if I beat him, we had a good chance to win the game."

On the other side, the five-foot-eleven Dixon battled John Stallworth, a quiet assassin. Dixon, though, loved to run his mouth during games and had a lot to say to every receiver he faced. Retorts were few in many years, particularly in 1987, when Dixon defended just seven passes all season as quarterbacks ignored his side. That's why the NFL Alumni selected him as the Defensive Back of the Year.

Like Minnifield, Dixon said he kept computerized data on every receiver and would watch tapes of upcoming wideouts on small TVs while traveling. Before Minnifield arrived, Dixon relied more on his talent to stop receivers. After all, that's how he quickly climbed the football ladder. He didn't even play football until his sophomore year at Theodore (Alabama) High School.

"My father didn't want me to play," Dixon said. "He thought it would interfere with my grades. I remember every day I used to stay after school and practice, knowing when I got home I would get a whipping. After about four of those, he realized I really wanted to play this game so he came to a practice with my mom, and we talked him into letting me play."

Within a year, colleges started calling, and Dixon, a receiver and cornerback in high school, used that raw talent to land a scholarship from Southern Mississippi. By the end of his freshman season, Dixon saw he could go even further.

"I said, 'Man, I'm good enough to get drafted around the fifth round,'" Dixon said. "After my sophomore year, I said, 'I can go in the first round if I work hard enough.'"

Dixon worked hard enough to be rated as the best pure cornerback in the 1981 draft by the *Sporting News*. When he finally was paired with Minnifield, Dixon combined athleticism with preparation to succeed.

"We were the most prepared corners in the game," said Dixon, who was switched to safety in '89, but returned to corner when Anthony Blaylock struggled. "We spent a tremendous amount of hours preparing and would start as soon as the game ended."

That probably helped prolong Dixon's career, which was cut short by injuries. Both he and Minnifield suffered from various muscle pulls. Some of the problems stemmed from their style and mind-set, which they carried into practice.

"Deep down, Hanford was so afraid of getting burned that he refused to let it happen," linebacker Clay Matthews said. "He played off this bravado. Some people didn't know how to take him, but I appreciated him because he worked so hard in practice, and that's why his career was cut so short. He ran his legs out. We went three or four years where we just played man to man every down, and in practice, he played like that. He just did not want to get beat. His bravado probably [turned people off], but once you got to know him, you realize he's just a guy who didn't want to get beat."

Dixon said, "We really made practice like a game-type situation. Those guys used to take it easy, and other defensive backs let them catch the ball. Not Frank and I. We really worked them. Our philosophy was, once they go against us, they were prepared to go against anyone."

43 **The Stalled Drive**
1990 vs. Buffalo

Browns 34, Bills 30
January 6, 1990

 Buffalo marched toward the end zone, determined to punish Cleveland once more. Not that the Browns needed more play-off agony. Especially not when it came like this: in the play-offs, with the lead, at home. That scenario haunted Cleveland the past three years, ever since Denver victimized the Browns under the same circumstances. Certainly, no one had forgotten the Drive. Here came its twin.

So there went Buffalo, toying with the Browns, dumping passes to running backs and creeping its way to the goal line. The Bills expected to send the Browns to yet another last-minute bitter play-off defeat, one that would be rehashed for months.

The Bills stood on the eleven yard line, running an offense the Browns couldn't stop. Nine seconds remained. This was Cleveland. This was the play-offs. This was the time to fall apart. Except it didn't happen. For once, the Browns received the breaks. For once, an opponent's running back, wide open in the end zone, dropped the ball. And the opposing quarterback tossed the late interception. After three years of play-off torture, Cleveland, and the 77,706 fans in attendance, finally had something to celebrate. Even if it was painful to watch unfold.

"It was like being at the blackjack table and having $5,000 down," receiver Webster Slaughter said afterward. "The dealer has the face card up, and you hate for him to turn the other one over."

That card, however, was an ace. At least for linebacker Clay Matthews. Talk about torture: Matthews had covered, or, rather, tried to cover running back Thurman Thomas all game. He failed. Thomas grabbed thirteen passes, tying an NFL record, and was all set to snatch his fourteenth when Matthews, standing on the one yard line, intervened.

Earlier in the game, Browns coach Bud Carson took Matthews off Thomas, opting for a defensive back. That failed, too, and Matthews returned to chasing Thomas out of the backfield.

When the Bills spread into their formation on the eleven, no one but quarterback Jim Kelly stood in the backfield. Matthews knew the play, mainly because he

Linebacker Clay Matthews saved the Browns with this last-minute goal-line interception to beat Buffalo in the play-offs.

had been beaten at least four times on it already. Thomas was the inside man in a three-receiver set.

"They called for a man-to-man defense, and I'm thinking, 'Oh, no,'" Matthews said. "I wasn't the most confident player on the field. [But] I know exactly what the play is. Thomas is going to go down and break out or break in. He broke inside, and I turned and ran."

Maybe Kelly didn't see Matthews. Or, perhaps, he figured the Bills were on a roll and couldn't be stopped, ignoring running back Ronnie Harmon's wide-open end-zone drop on the previous play. Whatever the reason, Kelly forced the ball over the middle at Matthews, who cradled the ball as he fell to his knee. Afterward, Thomas admitted being surprised to see Matthews line up across from him.

"What surprised me," Matthews said, "is that I beat Thomas to the point of the ball."

What pleased many is that Matthews held onto the ball. Just two weeks earlier in Houston, that apparently was asking too much. In that regular-season finale—with the Browns needing a victory to clinch a play-off spot—Matthews intercepted a Warren Moon pass in the fourth quarter with the Browns clinging to a 17–13 lead. Danger averted. Until Matthews decided to lateral to tackle Chris Pike. Four previous times, Matthews had pitched the ball to a teammate after an interception. Each time it worked—in 1987, he tossed the ball off to thirty-five-year-old end Carl Hairston after gaining thirty-six yards. Hairston rambled on for forty more.

"I never comprehended there was any downside to lateralling the ball," Matthews said. "Especially when you're four for four."

Make that four for five. Matthew's lateral to the six-foot-eight Pike sailed over his head, and the Oilers recovered. On the next play, Moon threw a touchdown pass. Lucky for Matthews, the Browns rallied to win.

"You make decisions and 99 percent of the time, you're comfortable with your decisions," Matthews said. "But after the Houston game I remember thinking, 'Yeah, I shouldn't have lateralled that one.' Maybe it wasn't the best of choices, but we had won the game. It was over.

"I went into a bookstore the next day, and some guy comes up and says, 'Are you Clay Matthews?' And I go, 'Yeah, how are you doing?' I'm always nice to people. And he says, 'What were thinking on that lateral?' Here I've got someone who never played the game questioning me. So it was good to come back the next game and do something good."

The Drive was foremost on owner Art Modell's mind when he hired Marty Schottenheimer's successor. No more last-minute collapses, declared Modell, who added he had never been involved in a more exhaustive search for a coach. With Bud Carson, Modell proclaimed he had found an attacking coach up to the final play. Schottenheimer, who resigned after the 1988 season, preferred to use an extra defensive back and a three-man rush late in games.

"That's what people knew Marty for," said safety Felix Wright. "When we were in close games, we went into a prevent. We weren't in a relaxed mode, but we would get away from things we were doing during the game. But we still had to perform. It wasn't Marty's fault. If we blitzed and got beat, people would still complain."

Carson liked to stay aggressive. That's how he helped mold Pittsburgh into a dynasty as the defensive coordinator in the 1970s. Players such as Joe Greene, Jack Lambert, Jack Ham, and Mel Blount certainly could make any coach look good. But Carson's schemes confounded opponents, and, in 1976, the Steelers recorded five shutouts in their last nine games to make the play-offs. He repeated his success with the Los Angeles Rams and later with the New York Jets.

Never mind the Jets' collapse against the Browns in '87; Modell was convinced Carson was his man. In fact, he said it would be his last coaching hire. Carson, fifty-eight when Modell hired him, never expected this day to come.

"I had given up getting here a long time ago," he once said. "So this is all a bonus to me now."

The players, though, still had to adjust to life without Schottenheimer, who quit after Modell told him to get an offensive coordinator. This clash of egos was a repeat of 1962 when Modell fired Paul Brown and replaced him with his exact opposite, Blanton Collier.

"I don't know who was wrong, but I know it hurt the team when Marty left," Wright said. "We had that winning tradition. But every coach has their own style, and one isn't better than the other. Bud was more the fatherly type. You could talk with him and joke around. Marty was more a disciplinarian and pretty serious. He was always to the point. You could talk to him, but more on a business level.

"We had more input with Bud. When we saw something on the field, we told Bud, 'This is what we're doing and this is what we have to do.' And he said, 'Do it.' With Marty, once a defense was called, we had our adjustments and that was it. With Bud, you could make battlefield adjustments. That gave the safeties a lot of leeway."

It helped that Carson knew how to massage a veteran team. That became important late in the season when the 7–3 Browns began to tumble. They tied Schottenheimer's Kansas City team then lost three straight games to nonplay-off teams Detroit, Cincinnati, and Indianapolis, scoring thirty-seven points in those games as quarterback Bernie Kosar was battered with boos. In the Colts loss, Kosar threw two interceptions, one of which was returned for a touchdown. During this stretch, Kosar went twenty straight quarters without a touchdown pass.

But Carson didn't panic. At the team's hotel the night before a home game against Minnesota, Carson addressed the team, reviewing the game plan and pointing out what it would take to win. It wasn't a pep talk. Carson said what he needed to then sat down.

"If he had given us a pep talk at that point, then we all would have known there was something wrong with this team," tight end Ozzie Newsome said.

The next day, Cleveland beat Minnesota in overtime and clinched its fourth division title in five years the following week at Houston.

"He was always very positive," tackle Cody Risien said. "He spoke reality."

The reality, in cornerback Frank Minnifield's mind, was that the Browns' defense was nearing the end of its dominance, despite evidence to the contrary. Cleveland forced eight turnovers in a season-opening 51–0 win over Pittsburgh, and Wright led the NFL with nine interceptions.

Four defensive starters—Minnifield, Matthews, tackle Michael Dean Perry, and linebacker Mike Johnson—made the Pro Bowl. And in eleven of sixteen games, the defense had allowed two or fewer touchdowns. Still, Minnifield saw signs of change.

"We had obviously been dethroned at that point," Minnifield said. "We had every different scheme imaginable and every different combination of coverages. We realized we could no longer just line up and kick someone's butt. We had to rely on sophistication of schemes to beat people. Three years earlier, we had but two defenses. Against the Bills, we probably had fifty. And it was necessary to have that many. We needed to outsmart the opponent. We were an old team at that point."

It showed against the Bills. Buffalo confused the Browns from the beginning by spreading them out, using a no-huddle attack and, often, four receivers. Cleveland had prepared for a two-tight-end, two-back set. At times, Matthews said, they didn't even have a defense called.

The Browns quickly saw Buffalo had no intention of slugging it out on the ground when Kelly hit receiver Andre Reed for a seventy-two-yard score in the first quarter. Cleveland joined the shoot-out as Kosar, emerging from the worst slump of his career, threw a fifty-two-yard second-quarter touchdown pass to receiver Webster Slaughter for a 10–7 lead. Kosar, who would complete twenty of twenty-nine passes for 251 yards and three touchdowns in the game, never saw the score thanks to a blitzing linebacker.

The fast-break pace continued as Kelly hit receiver James Lofton for a thirty-three-yard touchdown. Kosar answered with a three-yard touchdown pass to tight end Ron Middleton, giving Cleveland a 17–14 halftime edge.

Neither team slowed down in the third quarter. Each time the Browns bulked their lead to ten, the Bills stormed back. In the third quarter, Kosar hit Slaughter from forty-four yards out; Kelly connected with Thomas from six. Then came a play that broke the Bills' spirit, if only temporarily, and one that weighed on their minds as much as the game's final plays.

Browns safety Felix Wright upends Bills receiver Don Beebe, forcing an incomplete pass.

After Thomas's score, rookie returner Eric Metcalf, doubtful all week with a sore toe, scooted ninety yards for a touchdown—the Browns' first-ever kickoff return for a score in the play-offs—and a 31–21 lead with 4:23 to play in the third. The Bills had tried to kick away from Metcalf but failed.

"It was the biggest play in a game of big plays," Buffalo coach Marv Levy said later.

Yet it wasn't the decisive play as the Bills drove sixty-eight yards in eleven plays for a Scott Norwood thirty-yard field goal with 1:08 elapsed in the fourth. Again Cleveland took a ten-point lead as Matt Bahr booted a forty-seven-yarder midway through the quarter.

By this time, the Browns' defense had tried everything, abandoning their four-man rush for five-, six-, and three-man lines. None of them worked. Some blamed the field, which Bills defensive end Bruce Smith described as a "beach with sand painted green."

The home-field/sand advantage worked for Cleveland after Buffalo scored with four minutes left on a Kelly to Thomas four-yard pass. But Norwood missed the extra point.

"I planted my foot, and then it slid right out from under me," Norwood said. "The footing was terrible."

So, too, was the miss. Now, when the Bills regained possession on their own twenty-six with 2:41 remaining, they needed a touchdown to win. Kelly (twenty-eight for fifty-four, 405 yards, four touchdowns, two interceptions) ignored the crowd's ear-pounding cheers and drove the Bills downfield, toward the closed end. With each first down, the roars increased as the fans tried to derail this drive, hoping to erase their memories of another.

But with sixteen seconds left, Buffalo had a first down on the Browns' eleven. From there, Ronnie Harmon ran out of the backfield and into the left corner of the end zone. Safety Thane Gash was supposed to be there. He wasn't. Kelly spotted Harmon and floated a pass. And Harmon dropped it.

"It was a catchable ball," Wright said, "but under those circumstances, you never know."

Thomas, who had bickered with Kelly all season, said the quarterback had waited too long. No matter, nine seconds remained, and it was only second down. In the Browns' huddle, players shouted at one another, encouraging words mixed with vulgar ones.

"People got bent out of shape," Wright said. "We were saying, 'We can't allow this to happen to us.'"

They didn't. Matthews ended the game with his interception. Then he tossed the ball into the stands as the Browns earned their third AFC championship game appearance in four years. Each one ended the same way, and this was no different as Denver eliminated Cleveland once more. It would be the Browns' last championship appearance, and, midway through 1990, Carson would be fired.

A tiff between players and management hurt his cause as corner Hanford Dixon retired and the Browns gave his replacement Raymond Clayborne a $1 million contract. That prompted Minnifield, Wright, Johnson, and Matthews to hold out. None got better deals.

The Browns most successful era since the 1960s had ended. They ended their run in glory at the stadium, with a bit of luck and a crushing mistake by the other team. For a change.

	1	2	3	4	Total
Bills	7	7	7	9	30
Browns	3	14	14	3	34

FIRST QUARTER
B - Reed 72 pass from Kelly (Norwood kick). Bills, 7–0
C - Bahr 45 FG. Bills, 7–3

SECOND QUARTER
C - Slaughter 52 pass from Kosar (Bahr kick). Browns, 10–7
B - Lofton 33 pass from Kelly (Norwood kick). Bills, 14–10
C - Middleton 3 pass from Kosar (Bahr kick). Browns, 17–14

THIRD QUARTER
C - Slaughter 44 pass from Kosar (Bahr kick). Browns, 24–14
B - Thomas 6 pass from Kelly (Norwood kick). Browns, 24–21
C - Metcalf 90 kickoff return (Bahr kick). Browns, 31–21

FOURTH QUARTER
B - Norwood 30 FG. Browns, 31–24
C - Bahr 47 FG. Browns, 34–24
B - Thomas 3 pass from Kelly (kick failed). Browns, 34–30

44 **Clay Matthews**
Linebacker, 1978–1993

Number 57

 Young Clay Matthews headed across country, a first-round pick driving his wife's already aging Mercury Capri. He could afford better. He liked this. More than a dozen years later, Matthews still tooled around town in the rusted brown car, pounded by Cleveland's harsh winters.

By the early 1990s, the odometer was long broken, stuck on eighty-nine thousand miles. The air conditioner didn't work. Neither did the heater. Finally, after about eighteen years, Matthews bought himself something new. But he never stopped liking the Capri.

"I was comfortable with it," Matthews said.

The Browns were more than comfortable with Matthews. His career outlasted his Capri, though barely. Matthews played in more regular-season NFL games (232) than anyone else in franchise history and is the Browns' all-time leader with 76.5 sacks. His 279 games over nineteen seasons are the most by any linebacker. He made five Pro Bowls in sixteen seasons in Cleveland, a figure that doesn't measure his impact at outside linebacker.

"He was one of the greatest players to play the game," said former Browns coach Marty Schottenheimer. "When I came to Cleveland, I remember some people said he would never play, that he wasn't tough enough, and that he was a great athlete but not a football player. Boy, nothing could have been further from the truth. He had a standard of performance that was excellent, and he did it for an extended period of time. That's the portrait of greatness. He's one of the top three or four guys I ever had the privilege of coaching."

Matthews was easy for a coach to like. Even into his tenth season, Matthews worked on the scout team, providing a good look for the offense. Few starters do that. Fewer do this: Matthews also would play fullback or even quarterback against the second-team defense. Anything to stay on the field.

"I loved playing the game," said Matthews, who lasted three more years with Atlanta before retiring in 1996. "One of the few things I never understood is that there really aren't a lot of people who love playing the game. They love being a pro athlete, they love getting paid a big salary, they love the time off, and they love

doing a job that people are interested in. But there aren't a lot of people who love what they do. If you put them in an empty stadium and didn't pay them, there are a lot of people who wouldn't play. I loved playing. I loved competing. It was very easy."

Others saw Matthews's joy on the field.

"Clay always made the game fun," tight end Ozzie Newsome said. "He was always a kid playing football."

Speed never was his primary strength—Matthews ran the forty-yard dash in about 4.65 seconds—but he was rarely out of position because he understood the game. Certainly it was in his blood as his dad, Clay Sr., played four seasons with San Francisco in the 1950s. Clay Jr.'s brother Bruce has played sixteen seasons with the Oilers.

Their father rarely, if ever, discussed football strategy with his sons, who hold the all-time record for games played by brothers. The message he did deliver, however, stuck. Clay Sr. told his sons to be professional about their job, solve their own problems, and "refuse to lose." Clay Jr. carried those words to Cleveland, where he studied the game, watched film, and envisionied himself making certain plays. Few were in better shape, which explains why he missed just four games in his last eleven seasons in Cleveland.

"Clay would play around and joke with everybody," cornerback Frank Minnifield said. "But Clay would go home and study the game night and day to make sure he understood it. You didn't have to tell him anything twice."

For his first five seasons, Matthews said, he was content to grade out at 90 percent and finish with eight tackles or so. Every so often, though, he sniffed greatness. Then he craved more, elevating his expectations.

This is what followed: His first Pro Bowl bid in his sixth season, setting a standard that allowed him in his tenth season to be all-Pro and in his fifteenth to tie for the club lead with nine sacks. In 1989, Matthews was the Browns' only linebacker to play every down, and his last-second, goal-line interception of Buffalo's Jim Kelly saved Cleveland from another crushing play-off defeat.

"Once you had a game where you would get three-and-a-half sacks or an interception," Matthews said, "it got to the point where all you wanted to do was make big plays. As my career went on and on, I would get less and less satisfaction unless I had a couple big plays."

He also wanted to have fun, which explains his penchant for laterals after interceptions. His first four worked as teammates grabbed the ball and plowed forward for more yardage. Matthews's fifth flip failed, resulting in a fumble and, one play later, a Houston touchdown. The Browns rallied in the 1989 game to win, and Matthews's miscue was laughed off. Fortunately for Cleveland, he didn't try to lateral after intercepting Kelly two weeks later.

But having fun is why Matthews lasted, and it's why he basked in simple pleas-

Clay Matthews

ures, like driving remote control cars around the Browns' facility. Or by living in nice, but not luxurious, homes. And by working on cars, which Matthews would do Sunday nights after games. He couldn't sleep, so he'd head to a buddy's house and work on cars. Sometimes it was one of Matthews's old cars, such as his 1967 Camaro, '66 Ford Mustang, or '63 Jaguar. But they didn't fix that beat-up-on-four-sides '73 Capri, which still sits at one of Matthews's Cleveland-area car dealerships.

"We used to give him all sorts of grief," receiver Dave Logan said. "He was a playmaker, but he took noise from everybody because he'd drive that car and he was kind of a kooky guy. We used to kid him that he had the first dollar from his signing bonus. He was like the mad scientist."

A highly respected one, however.

"Clay never elevated himself above anybody," Minnifield said. "I'll bet you there's not a guy that didn't consider him a good friend. The thing I admired the most was his ability to deal with the media. I wish I had that type of wits about me when it came to the media. He kept the edge off and didn't receive the criticism the rest of us did because he answered all the questions. He didn't take them real serious and didn't take it as though they were pointed at him. He realized their role and had a good time at it. We knew Clay would come up with the right answer, and everyone would giggle and laugh and feel better."

The next stop for Matthews, who is a volunteer high school coach as well as a Little League coach in Agoura Hills, California, could be the Hall of Fame. Or it might not be. Either way is fine with Matthews, who said it doesn't weigh on his mind.

"A lot of people told me, 'You'll have a tough transition going back to being a regular person,'" Matthews said. "But the minute I retired, it was the easiest thing in the world. I went back to being a fan. I enjoy it. I would consider it an honor to be in [the Hall of Fame], but if not, I just loved playing. To have played for nineteen years is reward enough."

45 **My Quarterback Vinny**
1995 vs. New England

Browns 20, Patriots 13
January 1, 1995

They shouted for Bill to go, but only Bernie did. The fans voiced their opinions, gathering in hostile circles outside the Browns' locker room, loudly suggesting personnel changes owner Art Modell should consider. Like canning his coach.

Modell didn't budge. Bill Belichick was his guy. And quarterback Vinny Testaverde was Belichick's, so he disposed of Cleveland icon Bernie Kosar midway through the 1993 season. That turned the team over to Testaverde, whose confidence seemingly wobbled on a daily basis. Or even down by down.

Testaverde carried extreme baggage when he arrived in Cleveland, in 1993, after signing to back up Kosar. In six seasons in Tampa Bay, Testaverde went from winning the Heisman Trophy to being called "Interceptaverde" after years of struggling, not all of which was his fault. It didn't matter, though. Testaverde was Tampa's centerpiece, and the Buccaneers stank, finishing 28–67 during his tenure. Right or wrong, he carried the burden.

Testaverde came to Cleveland optimistic about starting fresh and said he would be Kosar's caddie. But Kosar struggled in '93, and when Testaverde guided the Browns to a comeback win over the Los Angeles Raiders in relief, speculation mounted as to who would be the starter. For two more weeks, it remained Kosar.

Then Testaverde started on October 17, leading Cleveland to victory over Cincinnati. He did the same the following week against Pittsburgh. But he hurt his shoulder in the win, and Kosar started the next game. It would be his last. After losing to Denver, Kosar was released, even though Testaverde would be sidelined for another three weeks. The Browns dropped all three games.

Now all Testaverde, fragile ego and all, had to do was replace a Cleveland legend, one who remained a presence despite now playing with Dallas—his number 18 Cowboys jersey was a top seller in Cleveland. The only way to rid himself of Kosar's shadow was by guiding a team to the play-offs. Then winning a game. Neither of which Testaverde had ever done, a fact often mentioned by fans and media.

"[Vinny's] confidence level wasn't there," said receiver Michael Jackson. "He was happy to have a new experience, but the fans wouldn't always allow that to

happen because they would talk about Tampa. Then there goes his confidence level. That guy had the potential to be a great quarterback. But I've seen his confidence rise and fall, and something you really don't need under center is instability as far as confidence goes."

One person who never suffered confidence lapses, at least not publicly, was Belichick. Now he was tying his reputation to Testaverde. But since Belichick took over a 3–13 team, in 1991, he hammered away at the roster, cutting loose numerous ties to the past. Then he ditched Kosar, citing diminished skills. Speculation raged that it was because Kosar had become bigger than the team and Belichick needed the control. Whatever the reason, Belichick, armed with a lowlight film of Kosar's bad plays, made the move. The fans fumed.

"It was the beginning of the end in Cleveland for Modell," *Cleveland Plain Dealer* writer Tony Grossi said.

The players, Jackson said, understood this: "If he let Bernie go, he wouldn't think twice about us."

After the last home game in 1993, a loss to New England, fans, some wearing Cowboy hats in tribute to Kosar, continued a postgame habit: They stood outside the Browns locker room chanting, "Bill must go! Bill must go!" The shouts carried into the upper deck, reaching ears all around the mammoth building. The Kosar hangover lasted into the next season as fans struggled to embrace the Browns, despite their winning six of their first seven games.

Part of the problem was the schedule, as none of the first six wins came against teams that would finish with winning records. Another problem, perhaps a main one, was Belichick, whose personality, *Akron Beacon Journal* columnist Terry Pluto once wrote, "would make the Boston Strangler seem like Mary Poppins." Also, Cleveland had not made the play-offs since 1989, its second longest drought in franchise history. But Kosar's ouster loomed in the minds of many.

"Bernie was hard to bury," said running back Earnest Byner, who re-signed with Cleveland before the 1994 season. "I don't think he'll ever be buried. It was a strain for the city to really take hold of the team [in '94]. I don't know if the Belichick era had left a real negative taste in their mouths, and that was probably true because of them releasing Bernie. But this was Bill's team, and everything was coming together."

Testaverde, though, began to shovel dirt onto those memories by winning games, as the Browns went 9–4 in games he started during the regular season, including a win at Dallas, to earn a wild card berth. He had occasional lapses, such as a four-interception game in a loss versus Pittsburgh. But sometimes he flashed greatness. Like against New England in the play-offs.

Testaverde wasn't the only Brown making his play-off debut. But Byner wasn't one of the neophytes. He had played on Cleveland's play-off teams, from 1985

Browns quarterback Vinny Testaverde, making his play-off debut, helped fans forget about Bernie Kosar, at least for a day.

to 1988, and later with Washington, where he won a Super Bowl. This was different.

"I didn't feel like that play-off game [against New England] was anywhere near the play-off games in the '80s," Byner said. "The energy wasn't there. Back then, the energy around that team was electric. I could feel the energy, and it got me wound up, even during the week. I didn't even want to leave the house at that time. During the '90s, it was nice, but the same kind of excitement wasn't there."

The play-off rookies disagreed.

"It was like being at a heavyweight championship fight," defensive end Rob Burnett said. "There was that kind of excitement and electricity in the air. I'll always remember it."

All eyes of the 77,452 fans at Cleveland Stadium, though, pointed at Testaverde. His teammates tried to deflect the pressure by stating their belief in him. They massaged his confidence with moves that were never required for Otto Graham, Frank Ryan, Brian Sipe, or Kosar. Linebacker Carl Banks told Testaverde to just play, saying they couldn't afford for their quarterback to go into a shell. The week of the play-off game, safety Eric Turner let Testaverde know the defense had confidence in him.

"Just hearing that gave me a good warm feeling that those guys were behind me," Testaverde said.

Before taking the field on New Year's Day, tackle Tony Jones pulled Testaverde aside and told him: "We'll protect you up front. Just relax." After that message, Jones said he gazed into Testaverde's eyes and saw a look unlike any he had seen from him before.

Testaverde had never been in this situation before. This is how he responded: twenty completions in thirty attempts for 268 yards, one touchdown, and no interceptions.

"Vinny didn't make the dumb mistakes that we expected," Patriots linebacker Vincent Brown said after the game.

Instead, he made all the right plays, completing eleven passes in a row during one stretch. Jackson was Testaverde's main target in this game. That in itself was news, given Jackson's volatile season. While the Browns worked on Testaverde's psyche, Jackson was trying to boost his own. He had been benched in the season finale for being a few minutes late for a team meeting. The fans turned on Jackson, who missed seven games because of injuries, and a few sent him nasty letters, one of which read, "I'll be glad when they get rid of you."

"I had been through a lot there," Jackson said. "When I got there [in 1991, the Browns] rid themselves of Webster Slaughter, Reggie Langhorne, and Brian Brennan. Those were mainstays, and the fans held me accountable. I tried to make them understand that I was only one guy, one they didn't even expect to make the team. It was hard for me to go out there knowing people didn't like me because of a move the organization made. I couldn't do anything right. Whenever I made a mistake, that's what was written up. Even if I had a good game, [the media] would write, 'Yeah, but he dropped this ball.'"

Nothing bad was written when Jackson caught seven passes for 122 yards against New England, the fourth-best single game receiving total in Browns history. Patriots cornerback Ricky Reynolds had tried to cover Jackson by himself. He couldn't. The coup de grâce: a diving thirty-six-yard catch before halftime. No points resulted, but the catch summed up his day.

"I talked a lot of noise beforehand," Jackson said. "I told [Reynolds] it would be a long day. We're friends and we talked a lot. It wasn't personal; that's just the way I am. My adrenaline was so high to where I'm thinking, 'I can't do anything wrong right now.' It was like, 'If I go for it, I'll come up with it somehow.'"

But it was a pass where he served as a decoy that gave the Browns a 10–7 second-quarter lead. Cleveland had taken a 3–0 first-quarter advantage when Matt Stover booted a thirty-yard field goal, his twenty-first straight that season.

New England, though, had a hot young passer in Drew Bledsoe, who had guided the Patriots to seven wins in a row. Their last loss: a 13–6 defeat in Cleveland. But Bledsoe had rolled since then with eleven touchdowns in those seven wins.

Though he would struggle all day, Bledsoe did complete a thirteen-yard pass to running back Leroy Thompson for a 7–3 lead. The Browns came back behind Testaverde. At the New England five yard line, he dropped back, hoping to hit Jackson in the left corner.

"But he was covered," Testaverde said. "The rush was coming, and I started to roll right."

Receiver Mark Carrier, in the end zone, ran with him. Only Reynolds, playing zone, stood between Testaverde and Carrier. So Testaverde tucked the ball and started to turn upfield. That suckered Reynolds, and Testaverde dumped a scoring pass to Carrier, who later admitted even he thought his former Bucs teammate would run for the touchdown.

Those who applauded the release of Kosar could point to this play as an example of why Belichick preferred Testaverde. If nothing else, he held a distinct athletic edge over Kosar.

The lead over New England lasted about seven minutes. A fake punt set up a twenty-three-yard Matt Bahr field goal with thirty seconds left in the half. Jackson's diving grab gave the Browns another scoring chance, but Stover's fifty-yard field-goal attempt was blocked by Mike Pitts as time expired.

The game remained tied at ten until late in the third quarter when Cleveland asserted control, embarking on a ten-play, seventy-nine-yard drive. One key play was also historical. Byner gained five yards on a third and five and became the Browns' all-time leading postseason rusher, surpassing former teammate Kevin

Running back Leroy Hoard snapped a 10–10 tie with this ten-yard third-quarter run.

Mack. But Leroy Hoard gave Cleveland a 17–10 lead on a ten-yard run with 2:21 remaining in the quarter.

The defense took it from there, constantly harrassing Bledsoe, also in his play-off debut. One sequence ruined his day. With 9:10 left in the game, defensive tackle Bill Johnson tipped a Bledsoe pass that linebacker Pepper Johnson intercepted, giving Cleveland a first down at the New England thirty-one. A conservative offense left Stover with a forty-nine-yard field-goal attempt, which he left short.

No problem. The defense would set him up again. Two plays after Stover missed, Bledsoe's pass over the middle was tipped by fullback Kevin Turner. The ball shot off his fingertips into Turner's arms at the Patriots' thirty-six. This time the offense moved the ball to the three where Stover kicked a twenty-one-yarder with 3:36 to go. All was safe. Or so it seemed.

New England marched sixty-three yards before facing a fourth down at the Cleveland fifteen. Patriots coach Bill Parcells elected for the field goal, and Bahr made it 20–13 with his thirty-three-yarder. Only 1:30 remained. But play-offs in Cleveland often meant drama. Once again the Browns kept their fans in the stands until the end when they failed to recover Bahr's onside kick. Actually, his first attempt bounced out of bounds and, after a five-yard penalty, Bahr tried again. This time it worked as Corwin Brown recovered at the New England thirty-six.

Bledsoe, though, could do nothing, due in large part to Burnett. On first down, Burnett crashed through the line and forced a bad throw. Four plays later, tight end Ben Coates broke free across the middle. But Burnett drilled Bledsoe into the ground, ending the game.

It was the Browns' last play-off win in Cleveland Stadium. Testaverde had made it happen.

"He was just a totally different guy," Jackson said. "We could see him thinking all year long about what to do and what not to do. We would always tell him, 'Man, don't worry and just go out and do what it takes to win. Don't try to win it yourself.' After that game, it was like, 'Damn, I can do this.' He was like a kid learning to walk. You see an excitement in a person's eyes when they find out they can do something that people had convinced them they shouldn't think they could do. That's what I saw in him. That filters down to the other players."

The Browns wanted to play their next opponent, Pittsburgh, immediately. Never mind that the Steelers had defeated them twice, intercepting Testaverde six times in two games. They dominated visiting Cleveland again, winning the first play-off game between the teams, 29–9.

Testaverde's numbers reflected the final score: thirteen for thirty-one, 144 yards, one touchdown, and two interceptions. In truth, two dropped passes on the first possession spelled doom.

"He was as talented as any quarterback in the league," Burnett said. "[But] he had trouble when all the burden was on him."

It didn't matter what the offense did because the defense couldn't stop Pittsburgh's running game, allowing a franchise-high 238 yards rushing.

"As happy as I was after the New England game, I was as low as an ant in the dirt [after losing to Pittsburgh]," Burnett said. "The play-offs were a good time and exciting. But it didn't last that long."

Nor would the Browns, at least Modell's version, last much longer in Cleveland.

	1	2	3	4	Total
Patriots	0	10	0	3	13
Browns	3	7	7	3	20

FIRST QUARTER
C - Stover 30 FG. Browns, 3–0

SECOND QUARTER
N - Thompson 13 pass from Bledsoe (Bahr kick). Patriots, 7–3
C - Carrier 13 pass from Testaverde (Stover kick). Browns, 10–7
N - Bahr 23 FG. Tie, 10–10

THIRD QUARTER
C - Hoard 10 run (Stover kick). Browns, 17–10

FOURTH QUARTER
C - Stover 21 FG. Browns, 20–10
N - Bahr 33 FG. Browns, 20–13

46 **The Dawg Pound**
1985–1995

 Together they hatched a plan to inspire their defensive line. It involved barking. So, in the huddle one day in training camp, cornerbacks Hanford Dixon and Frank Minnifield stood inches from their linemates and started woofing, hoping this would somehow send them crashing through the line and into the quarterback's face.

That's all Dixon and Minnifield hoped to accomplish. Next thing they knew, the fans started barking. Then they wore dog masks. And dog bones. And Milk-Bone necklaces. And T-shirts. And the stadium's bleacher section was renamed the Dawg Pound.

An entire city barked with them, creating an identity that lived on, especially in the bleachers, even after Minnifield and Dixon left town. Winning boosted the Pound's image, and the Browns did their share of that in the late 1980s, advancing to three AFC championship games. It's hard to create a frenzied atmosphere with a losing team. But the Browns strung together their best seasons since the 1960s. Minnifield and Dixon soon found themselves on a poster with their respective nicknames, "Mighty Minnie" and "Top Dog."

"One of the proudest moments I had in Cleveland Stadium," Minnifield said, "was when fans showed up in dog masks and started throwing dog biscuits. It felt like home then. We'd go to Houston, and if we beat them, we'd get beer and everything thrown on us. The Dawg Pound really gave us a home-field advantage."

"We said, 'It's out of control,'" said Dixon, who is the originator of the "Dawgs" nickname and deserves the credit for getting everything started. "But it was great. It just blew up so fast, I wish I had trademarked that thing."

He would have made a mint. It started like this: One day in training camp, Dixon thought of ways to motivate the line, which was devoid of big-name players. Coach Marty Schottenheimer had been pleading with the line to be the big dogs on defense.

Dixon stretched it further.

"I started thinking, 'A quarterback is like a cat, so we'll make our line the dogs,'" Dixon said. "We all started barking at the line, and the fans were so close, they just picked it up and started barking at the entire defense. Before that day was up, the whole defense was called, 'The Dawgs.' By the time we played a game at the stadium, it was there."

Cleveland's famous Dawg Pound was always full of people and energy, including D-Dawg in his customary 29 jersey with Dawg mask.

From the first barking in 1985 through the last home game in 1995, the Dawg Pound endured. Others in the stadium wore masks and barked and had all the Dawg paraphernalia, but the bleachers became the Pound, mainly because of its proximity to the field. Also, they were the cheapest seats and often drew a rowdier bunch. Before the Dawg craze, the Browns sold two thousand season tickets in this ten-thousand-seat section in the east end zone. By 1990, that number jumped to six thousand.

"We drew a lot of energy from the entire stadium," Dixon said, "but especially from the Dawg Pound."

The players acknowledged these fans every game, racing to the open end to slap hands before games, or bending over the railing for a round of back slapping after a score. When noise was needed, they waved to the Pound.

After the Browns last-ever game in the stadium, before owner Art Modell bolted for Baltimore, nearly twenty-five players spontaneously ran to the Pound to shake hands and pat the fans' backs, to console and thank them at the same time.

"They were the backbone of our support system," said defensive end Rob Burnett. "We knew we could count on them for rowdiness when we needed it."

Opposing teams, backed up into the end zone by the bleachers, would get pelted by Milk-Bones, especially during TV time-outs. They also had to dodge snowballs and an occasional battery. This didn't start with the Dawg Pound as, in 1978 against Houston, a controversial pass interference call on cornerback Ron Bolton prompted bleacher fans to toss beer cans at the officials and the Oilers. The officials moved the teams to the other end.

Twice during the Pound era, officials switched a team's direction for fear of these fans hurling too much debris. The Browns won both games, against Denver and Houston.

"They're 2–0 in my book," Minnifield said. "They killed the psyche of opposing teams and destroyed them mentally."

They didn't destroy Denver quarterback John Elway, who led a ninety-eight-yard death march toward the Dawg Pound in the 1986 season AFC championship game. Browns quarterback Brian Sipe tossed his infamous interception at this end in the 1981 play-off loss to Oakland. But those old enough remembered Lou Groza's kick toward this end zone to win the 1950 championship.

The Pound provided controversy, too. Against Cincinnati, in 1985, Minnifield leveled receiver Cris Collinsworth, then stood over him and barked as Collinsworth lay injured. Soon, radio talk shows were filled with angry callers, upset over the way Cleveland, because of the Pound, was portrayed. So Minnifield made a few calls as well, defending the Pound. But he never identified himself.

"I said I was totally in favor of the Dawg Pound," he said. "And I was in favor of them throwing biscuits. When we went to Denver, they'd throw snowballs at us, so I didn't have a problem with a little biscuit coming onto the field. Art Modell didn't like the image of the Dawg Pound. He didn't say anything about that, but he never openly supported the Dawgs. But he had a good time when we were winning and the money was rolling in."

After the 1986 season, the Browns sent a letter to season-ticket holders, signed by several players, including Dixon and Minnifield, asking fans not to throw things on the field.

"We started getting to where a few dog bones became many bones and some bones wrapped with a battery," former Browns Vice President of Public Relations Kevin Byrne said. "So we had to slow it down."

It didn't work. During a 28–23 win over Houston, in 1988, bleacher fans pelted a television cameraman, knocked unconscious in a collision, with snowballs. That prompted *Cleveland Plain Dealer* columnist Bill Livingston to write, "All of the creeps who threw snowballs from the Dawg Pound—my, weren't you picture postcards for this city's renaissance. These jerks may be a minority, but they have a disproportionate effect on the game. . . . Please go throw yourselves in the lake with an anchor around your neck."

But a few snowball-slinging fans didn't diminish the Pound's popularity. Soon some fans became celebrities. Vince Erwin as D-Dawg was on *Browns Insider* for one season and, in 1993, was part of a feature on the Pound by an English TV station. Fans requested autographs and snapped pictures of him with their kids. Of course, he always had to wear his mask. That was his gig.

Then there was John Thompson, aka Big Dawg, who became profiled time and again after Modell moved the franchise. Even baseball's home run champ and longtime Browns fan, Hank Aaron, donned disguises and sat in the Pound.

But it was the anonymous fans who provided the bleachers' backbone long before it became a fashionable place to sit. It was a group of no-names in section sixty-one who picked up on the Dawg theme and started bringing a doghouse. Naturally, it had beer inside. Erwin took it from there, buying his famed wolf mask and waving his cowbell, a leftover from the Brian Sipe years. Erwin's fond memories don't center around the fame he gained.

"It was a lot like a family there," said Erwin, a season-ticket holder since 1978. "We'd go to preseason games and we wouldn't watch the games. We were interested in what was going on in everyone's lives. It was sort of like a homecoming."

The anonymity added spice. In 1985, an older, gray-haired man—a long-time season ticket holder—tired of hearing a Raiders fan hollering and insulting Cleveland. So the old man stood up and punched the Raiders fan, who fell to the ground. The old man stood over him and barked.

Pity the mouthy Steelers fan. Thompson told *Sports Illustrated,* in 1995, of a time when the Steelers were in town and "we had a huge bonfire using stuff we ripped off fans, like Starter coats and stuff. Those are expensive, like a hundred bucks, and here we were burning them to keep warm and roast weenies."

They also kept the players entertained.

"A few times we'd stop on the field and watch the fights in the stands and in the Dawg Pound," Minnifield said. "We'd say, 'Someone said the wrong thing in the Dawg Pound.' I don't remember any fight in particular, but they were all good fights."

Receiver Michael Jackson said, "It was like Mardi Gras at a football game. The Dawg Pound reminded me of the inner city. It was like the rest of the stadium was the county and the Dawg Pound was the inner city where the rowhouses are and where they had gang-infested areas. We didn't have to worry about people coming in from other towns and displaying team logos and colors in the Dawg Pound. They were into the game as much as we were."

Another fan, Todd Baldau, recalled his first Pound experience: A controversial

The Dawg Pound was always on hand to celebrate a touchdown, as receiver Webster Slaughter learns in a 38–3 win over Atlanta in 1987.

pass interference call caused him to rush from his third-row seat to the front railing where he shouted at the officials. To his right stood a man wearing an orange jacket with the words "Event Staff" on them, someone who should have been keeping peace in the stands. Instead, he joined Baldau in hurling obscenities.

The bleachers provided the best chance to get on TV after a field goal or extra point. It was also the best spot to snag a football that sailed over the net. Long before any nicknames, one fan, sitting in the middle of the bleachers, came prepared. When an extra point reached the stands, a fan threw the ball in his direction. He caught it and stuffed it in a bag, then pulled out an old, beat-up ball and whipped it in another direction, taking the cops with it.

The police eventually revised their ball retrieval system—they would kick anyone out who threw the ball—but no one could stamp out the enthusiasm.

"Whenever a team was backed up there on offense, the noise was ridiculous," Burnett said. "I got a kick out of it. When it's December and the wind whips off the lake and you look up and see half-naked people screaming and hollering, it's like, 'Wow. I didn't know things like that existed.' I smelled a whole lot of different things coming out of there, a lot of illegal things. I saw breasts. That was more shocking. I was just looking up to see all the people, and all of a sudden a girl on some guy's shoulders pulled her shirt up. I was like, 'Whoa.'"

Safety Felix Wright often became lost in the Pound, running up the short embankment directly beyond the end zone after defending a pass.

"I remember once coming back with an armful of beer spilled on me," said Wright, who later played an exhibition game in Cleveland with Minnesota in 1992. "You never knew what to expect when you were up in there. Before the game, it was cool. During the game, you never knew because you've got both teams there and the fans are trying to distract the opposing team. So when they threw that beer, they probably intended to hit the other guy and ended up hitting me. Opponents hated coming into the stadium. It wasn't nice, and they got harrassed. It was a great place to play, but you had to be on the right side."

If you were, the Pound treated you as its own puppy. The fans reveled in the nickname, and, though Dixon started the hysteria, the fans escalated it. When the craze fizzled in the early '90s, talk show host Greg Brinda said those who continued to dress in Dawg garb considered themselves "the true Browns fan and the symbol of Browns fans." But barking returned with winning, thanks to fans hungry for a wild time. Will it continue? Wright says no. Others say it will.

"The great thing with the Dawgs is that, in typical Cleveland fashion, [the organization] never promoted it," Byrne said. "It evolved by itself. We didn't push it. When they come back, the Browns will still be the Dawgs and there will be a Dawg Pound. The fans took it on as their own, and we had a great time with it."

47 **Sad Farewell**
1995 vs. Cincinnati

Browns 26, Bengals 10
December 17, 1995

Pain covered faces once hidden by Dawg masks. Grown men cried. This wasn't a football game; it was a funeral. An angry one. Cherry bombs exploded, leaving Cleveland Stadium in a smoky haze. Fans sawed off their seats and tossed them over the railings, sometimes hoisting entire rows. A fire burned in the bleachers. A hole burned in their hearts.

The Browns were moving. What difference did it make whose fault it was? Someone would get the blame. So the emotion once used for cheering the Browns was used to bury them in their last game at the stadium.

"We were concerned about safety, and we had told the security people to get the players off the field as soon as you can," recalled Kevin Byrne, then the Browns' vice president of public relations. "We didn't want to jeopardize them."

The officials were concerned, too. With two minutes left in the game, they turned the teams around to drive toward the closed end zone.

Cleveland receiver Michael Jackson was digesting the proceedings when an idea popped into his head. He said he began telling teammates: "Don't shake hands with the Bengals. When the game ends, run to the Dawg Pound to show appreciation."

Some players balked. They hadn't enjoyed being booed during the second half of the season, after owner Art Modell had announced he was moving the franchise to Baltimore, and wanted to leave the field immediately. Jackson remained firm.

"I was like, 'No, I'm going to show appreciation because this is a great place to play ball,'" Jackson said. "I told them, 'Hopefully, at some point they will get a team or maybe we won't have to leave.' I knew it would help."

The crowd of 55,875 counted down the final seconds—in between chants of "Modell sucks!"—and many positioned themselves to storm the field. Dog biscuits, ice, and toilet paper were hurled at security guards.

Then it happened. Jackson, running back Earnest Byner, defensive end Rob Burnett, quarterback Vinny Testaverde, center Steve Everitt, and receiver Derrick Alexander raced to the bleachers. Others quickly followed. Soon, nearly twenty-

Browns center Steve Everitt and his teammates said a tearful goodbye to the Dawg Pound after the last game in Cleveland Stadium.

five Browns were in the end zone thanking, and consoling, jilted Cleveland fans. Burnett hopped into the stands. Byner, who said he didn't hear of Jackson's plans, ran the length of the Pound slapping hands.

"People were crying; they didn't want to let you go," Byner said. "We were hugging people, shaking hands. People were saying thanks for the memories. At that point, it was nice."

It might have prevented bedlam.

"Everyone was calm," Byrne said, "and it became an emotional farewell rather than a nasty one."

Only four months earlier, Clevelanders braced for a special sports year. The Indians had the American League's best record, and the Browns were coming off a second-round play-off appearance. They figured the next step was the AFC championship game. And beyond. Some experts agreed, as *Sports Illustrated*'s Paul Zimmerman predicted a Cleveland-San Francisco Super Bowl. Zimmerman figured this team was headed in the right direction. Turns out they were headed east to Baltimore.

On October 30, Cleveland celebrated the Indians' first World Series appearance since 1954 with a downtown parade. Now their attention would turn to the Browns, who had just evened their record at 4–4 with a win the day before at Cincinnati. Time remained for a turnaround.

But within days speculation raged about a possible Browns move, with good reason. Modell had signed an agreement, on October 27, to relocate the team to Baltimore—ten days before the city would vote on funding for stadium refurbishments—a transaction he had denied making for more than a week. Before the Browns hosted Houston, on November 4, amid the rumors, Modell said, "How can there be a reaction? Nothing's happened, has there?"

It was a move Modell had said he would never do. That March, when asked about the Rams moving from Los Angeles to St. Louis, Modell said, "You can't have clubs jumping for the big bucks and deserting a marketplace at a whim."

As late as July, Modell was quoted as saying he didn't want to discuss the stadium situation until after the season. He didn't want any distractions. Guess what he got.

"The organization had told us we weren't moving," said Jackson, who whipped three footballs into the stands after the win over Cincinnati. "We were introduced to it through the papers; we were just like the fans. They knew before us. We were at practice when the newspapers came out. We were like, 'Man, that's not happening.' Then one day a team meeting was called, and Art told us we were moving to Baltimore. We knew it would be a long season."

It was. On November 6, Modell stood on a podium in Baltimore and announced the move. Modell said he had no choice, and his supporters blamed the politicians, saying they dragged their feet and took care of the Indians and Cavaliers before the Browns. Critics blamed it on his own financial bumblings, such as a $5 million signing bonus to receiver Andre Rison, in 1995, and said he never gave the fans a chance to save the team. And, they said, he lied to them. Again and again. Either way, it was bad for the team. The Browns lost their next six games en route to a 5–11 finish.

"It was very distracting," Burnett said. "We heard about it so much. You couldn't watch any part of the news telecast without hearing about it ten to thirty times. At the supermarket, with your neighbors, everyone in the world who knew you were part of the situation had a question. After a while, the questions became repetitive, and it became a pain in the ass. It was a very strange season."

Confusion reigned before the home finale against Cincinnati. The league wouldn't vote on the move until January, and Cleveland Mayor Mike White had mobilized his troops in hopes of blocking Modell. This created a glimmer of optimism that maybe the league would force Modell to sell so the team would remain in Cleveland.

Still, many expected this to be the franchise's final game at the stadium. The players, though, tried to concentrate on the game. That's what Byner was doing, and he did so even more when coach Bill Belichick told him the night before the game that he would be the featured back. Starter Leroy Hoard was hurt. Later that night, Byner, then thirty-three, gathered the other running backs, and they held hands and prayed.

"I had a good night's sleep," he remembered.

He would need it. Byner hadn't surpassed one hundred yards since 1992 with Washington. But he would do so this day, finishing with 121 yards on thirty-one carries to go with thirty-six yards on seven receptions.

"I thought I was going to die," he said. "[But] once I got my second wind, I was ready to settle in and play."

Perhaps it was fitting that Byner had one of his best days in his last game in Cleveland. He had long been a fan favorite since making the team as a tenth-round pick in 1984. Byner began his career as a special-teams player, but his impact grew. In a win at Buffalo his rookie season, Byner scooped up a fumble on a rain-soaked field and ran fifty-five yards for a touchdown. Against Houston in the season finale, he ran for 188 yards.

The next season, he did even more. In a play-off loss at Miami, Byner rushed for 166 yards and two touchdowns. Byner could do a little of everything: block, run, catch. That's why coaches liked him, and it's why he stuck around. Fans loved his feistiness, even if it sometimes irritated teammates.

"I would fight guys," Byner said. "I probably alienated some because of my temperament. That was just me. When we played Miami in the play-offs, they

Running back Earnest Byner and quarterback Vinny Testaverde powered the Browns'
offense in their first win since the move was announced.

held me out of drills because they knew how fired up and crazy I would be in them."

Then came The Fumble in the AFC championship game loss at Denver, on January 17, 1988, when Byner was stripped of the ball just before crossing the goal line for the game-tying score. The next year, he received two crucial unsportsman-like conduct penalties in a play-off loss to Houston. That off-season, he was shipped to Washington for running back Mike Oliphant. When Byner returned, in 1994, he did so with a Super Bowl ring courtesy of the Redskins.

"That first year back, I could feel the level of love and respect that people had for me," he said. "I felt like I was brought back to the Browns because it was destiny's way of saying, 'You've been all right. Through The Fumble and The Drive and all the personal foul penalties. And even though you've been with the Skins for five years, you've still been all right with the Cleveland people.' I remember, as the [last] game was winding down, sitting on the bench and looking around the stadium and going through different memories and rehashing my career in Cleveland Stadium."

Quarterback Vinny Testaverde, playing with a hip pointer, had a strong game, too. He had been benched for three games during the season, yet responded with one of his better statistical years, with seventeen touchdowns, ten interceptions, and his highest quarterback rating, 87.8. His hot play continued in this game as he completed twenty-two of thirty-two passes for 241 yards. Testaverde threw a one-yard touchdown pass to tight end Frank Hartley and a sixteen-yarder to receiver Keenan McCardell. Later, Testaverde threw a victory salute as he ducked into the dugout one last time.

The defense smothered Cincinnati quarterback Jeff Blake. The Pro Bowl performer completed only twenty-two passes in forty-six attempts for 257 yards and one interception. The Bengals never had a chance, and their lone touchdown came with 6:51 left in the game. The special teams chipped in with four Matt Stover field goals, three in the second half.

"We wanted to play hard for the fans," Testaverde said after the game, "to try and pull off a win for them."

After returning from the Pound, Tony Jones knelt at midfield, giving thanks, he said, for playing in Cleveland for nine years. In the locker room, he said, "I never wanted the day to be over."

The fans' voice was heard. So, too, were their sounds of constant seat ripping, which Jackson said sounded like "pistols going off." They littered the stadium with anti-Modell signs—though one supportive banner read, "Thanks for the 34 years of memories." That sign, however, was hanging long before fans passed through the gates, suggesting the organization displayed it. Many fans carted away pieces of the stadium as souvenirs. Byrne said at least two hours after the game, he still heard the sawing.

The fans' anger was directed at one man, owner Art Modell, who stayed away from the final game.

"For those of us in the organization, it was surreal," Byrne said.

Among other things.

"It was sad, real sad," broadcaster and former tackle Doug Dieken said. "The saddest part was the people that were there and how they were hurt. They'd thank you and be in tears. It was humbling to see how much of what you had done meant to these people. Any time you have something that helped so few and hurt so many, it ain't right. The frustration and the anger . . . you couldn't blame anyone for what was going on. You could see the stadium being dismantled because you knew these people were hurting. They were innocent bystanders. They had been loyal for fifty years, and then they got the carpet pulled out from underneath them just because someone doesn't know how to manage their money. It was sad."

Long after most fans had departed, Burnett headed to his car. There stood four of his friends with a whole row of seats. Then he got a surprise.

"Everything had settled down, and we're getting out of there when a three-hundred-pound bearded man with snot coming out of his nose gave me a hug," Burnett said. "He said, 'We're going to miss you guys.' It scared me at first, then I thought, 'You'd never think a guy like that would be [in tears].' It broke a lot of hearts."

The hearts would begin to mend as the NFL, in an uprecedented move, guaranteed Cleveland a team by 1999. The colors and nickname remained, while the old franchise became the Baltimore Ravens. Cleveland had fought for a new team and won, displaying the energy that once surged through the players—even in the last game.

"It was an emotional day out there," Testaverde told reporters afterward. "We're going to reflect back on it, and there's going to be a hole inside of us. Something's going to be missing, and it's that we're not going to be playing here anymore."

	1	2	3	4	Total
Bengals	0	3	0	7	10
Browns	0	17	6	3	26

SECOND QUARTER
Cle - Hartley 1 pass from Testaverde (Stover kick). Browns, 7–0
Cin - Pelfrey 30 FG. Browns, 7–3
Cle - Stover 37 FG. Browns, 10–3
Cle - McCardell 16 pass from Testaverde (Stover kick). Browns, 17–3

THIRD QUARTER
Cle - Stover 42 FG. Browns, 20–3
Cle - Stover 19 FG. Browns, 23–3

FOURTH QUARTER
Cle - Stover 35 FG. Browns, 26–3
Cin - Bieniemy (Pelfrey kick). Browns, 26–10

Afterword

Other cities have lost teams before. Other cities have watched politicians and owners bungle a good situation, forcing a franchise to flee. This will happen again. But what happened when Cleveland lost a team might not.

After owner Art Modell announced his move, in 1995, the fans took control once they wiped away the tears. Within a week of hearing Modell's plans, the citizens of Cleveland passed a proposal for improvements to Cleveland Stadium, hoping that would sway the league to block Modell.

The Browns' fans bombarded the other twenty-nine NFL teams with thousands of faxes, clogging machines for hours. They rallied on Capitol Hill and congregated at the owners' meetings in Dallas. Electronic signs flashed, "Stop Art Modell" all over town, twenty-four hours a day. Big Dawg, John Thompson, showed up on show after show.

While Modell and the players would still leave, the history, colors, and team name stayed behind. Never before had the NFL agreed to such a deal. Also, the league guaranteed Cleveland a team by 1999. By mid-1998, more than fifty-two thousand season tickets had been sold and the loges had nearly sold out, giving new owner Al Lerner, on whose plane Modell signed his agreement with Baltimore, a strong base.

"When it's all said and done, it was a case of the voices finally being heard," said *Cleveland Plain Dealer* writer Tony Grossi. "If not for these people and that passion, this never would have happened."

During the opening week of 1996, the first year minus a team, hundreds of Browns fans congregated in a parking lot near the stadium to tailgate, reminisce, and then head home—without a game to attend.

"Everybody can say Green Bay is a great city and Pittsburgh is a great city and Philadelphia is a great city," former Browns coach Sam Rutigliano said, "but Cleveland has now proved it, because none of them were tested. I'm not sure in the history of professional franchises that anyone has ever said, 'You're not moving the team colors. You're not moving the name. You're not moving the tradition.' The Rams went from Los Angeles to St. Louis, and L.A. doesn't have a team and they don't give a crap. Not here.

"I think today [Modell] regrets destroying all the things that meant the most to

This sign at the last game in Cleveland Stadium proved correct after the fans led an emotional campaign to save the Browns.

The Browns' new home, sits on the same site as their old one, in downtown Cleveland near Lake Erie.

him. Knowing him as well as I do in my heart of hearts—he's a stubborn guy—I know deep down that's what he feels."

When broadcaster Gib Shanley tired of the Move talk, he said fans should "get a life. It's not the end of the world."

"It's not the fans' team," Shanley said.

He's right, of course, from a business standpoint. And Shanley said he talked to numerous attorneys who said they would have done the same thing as Modell. But making his sweetheart deal with Baltimore didn't make him a good businessman. Rather, it showed what a bad one Modell was for messing up a situation in which seventy-eight thousand fans routinely filled an aging stadium.

And consider this: The fans bought into the product long ago, making it one of the NFL's most desirable franchises. Owners ask fans to invest time, money, and emotion—without the latter, money isn't spent—and tell them it is their team. That they help the team win. That they are important. And then everyone says, "Sorry, it's just a business." No one's buying it.

"When I heard they were moving, I remember being devastated," linebacker Clay Matthews said. "Not for me, but for all those people over the years who came up to me on a Monday and were depressed. The guy in the market, the people in the mall. The players would survive. The owner would survive. But I was thinking about those fans who had given so much and how it hurt them. That's why [getting an expansion team] is so great. Sink or swim, you're not getting anyone else's dead weight."

"Art Modell left," cornerback Frank Minnifield said, "but the Browns never left. They'll always be in Cleveland. The NFL won't be whole until the Browns are back on the field."

A clock in Tower City has counted down the days until the Browns returned. A 40-by-160-foot mural on a downtown parking garage screams for attention. Paul Warfield, Jim Brown, Lou Groza, and Otto Graham are painted alongside a future star and the line: "More Heroes To Be Named Later."

"The greatest thing that happened," Warfield said, "is that these fans fought and got a commitment from the NFL. Now you can feel the excitement in the area. A new chapter has begun. I'm happy to see football return, and whatever I can do to see that it gets back to where it was, I'll do."

Will it be the same? Who knows. In some ways, no, how can it be? After all, the stadium has been demolished, replaced on the same site by a new one. The 72,800-seat open-air stadium will have a section nicknamed the Dawg Pound, but that moniker was earned in Cleveland Stadium, not given.

But in other ways, this is more of the fans' team, and maybe it will be even better. It will have two color video scoreboards, three times as many restrooms as in the old building, and exotic coffees. Imagine serving a fancy java blend in the old Dawg Pound—and surviving. Seats will be angled toward the field, which, by the way, will be natural grass. And there will be no pillars. Hallelujah.

The new place will be nicer. For a cost of approximately $250 million—$246.5 million more than its predecessor—it should be state of the art. But the only way it can match the aura of Cleveland Municipal Stadium is if the new team heeds the words of the Browns' greatest ambassador, Lou Groza. No one represents the Browns' greatness more than Groza, the only person connected to every Browns championship and all but one of the other thirteen Hall of Famers. Like many former players, he wept when they left, but he has since dried his tears. Now he has advice for the new team.

"I hope it's a winner," Groza said. "That's the tradition of Cleveland football. It's there and it's been established."

Reference Material

Appendix A
Cleveland Browns All-Time Team

Picking an all-time Browns team is, clearly, difficult. Especially on defense, as most of the offensive positions were obvious, thanks to the presence of seven Hall of Famers. Only two Hall of Famers played on defense. But with help from numerous former players and media members, here's our list of the greatest Browns of all time.

Defense

DE	Len Ford
DT	Walter Johnson
DT	Jerry Sherk
DE	Bill Glass
MG/MLB	Bill Willis
LB	Clay Matthews
LB	Jim Houston
DB	Frank Minnifield
DB	Hanford Dixon
DB	Thom Darden
DB	Warren Lahr

Offense

LT	Dick Schafrath
LG	Jim Ray Smith
C	Frank Gatski
RG	Gene Hickerson
RT	Mike McCormack
TE	Ozzie Newsome
WR	Dante Lavelli
WR	Paul Warfield
QB	Otto Graham
RB	Jim Brown
RB	Marion Motley

Special teams

K	Lou Groza
P	Horace Gillom
PR	Bobby Mitchell
KR	Greg Pruitt

Coach

Paul Brown

Tackle Lou Groza appeared in more memorable games than any other Brown.

Appendix B
More Memorable Browns Games at Cleveland Municipal Stadium

September 6, 1946: Browns 44, Seahawks 0

The Browns won their first-ever game, defeating the Miami Seahawks in the All-America Conference opener. Cliff Lewis made his first and last start at quarterback for the Browns in front of 60,135 fans. But the Browns lost money: Miami skipped town without paying any of its bills, leaving Cleveland to cover its hotel debt. By next season, the Seahawks were relocated to Baltimore.

The Browns went 7–1 at home, including a 14–9 win over the New York Yankees in the championship. Quarterback Otto Graham completed sixteen passes for 213 yards to lead the Browns in front of 40,469 fans.

December 19, 1948: Browns 49, Bills 7

Cleveland became the second team in pro football history to finish a season undefeated after manhandling Buffalo in front of 22,981 frigid fans. No other team finished with a perfect record until Miami went 17–0 in 1972.

The Browns extended their unbeaten streak to eighteen after opening a 28–0 lead against the Bills. Each winning player received $594.16. Cleveland's biggest test this season came when it had to play three games in eight days—all on the road. The Browns defeated New York 34–21 on a Sunday, followed by a 31–14 win over Los Angeles on Thanksgiving Day. Three days later, with Graham hobbled by a bad knee, they beat San Francisco 31–28. Two weeks earlier, on November 14, the Browns beat the 49ers, 14–7, in front of 82,769 fans—setting an attendance record for a pro game.

November 25, 1951: Browns 42, Bears 21

Cleveland receiver Dub Jones tied an NFL record with six touchdowns in front of 40,969 fans. Assistant coach Blanton Collier informed coach Paul Brown from the press box that Jones was one touchdown from tying the record set by Ernie Nevers of the Chicago Cardinals in 1929.

But it took quarterback Otto Graham to change a play call for Jones to score his last touchdown. Graham told Jones to run a post, and they connected for the score. Legendary Bears coach George "Papa Bear" Halas spent the day screaming from the sidelines, which annoyed Browns linebacker Tony Adamle. While Halas protested one call, Adamle walked over, tapped him on the shoulder, and said, "Would you please get the hell out of here!"

November 24, 1957: Browns 45, Rams 31

Jim Brown showed the NFL what it could expect for the next nine seasons with one of the greatest single-game performances in history. The twenty-one-year-old rookie rushed for an NFL-record 237 yards on thirty-one carries, and scored four touchdowns, including a sixty-nine-yard dash. A crowd of 65,407 watched.

The Browns trailed 28–17 in the third quarter when they erupted, thanks to Brown's running and Milt Plum's passing. The backup quarterback completed six of nine passes for sixty-two yards. Halfback Lew Carpenter chipped in with seventy yards on fifteen carries. Brown would lead the NFL in rushing with 942 yards. He would later tie this single-game record, which has since been broken, in a 1961 home victory over Philadelphia.

November 2, 1969: Browns 42, Cowboys 10

A record crowd of 84,850 saw Cleveland improve to 5–1–1 with an upset win over Dallas. Browns linebacker John Garlington recovered a fumble on the Cowboys' first possession, setting up a forty-eight-yard touchdown pass from quarterback Bill Nelsen to receiver Paul Warfield. Cleveland built a 28–3 halftime lead.

Nelsen finished eighteen of twenty-five for 255 yards, but the big story was the defense, which finished with six sacks and three interceptions. Cleveland proved this win was no fluke when it beat host Dallas 38–14 in the '69 play-offs.

November 19, 1972: Browns 26, Steelers 24

With 1:58 left in this first-place battle and Pittsburgh leading 24–23, Browns kicker Don Cockroft sliced a twenty-seven-yard field goal. But he got another chance, thanks to linebacker Dale Lindsey's stop of quarterback Terry Bradshaw on third and short. Quarterback Mike Phipps drove the Browns downfield, and, with thirteen seconds remaining, Cockroft kicked the twenty-six-yard game-winner before a crowd of 83,009.

Pittsburgh overcame a 20–10 halftime deficit, in part because of rookie running back Franco Harris's seventy-five-yard touchdown run. Harris gained 136 yards, while Leroy Kelly led the Browns with 107. The victory, Cleveland's fourth straight, left the teams tied in the AFC Central with 7–3 records. The Browns won four of their next five, but their only loss was at Pittsburgh, costing them the division title. They finished a game behind the Steelers.

September 26, 1977: Browns 30, Patriots 27 (OT)

The Browns made their first *Monday Night Football* appearance in four years a memorable one. Quarterback Brian Sipe's pass to running back Greg Pruitt tied the game at 24 midway through the fourth quarter. Then kicker Don Cockroft snapped the tie with fifty-five seconds left, kicking a thirty-seven-yard field goal.

But New England wasn't finished. The Patriots' John Smith sent the game into overtime with a last-second field goal. Cockroft trumped his heroics, however, with a thirty-five-yard kick 4:45 into the extra session, sending 76,418 fans home happy.

November 18, 1979: Browns 30, Dolphins 24 (OT)

The Kardiac Kids did it again, leaving both teams with 7–4 records after a game in which the lead changed hands six times. Miami led 24–17 with 1:29 remaining when quarterback Brian Sipe threw thirty-four yards to tight end Ozzie Newsome. It was the second time they connected for a touchdown in this game.

The Browns won the toss in overtime, and Sipe hit receiver Reggie Rucker for the game-winning thirty-nine-yard touchdown pass. Rucker finished with nine catches for 177 yards, five short of Pete Brewster's then team record for receiving yards in a game. Sipe finished with 358 yards passing and surpassed ten thousand yards for his career.

November 23, 1986: Browns 37, Steelers 31 (OT)

Second-year quarterback Bernie Kosar lifted the Browns to their first season sweep of Pittsburgh since 1969 when he hit receiver Webster Slaughter on a thirty-seven-yard touchdown pass on Cleveland's second overtime possession.

Kosar completed twenty-eight passes in forty-six attempts for 414 yards, two touchdowns, and an interception and earned AFC player of the week honors. After the game, NBC wanted an on-field interview. Kosar told them to talk to Slaughter instead. When NBC persisted, Kosar agreed, but midway through his third short answer, he took off the headset and said, "Thanks, guys. Gotta go." And joined his teammates in the jubilant locker room. The win, in front of 76,452 fans, boosted the Browns' record to 8–4 en route to a 12–4 finish.

October 24, 1993: Browns 28, Steelers 23

Pittsburgh moved the ball with ease and held Cleveland's offense to two touchdowns. But the Steelers couldn't solve Eric Metcalf. He tied an NFL record with two punt returns for touchdowns as Cleveland won in front of 78,118 fans.

Metcalf's first score, a ninety-one-yarder, gave the Browns a 14–0 second-quarter lead. Quarterback Vinny Testaverde, who would later leave the game with a shoulder injury, had passed sixty-two yards to receiver Michael Jackson for the first score. But Pittsburgh responded with two touchdowns, tying the game at halftime.

The Steelers took a 23–21 lead in the fourth quarter on a twenty-nine-yard Gary Anderson field goal with 7:51 to play. Then, with 2:05 remaining, Metcalf struck again, racing seventy-five yards for another score. Metcalf, who finished with 237 total yards, became the first player ever to score on two returns of seventy-five yards or longer.

Everything seemed right for the Browns as they improved to 5–2 and led the Steelers by one game in the AFC Central. But a week later, they lost to Denver and coach Bill Belichick released quarterback Bernie Kosar. They finished 7–9.

Bibliography

Books

Brown, Jim, with Steve Delsohn. *Out of Bounds.* New York: Kensington Publishing Corp., 1989.

Brown, Paul, with Jack Clary. *PB: The Paul Brown Story.* New York: Atheneum, 1979.

Byrne, Steve, Jim Campbell, and Mark Craig. *The Cleveland Browns: A 50-Year Tradition.* Champaign, Illinois: Sagamore, 1995.

Clary, Jack. *Great Teams, Great Years: Cleveland Browns.* New York: Macmillan Publishing Company, 1973.

Cormack, George. *Municipal Stadium: Memories on the Lakefront.* Berea, Ohio: Instant Concepts, 1997.

Hodermarsky, Mark. *The Cleveland Sports Legacy Since 1945.* Cleveland: Cleveland Landmarks Press, 1991.

Leuthner, Stuart. *Iron Men.* New York: Doubleday, 1988.

Levy, Bill. *Sam, Sipe and Company: The Story of the Cleveland Browns.* Cleveland: J. T. Zubal and P. D. Dole, 1981.

McDonough, Will, et al. *75 Seasons, The Complete Story of the National Football League, 1920–1995.* Atlanta: Turner Publishing, 1995.

Pluto, Terry. *When All The World Was Browns Town.* New York: Simon and Schuster, 1997.

Strother, Shelby. *The NFL Top 40: The Greatest Pro Football Games of All Time.* New York: Viking Penguin, 1988.

Zimmerman, Paul. *A Thinking Man's Guide to Pro Football.* New York: E. P. Dutton, 1970.

Magazines

Browns News/Illustrated

NFL GameDay Magazine

Sports Illustrated, August 26, 1985; December 4, 1995

Newspapers

Akron Beacon Journal

Baltimore Sun

Cleveland Plain Dealer

Cleveland Press

New York Times

Pittsburgh Press

USA Today, July 28, 1998.

Record Books and Guides

Cincinnati Bengals Media Guide. Cincinnati: C. J. Krehbiel, 1995, 1998.

Cleveland Browns Media Guide. New Washington, Ohio: The Herald Printing Company, 1946–1995.

Dallas Cowboys Media Guide. Dallas: Dallas Cowboys, 1995.

Houston Oilers Media Guide. Houston: Technigrafiks, 1995.

Indianapolis Colts Media Guide. Indianapolis: Sport Graphics, 1996.

New York Giants Media Guide. New York: New York Giants, 1994.

The Official National Football League 1998 Record and Fact Book. Los Angeles: National Football League Properties, Inc., 1998.

Pittsburgh Steelers Media Guide. Pittsburgh: Pittsburgh Steelers, 1997.

San Francisco 49ers Media Guide. New Washington, Ohio: The Herald Printing Company, 1998.

Washington Redskins Media Guide. Landover, Maryland: Chroma Graphics, 1998.

Videos

The Cleveland Browns: Fifty Years of Memories. New York: NFL Films Video, PolyGram Video, 1996.

Restore the Pride: Cleveland Browns Video Yearbook. New York: NFL Films Video, PolyGram Video, 1992.

A Winning Tradition: The Cleveland Browns 1964, 1965, 1967, 1968, 1969. Los Angeles: NFL Films Video, Fox Hills Video, 1988.

Web sites

www.clevelandbrowns.com

www.ohio.com

Photo Credits

Browns News/Illustrated: pp. 203, 210, 244, 259
The City of Cleveland: p. 285
Cleveland Public Library: pp. 12, 32, 37, 100, 112, 128, 155, 158
Cleveland State University: pp. viii, 10, 18, 21, 25, 28, 39, 40, 48, 52, 56, 59, 62, 68, 72, 76, 80, 92, 96, 102, 104, 108, 116, 120, 124, 132, 137, 140, 142, 150, 162, 166, 170, 173, 178, 182, 186, 191, 194, 197, 199, 207, 232, 289
Diamond Images: pp. 262, 266, 279, 281, 284
Kuntz, Ron: pp. 214, 218, 221, 226, 230, 250, 254, 270, 273, 276
McNamee, Wally: pp. 82, 88
Willoughby News Herald: pp. 14, 236, 241

Note: The Cleveland State University Archives is home to numerous pictures from the *Cleveland Press.* The following photographers have pictures in this book: Frank Aleksandrowicz, Fred Bottomer, Timothy Culek, Byron Filkins, Ron Kuntz, Larry Nighswander, Ernie Noble, Paul Tepley, and Jim Welch.

About the Author

John Keim is a Lakewood, Ohio, native who has covered the Washington Redskins for the Journal Newspapers since 1994. He has coauthored two other books, *America's Rivalry: The 20 Greatest Redskins-Cowboys Games* and *Hail to RFK! 36 Seasons of Redskins Memories.* He is a correspondent for *Pro Football Weekly,* and his work has also appeared in *Sport Magazine* and *Joe Theismann's Pro Football Yearbook.* The Ohio State graduate and former *Willoughby News Herald* intern lives in Chantilly, Virginia, with his wife Kerry and sons Matthew and Christopher.

About the Book

Legends by the Lake was designed and typeset on a Macintosh in QuarkXPress by Kachergis Book Design of Pittsboro, North Carolina. The typeface, Meridien, was designed by Adrian Frutiger in 1957 for the French foundry Deberny & Peignot.

The book was printed on 60-pound Cougar Opaque Smooth Finish and bound by Braun-Brumfield, Inc., of Ann Arbor, Michigan.